PROPHECY AND CANON

A Contribution to the Study
of Jewish Origins

UNIVERSITY OF NOTRE DAME
CENTER FOR THE STUDY OF
JUDAISM AND CHRISTIANITY
IN ANTIQUITY

Number 3

Prophecy and Canon

A CONTRIBUTION TO THE STUDY
OF JEWISH ORIGINS

Joseph Blenkinsopp

Frederick A. Niedner

UNIVERSITY OF NOTRE DAME PRESS

NOTRE DAME   LONDON

Library of Congress Cataloging in Publication Data

Blenkinsopp, Joseph, 1927–
  Prophecy and canon.

  Includes bibliographical references and indexes.
  1. Bible. O. T.—Canon. 2. Bible. O. T.
Prophets—Relation to the Pentateuch. 3. Bible.
O. T.   Pentateuch—Relation to the Prophets.
I. Title.
BS1135.B57   221.1′2   76-22411
ISBN 0-268-01522-8

For my colleagues in
the Department of Theology at
the University of Notre Dame

Contents

Preface

THE FOLLOWING WORK HAS GROWN OUT OF A PRO-
gressive uneasiness and dissatisfaction with Old Testament
studies. Perhaps in no other area has such intense and sustained research led to such widespread disagreement. No body
of literature in ancient or modern times has attracted such a
vast concentration of effort, given rise to such learned in-
genuity and virtuosity, and been subjected to such micro-
scopic inspection. All of this, however, has only served to
emphasize a fundamental lack of clarity with respect to the
subject matter of the discipline as a whole. The highly specific
viewpoints which have dictated the selection and arrangement of the material make it impossible to describe the Old
Testament simply as a history of Israelite or early Jewish literature. Attempts to give an account of the subject matter as a
whole which take cognizance of these viewpoints traditionally
fall into either a chronological or thematic model. They are
therefore entitled either a History of the Religion of Israel or a
Theology of the Old Testament. In both cases one is faced
with severe methodological problems. For, as I will argue,
there is no one "religion" of Israel. What these writings attest
to is rather a plurality of "religions" or religious viewpoints,
generally quite diverse and sometimes mutually exclusive.

As for the theologies of the Old Testament, one would have
to assume the intention of giving a theological account of the
Hebrew Bible as a whole, including its internal structure, the
relation between its parts and the like. In point of fact, however, this is rarely attempted. What usually happens is that
the writer reorganizes the biblical material in such a way as to
give prominence to themes which are important to him per-

sonally or confessionally. In the process the Hebrew Bible as such is left unexplained.

Any attempt to give an account of the Hebrew Bible, including its shape, structure and internal arrangement, must come to terms with the issue of canonicity. In other words, if the canon reflects the developing self-understanding of the group within which it came into existence, it will have to be considered an important ingredient in any chronological or thematic account of the religion of Israel and early Judaism. It may even prove to be the key in working out a theology of the Old Testament which really takes seriously the material in the form in which we now have it. Such, at any rate, would be a hypothesis worth exploring, and it is one which I take seriously in the present work. I am therefore not just interested in giving another account of the development of the canon. My purpose is rather to suggest some ways in which a reconsideration of the canon of the Hebrew Bible might bear on Biblical Theology and on our understanding of Judaism during the period of its emergence and earliest development.

This last point is particularly relevant today. Most scholars who have written on the question have directed their attention to the Hebrew Bible as a component of the Christian biblical canon. While this is understandable for a Christian scholar, it has had the unfortunate effect of collapsing the problem of canonicity into the quite different problem of the relation between the testaments. In the following study, therefore, I have concentrated exclusively on the Hebrew Bible as the canonical scriptures of Judaism. I have done this for the practical reason that, as I see it, the issues involved in canonicity can best be worked out in this way. This is not, however, the only reason nor is it the most important one. As a theologian, I would decisively reject any Christological reading of the Hebrew Scriptures which, in effect if not in intent, deprives the experience of Israel and indeed of Judaism of any real theological significance in its own right. Exclusively Christological understandings of the Hebrew Scriptures lead in a direct line to neglect of the theological problem posed for Christians by the ongoing existence of Israel (inclusive of the land of Israel) and, paradoxically, to an impoverishment of

Christian theology. How many Christian theologians take Jewish teaching on such matters as tradition, religious authority or ethics seriously in working out their own positions?

I am happy to express my debt of gratitude to those scholars who have reopened discussion of the long neglected canon and whose contribution is acknowledged in due course in the present work. I am also indebted to the University of Notre Dame which granted me a leave of absence and generous financial support, thus enabling me to complete the first draft. The dedication to my colleagues in the Department of Theology is intended as a small expression of my esteem and friendship.

Except where otherwise indicated, quotations are from the New English Bible.

Joseph Blenkinsopp
University of Notre Dame

PROPHECY AND CANON

A Contribution to the Study
of Jewish Origins

1: The Hebrew Canon

I. Law and Prophecy in the Canon

ONE OF THE DEEPEST ENIGMAS OF HISTORY IS THE CON-
tinuous existence of the Jewish people over a period of some
3,300 years from the labor camps of Rameses II to those of
Hitler and beyond. All sorts of explanations have been offered, some emphasizing socio-political and economic causes,
others appealing to less tangible factors such as tradition and
the sharing in a common memory. It may be true, as Isaac
Bashevis Singer once said, that Jews suffer from many collective ailments but not from amnesia; yet there have been other
societies which have lived by tradition and have nevertheless
lost their identity and ceased to exist. For Toynbee the distinguishing mark of Israel was rather the ability to come up with
radical innovations capable of surviving changes in social and
political organization.[1] If this is so, it would seem to imply two
things: the emergence of a tribal federation in the pre-state
period, whose ideal form of life was expressed in its myth and
laws; the phenomenon of free prophecy during the period of
the state, which assured the survival of this ideal form. The
former constituted a normative order over against the changing
social and political patterns encountered throughout the history, while the latter enabled this order to survive even the
destruction of the state and adapt itself to other conditions. In
this historical process the crucial factor came to be the relation
between normative order and prophecy. To understand this

1

relationship would therefore seem to hold out the promise of better understanding the enigma of Judaism.

An obvious place to begin would seem to be the Hebrew canon in which law and prophecy are juxtaposed. This juxtaposition itself constitutes a historical and theological problem of the first order. The history of prophecy, the kind represented in the second part of the canon, is coextensive with that of the monarchy. With the end of national independence in the sixth century B.C.E., it was eclipsed or, more exactly, began to undergo a thorough transformation. The decades preceding the collapse of the state saw prophecy undergoing a profound crisis. It is no accident that about the same time a written law with its interpretative framework was officially promulgated. One of the principal arguments of the present study will be that tension between normative order (from that time known as Torah) and prophecy is a constituent element in the origins of Judaism. What I will try to show is that the present form of the Hebrew canon reflects a certain way of dealing with this tension. The first and most important stage will be to demonstrate that there exist connections both overt and hidden between the final stages of the formation of the Torah-canon or Pentateuch and the eclipse of free prophecy (chapters 2, 3 and 4). It will then be argued that the emergence of the prophetic canon represents an unanticipated restoration of equilibrium between normative order and prophecy (chapter 5). The third part of the canon (the Writings), finally, will be shown to result from the transformations undergone by prophecy during the period of the Second Temple (chapter 6).

It will soon become clear that I am not concerned to take the reader once again through the history of the formation of the canon, a subject on which all the relevant information, patchy as it is, is easily accessible. What needs to be done, and what I hope to do, is to take the formation of the canon as an important chapter in the history of nascent Judaism. Granted the legitimacy of this approach, it must seem strange that one can go through any number of theologies of the Old Testament and histories of the religion of Israel without finding any significant treatment of the problem of canon.

It must also be said, for the sake of clarity, that I do not intend to deal with the Hebrew Scriptures as a constituent element of the Christian canon nor with the formation of the Christian canon itself.[2] It is understandable that Christian scholars should treat the Hebrew Scriptures as part of the Christian canon, but it must be understood that this approach carries with it certain disadvantages. Most obviously, the problem of the canon itself, which I have restated as that of the relation between normative order and prophecy, tends to get lost in discussion on the relation between the Old and New Testaments. It would also tend to obscure the important consideration that conflicting claims to authority are involved at every stage of the formation of a canon. It would, finally, make it more difficult to understand the nature of the claims which determined the self-understanding of nascent Christianity as it severed itself from the parent body of Judaism. This is not to deny the legitimacy of a Christian reading of the Hebrew Scriptures. It may, however, be taken as a warning against reading them in a way which would end up ignoring Judaism as a theological problem for the Christian.

We may dispense with etymologies and original meanings and begin by saying that a canon is generally taken to be a collection of writings deemed to have a normative function within a particular community. We must not exaggerate the official character of the writings which came to be known as the Hebrew Scriptures. Law codes were officially promulgated at least twice in the course of the history, during the reign of Josiah in the latter part of the seventh century B.C.E. and during the mission of Ezra some two centuries later. But there is no evidence that the contents of the canon as a whole were ever officially established during the period in question, and that such a decision was made by the Jewish leadership at Javneh (Jamnia) at the end of the first century of the era is a myth of Christian scholarship without documentary foundation.[3] Any group which has arrived at a certain level of consistency and complexity will evolve its own norms, thereby providing a sense of identity and determining what is and is not consistent with membership in it. Whether the group-myths ever get to be written down will depend on a wide range of possible factors which can generally be investigated. In the case of Israel and early Judaism (as in that of early Christianity) we will argue that the decisive factor was the need to resolve conflicting claims to authority, the point at issue being the interpretation of the received corpus of tradition. This may not lead us to view writing, with Lévi-Strauss, as an instrument of oppression and control,[4] but it should alert us to the possibility that it will embody claims of a polemical and tendentious nature.

It is tautological to say that in Israel, as in other traditional societies, what was normative in general was ancient tradition. While we never come across this tradition in the pure state, almost everything we find in the Hebrew Scriptures presupposes its existence. In this case, as in others, it took the form of a providential history of divine deeds and disclosures and an ancient deposit of custom and law. If it were possible to think of a group more or less exempt from historical vicissitudes, as is perhaps the case with certain primitive societies, living according to such a tradition would present no major problems. But as soon as political and social pressures begin to make inroads, impose strain and anxiety and corrode the inherited sense of identity, then at that point appeal to tradition begins to be problematic. When that happens it is predictable that many will react by ignoring the new situation more or less consciously and by appealing to the tradition with even greater insistence and urgency. Others will simply abandon the tradition and seek out other forms of legitimation. Others again will acknowledge that they are living in a changed world and will try to reinterpret the tradition in the light of the new situation and in a way which will make adaptation possible without severing the links with the past. This last, we may suppose, is the most difficult and hazardous of the alternatives.

What we would anticipate happening in any situation of this kind did indeed happen in the historical experience of Israel. At this point only the briefest sketch will be necessary.

According to the orthodox critical position, always subject to revision, the earliest of the large-scale complexes in the Pentateuch or Hexateuch is the Yahwistic (Jehovistic) work

(J) which was put together during the United Monarchy or at least not later than the ninth century. With all its nationalistic and dynastic fervor, it betrays the anxiety and stress induced by the passage to a new and threateningly secular form of political organization, namely, monarchy. It is no accident that the historical phenomenon of prophecy is attested in Israel from that time. A sense of historical crisis only became really acute, however, with the direct threat to national existence posed by the Assyrian drive to the Mediterranean in the eighth century, and it is likewise no accident that the writing down of prophetic oracles dates from that time, the first direct attestation being in Isaiah. It was during temporary respite from this pressure from outside, first under Hezekiah towards the end of the eighth and beginning of the seventh century, and later under Josiah in the last quarter of the seventh century, that positive attempts were made to reorganize the life of the nation on the basis of a more thorough assimilation of the tradition in written form. It is to these attempts that we owe, respectively, the Yahwistic-Elohistic national epos (JE) and the promulgation of the Deuteronomic law. With the ascendancy of the neo-Babylonian empire following hard on the collapse of the Assyrians came the greatest crisis of all, resulting in loss of national independence. It is no accident that these years witnessed the greatest concentration of prophetic activity. Nor is it surprising that at this time prophecy became more deeply problematic than ever before.

First the prospect and then the actual experience of total political disaster provide the clearest instance of the tradition coming under severe pressure from outside. Writings extant from the last decades of independent Judah and the early exilic period clearly attest to such a situation and attempt to respond to it in different ways. It must be borne in mind, though, that such responses represent the views of small groups or individuals. Much more widespread must have been the attitude of those settlers in Egypt who were quite clear as to the cause of the disaster and the line of action to be taken:

We will not listen to what you [Jeremiah] tell us in the name of the LORD. We intend to fulfil all the promises by

which we have bound ourselves: we will burn sacrifices to
the queen of heaven and pour drink-offerings to her as we
used to do, we and our fathers, our kings and our princes, in
the cities of Judah and in the streets of Jerusalem. We then
had food in plenty and were content; no calamity touched
us. But from the time we left off burning sacrifices to the
queen of heaven and pouring drink-offerings to her, we
have been in great want, and in the end we have fallen
victims to sword and famine. (Jer. 44:16–18)

While many, then, abandoned the tradition for another form
of legitimation (one that had been a rival to the tradition for
centuries), others, inspired by state prophets like Hananiah
(Jer. 28), continued to appeal to the tradition with its assur-
ances of divine protection and blessing as if nothing had happened. Only a few, it seems, were able to face up to the
propect of destitution while remaining faithful to the tradition. The price they had to pay—and this is always the
case—was a painful re-evaluation of the tradition in the light
of a new situation. It seems safe to assume that this was the
position advocated by institutionally unattached prophets like
Jeremiah, perhaps by him alone.

   I have taken the position that free prophecy made possible
the survival of the normative order by opposing the tendency
for that order to be assimilated to current institutional patterns. Such a position involved opposition to the claims of
controlling elites to represent the tradition and embody it in
certain prescriptive forms to which absolute allegiance was
due. Hence it is no surprise to find Jeremiah opposing not only
state prophets like Hananiah but also those scribes who
claimed authority to provide a prescriptive version of the
founding events and the laws in writing.[5] The basic issue was
the claim to mediate and interpret the tradition in light of the
contemporary situation. The evidence seems to suggest that it
was at least partially in reaction to claims made by prophets
detached from the state institutions, including the cult, that
official versions of the archaic normative order first came into
existence. Since these versions reach their fullest expression
in the Pentateuch, we should be able to test the hypothesis by

examining carefully the final and decisive stages in the formation of the Pentateuch. This testing will occupy us in the chapters that follow.

At this point we link up with the debate which has been going on for centuries on the relation between law and prophecy in Israel.[6] In both Jewish and Christian scholarship the traditional view held that the law was absolutely antecedent to the prophets and that the function of the latter was primarily the exposition of the law. With varying nuances this view held down into the nineteenth century when, as a result of the labors of Ewald, Vatke, Wellhausen and others, the order was reversed. It was basic to Wellhausen's position, presented with great skill and flair in his *Prolegomena,* that the formulation of the laws came later than the prophets, that therefore the prophets were not exponents of the law, but that on the contrary their labors made the law possible.[7] It is widely assumed that this new position was dictated by a Hegelian philosophy of history which was all-pervasive in nineteenth-century German academic circles, and that simply to state this is enough to disqualify it. In point of fact, however, Wellhausen's arguments are drawn from detailed critical exegesis and can be refuted only on the same grounds. Moreover, it soon becomes apparent to anyone reading the *Prolegomena* today that he drew his inspiration as much from German Romanticism as from Hegel, and nowhere is this more in evidence than in his negative evaluation of religious institutions and his view of the prophet as a "religious genius."[8]

A century after Wellhausen the emphasis has shifted once again, though we have no guarantee that we have reached anything like a definitive solution. Certain advances have, however, been made. We are now, for example, more careful to distinguish between the origins of the laws and their later formulation and promulgation. Much of the ritual legislation in the Priestly work (P), in particular, has been shown to be genuinely ancient. As for the prophets, they are now seen to be dependent at the very heart of their message on the archaic heritage of covenant and covenant law. Their accusations correspond, sometimes verbally, with laws which show every sign of antiquity, and their condemnations follow closely the curses attached to practically every kind of alliance in the ancient Near East.

It is apparent, then, that there is no simple answer to the question: which came first, prophecy or law. The covenant institution and its attendant laws antedated the prophetic movement, though their antiquity cannot be established by appeal to Hittite vassal treaties.[9] Free prophecy was well established before the time of the Deuteronomic and Priestly scribes whose monument is the Pentateuch. To put it more pointedly, the prophetic contradiction of current assumptions about the tradition had already created its own momentum, indeed its own interpretative tradition, before the rise of legal scribalism. The further position maintained here is that it was the prophetic claim to mediate the tradition or, conversely, to interpret the present in light of the past, which played a significant role in bringing about official and prescriptive versions of the ancient laws and founding events. Beginning with Deuteronomy, which for the first time speaks not of laws but of *the* Law, these reached final and definitive form in the Pentateuch. Prophecy stood for openness in relating tradition and situation. When, for example, Amos proclaims that Israel is now on the same level as Ethiopians, Philistines and Syrians (9:7–8), he is saying that the past can change in relation to the present, that there always exists the possibility of a new reconstruction of the past. Clerical scribalism could not ignore this kind of claim and it did not try to do so. On the contrary, its products (especially Deuteronomy) are at many points deeply indebted to prophecy. To state briefly what will be dealt with at length in subsequent chapters, clerical scribalism met the prophetic claim not by confrontation but by assimilation and redefinition, seeking to bring prophecy within its own institutional grid. I am not for a moment ascribing cynical self-interest to these Torah scribes, for it is clear that they were persuaded of their own legitimacy and of the inability of prophecy to provide a sound basis for the life of the community. It remains true, however, that the claim implicit in the work of the clerical and legal scribes came to be seen in the course of time as incompatible with that of the free prophets.

As Wellhausen put it, once you have the transcript of the original revelation at Sinai, sporadic prophetic revelations become superfluous.

It is only when we have dealt with the Pentateuch in its relation to prophecy that we can go on to the further problem of the unanticipated extension of the canon by a collection of prophetic writings. This, too, constitutes an important aspect of the religious history of early Judaism and one almost entirely neglected. Insofar as it also raises the problem of canonicity within the canon, it will inevitably force us to take a closer look at the arguments advanced in support of the theological status of the biblical canon as a definitive norm of faith.

II. The Present State of Canon Study

The traditional place for the study of the canon has been, and in fact generally still is, within Introduction to Biblical Studies. Given the predominantly literary emphasis in Biblical Studies, the result has been that the formation of the canon has not been seen as an important chapter in the religious and social history of early Judaism. Indeed, it has not even been taken seriously by the practitioners of Biblical Studies as an essential aspect of the exegesis of texts. Everyone knows about form criticism, redaction criticism, traditiohistorical criticism and several other more recent and tentative approaches to the exegete's craft. But as yet few exegetes take seriously what we may now call canon criticism as the study of the decisive phase in the development of the tradition and therefore in the religious history of which the individual text is a part. This must be considered a serious omission if we are prepared to concede: first, the importance of the location of a text within an ongoing tradition; and second, that canon implies the attempt to impose a definitive shape and meaning on the tradition as it comes to expression in texts.

Part of the problem has to do with excessive emphasis on the "original meaning" of texts in modern critical exegesis. The culprit, one suspects, is an overly heavy and often unim-

aginative use of form criticism, giving the impression in some
instances that form criticism is practically co-extensive with
literary criticism. The irony of the situation is that form criticism, with its attempt to locate the *Sitz im Leben* of a text,
provides a valuable starting point for the reconstruction of the
social world from which the text comes. But to this we must
add the task of reconstructing the different social, intellectual
and religious situations of which the text in its ongoing reinterpretation and reappropriation is a part. To speak, then, of
the historical location of a text implies more than its original
meaning, presuming that this is identifiable. It must also take
account of its open-ended future within an ongoing tradition.

An example may help to illustrate some of the more obvious
shortcomings of the "original meaning" brand of exegesis. In
Ex. 4:24–26 we read how Moses was saved from death at the
hands of Yahweh by the prompt action of his wife in circum-
cising her son. Following the commentaries, we will duly
reach the conclusion that this contains an etiology of circumcision as originally an apotropaic rite preparing for marriage.
At this time it was, of course, administered no earlier than
puberty. The obviously secondary role of the son alongside
Moses points to the historical development leading to infant
circumcision, a situation presupposed in the Priestly work
(Gen. 17:12; Lev. 12:3). To the extent that these deductions
are correct (and we may add that there is still much left
unexplained) we shall have won from the text information of
some historical and sociological interest. But we shall as yet be
completely in the dark as to why this text is located where it
is, what it is doing there, what function it might have in the
larger context to which it belongs. We may then go further
and assign it, with all due reserve, to J, or at least to JE, which
would at once put us under obligation of asking what function
it has in this larger literary context. We would then have to
note that the incident takes place while Moses is returning
from Midian to Egypt to carry out his mission to Pharaoh, and
the inference would perhaps be that circumcision was in some
way essential to the success of the mission. But with this
conclusion our work is not yet done, for we know that JE came
to be incorporated into an even broader literary context by the

priestly-scribal school several centuries later. Hence we must
go on to note that according to P circumcision had been
established long before as a sign of the covenant (Gen. 17).
How then could Moses assume the leadership of the people,
with whom God had sealed his covenant in their very flesh,
with his own son uncircumcised? A reading of the literature of
the exilic period shows what importance circumcision had
assumed for the dispersed communities. To them the message
of this small pericope must have carried a new urgency: how
much store must be placed on circumcision when its neglect
was enough to turn their God from a friend to an enemy?

Later Jewish interpretations of a more or less official nature
highlight the disadvantages of limiting oneself to canonical
meanings. Thus, the targumic tradition finds in the text an
attestation of the vicarious efficacy of sacrifice epitomized in
the shedding of blood.[10] As with the Akedah or Binding of
Isaac (Gen. 22), such a rereading opens up a richer vein of
meaning than is attainable by use of the form critical method.

Redaction study also must take account of the canon as
context. The reason is, of course, that canon implies a positive attempt to give form, structure and meaning to traditional
material by placing it in a particular context. On this point,
an example of somewhat wider significance than the preceding may be introduced. In his well-known essay "The Form-
Critical Problem of the Hexateuch," first published in 1938,[11]
von Rad set out to apply the form critical method to the
Hexateuch as a whole. He was moved to do this, he tells us,
by his conviction that analysis of sources and examination of
individual passages had led further away from the final form
and overall meaning of the Hexateuch. The Hexateuch, he
maintained, could be considered an elaboration of a distinct
genre, the historical credo, found in a more succinct form in
such credal statements as accompanied the offering of
firstfruits (Deut. 26:5–10). Hence, it is possible and necessary
to examine it form-critically, determine its *Sitz im Leben* and
trace its development from an original cultic form to the
baroque elaboration of its final shape and structure.

This is not the place to discuss von Rad's essay in any detail.
It is well known, has been very influential particularly among

American scholars, and has been subjected to some searching
criticism over the last several years.[12] One cannot help asking, though, whether this is really a *form-critical* explanation
of the Hexateuch. As generally understood, form criticism
deals with material traditioned orally which has found its way
into writing. Such is the case with much, but by no means all,
of the material in the first six books of the Bible. To speak of
the Hexateuch as a "form" in anything like the sense in which
the term is used by Gunkel, Gressmann, Bultmann or Norden
must seem rather abusive. It is also by no means clear that this
complex can be adequately explained as a development from a
historical credo. Apart from other problems, it leaves unexplained the considerable amount of material in it which is
neither historical nor credal.

The main problem with von Rad's essay from our present
perspective, however, is the following. Whatever arguments
can be marshalled in favor of a Hexateuch or a Tetrateuch,
what emerged finally was a Pentateuch, and it is this that we
have to explain. This is not to deny that to speak of a
Hexateuch may be an appropriate way of describing a certain
stage in the formation of the traditions. But to leave out of
account the final form, which is a Pentateuch and nothing
else, exposes one to the risk of misrepresenting much of the
material contained in it. For each reshaping of the whole
necessarily affects the internal relation between the parts and
the function and, therefore, significance of each.

Turning to another very influential study, Martin Noth's *A
History of Pentateuchal Tradition*, first published in 1948,[13] we
also find no reference to canon and the related questions we
have been discussing. Like von Rad, Noth sees the cult as
playing a decisive role in the formation of the primary traditions identified as the leading of Israel out of Egypt and
guidance into the arable land (p. 253). These and related
traditions were already more or less fixed in the pre-state
period so that the literary activity of the editors J, E and P
added nothing substantial either in content or point of view
(pp. 248, 250f.). He admits that scholarship must take account of the total context, namely, the Pentateuch, and he
acknowledges the fact that the history of the traditions is an

essential part of the history of Israel (pp. 250, 252). It remains questionable, however, whether the editorial and scribal activity which eventuated in the Pentateuch made as little difference as he maintains. To take an important example: he notes that P omitted the theme of guidance into the arable land, bringing the story to a close with the death of Moses instead, but he does not go on to ask what occasioned this decisive structural alteration and how it affects a reading of the story as a whole. As for the beginning of the story, he works with the common assumption that it starts with the exodus from Egypt but does not feel it necessary to explain why in point of fact the starting point is not the exodus but the creation of the world.[14] Here as elsewhere, then, the history of the traditions must include the editorial history which resulted in the Torah-canon. Both are part of the history of late Israel and early Judaism.

In recent years there have been welcome signs of a revival of interest in the canon as a historical and religious datum. It seems likely that this has arisen out of the collapse of the so-called "Biblical Theology movement" and the concomitant failure to discover a principle of unity running throughout the biblical material—whether the sovereignty of God, the covenant, a particular view of history (*Heilsgeschichte*) or something else.[15] Without trying to evaluate this most recent development as a whole, for which the time is not yet ripe, some indication of the kinds of issues which are being raised ought to be given.

The late Professor George Ernest Wright took the view that the Old Testament canon was the result of an ad hoc decision of the community which amounted to an artificial cutting off of a living tradition. It appears, however, that this general statement was meant to refer only to what he called the marginal books, the inclusion or exclusion of which would make little theological difference anyway. In other words, *Tôrāh* and *Nᵉbîʾîm* provided the interpretative principles according to which the *Kᵉtûbîm* were to be read. Thus there is an "authoritative core" within the canon, and Wright went on to say that each age chooses its own "canon within the canon" according to its perception of what is more or less important and relevant. Thus, classical Judaism finds this core in Torah while scholarship in the early modern period tended to identify it with the prophetic literature. Luther (to move into the Christian canon) found it in Romans while devaluing James, and so on.[16]

While it is obviously true that different ages emphasize different parts of the Bible, to go on to speak of a "canon within the canon" may have the unfortunate effect of leading us to overlook the primary task of understanding the actual historical canon. Further, we do not give an adequate account of its formation in terms of an ad hoc decision, or an "almost artificial" decision (p. 169) made by the community; quite apart from the fact that we know of no point in the formation of the Hebrew canon where such a decision was made. It would be more exact to say that canonicity happens *within* the history and interpretation of the tradition and, as I shall argue, out of conflicting claims to mediate it.

We find a rather different approach in the work of B. S. Childs, especially in his recent book, *Biblical Theology in Crisis.*[17] After tracing the rise and fall of the Biblical Theology movement, he shows up the failure to identify a principle of unity which holds together all of the Christian Bible. His solution is to propose the thesis that "the canon of the Christian church is the most appropriate context from which to do Biblical Theology" (p. 99). Steering clear of Wright's "canon within the canon" and his explanation in terms of ecclesiastical decision, he rightly points out that the formation of the canon is inseparable from the process of critical reinterpretation from which certain writings emerged as canonical and others did not (p. 106).

There are many good things in Childs' book which badly needed saying. It was high time, for example, that someone actively engaged in biblical scholarship spoke out against the hubris of the historical-critical method with its unspoken supposition that the entire previous history of biblical interpretation is to be judged by its standards and inevitably found wanting. It was also opportune to point out some of the ambiguities involved in appealing to the "original meaning" as primary. The practice of form criticism offers many advantages but it cannot lead to an understanding of a passage in context. Childs' emphasis on canon as context provides a valuable way of integrating the historical-critical with other methods and of taking in the entire history of a tradition rather than just its point of origin.

It will be clear from what has been said earlier that the main problem with Childs' view of canon is that it speaks of the Hebrew Scriptures only as a component of the Christian canon and therefore tends to reduce the problem to that of the relation between the testaments. We have seen that canonicity is inseparable from conflicting authority-claims, that these claims are about the right to provide a normative version of the tradition, and that the emergence of Christianity is intelligible only within the formulation and resolution of such claims. The more firmly a claim of this nature is pressed by the religious and intellectual elite in control the greater is the tendency towards sectarianism; and the emergence of sects during the Second Temple period, whether it is dated from the Seleucid epoch or a much earlier time, rests in the last analysis on conflicting hermeneutics with respect to early tradition.[18] What in fact controlled the self-understanding of early Christianity as a Jewish sect[19] was above all an alternative understanding of what Israel was meant to be, an understanding based on its own interpretation of certain biblical texts.

The question may also be asked (and this is not a criticism of Childs) whether the view that only a Christ-centered interpretation of the Old Testament is theologically possible is not itself theologically open to question. It may be asked, in other words, whether there may not be ways of postulating ultimacy of Christ which, in effect if not in intent, rob the history of religions and the history of Judaism in particular of real theological significance. Or whether it may not be possible to over-value Christology at the expense of the logically and theologically prior doctrine of the Trinity.[20]

An even more recent call to "canonical criticism" comes from James A. Sanders in a small book with the title *Torah and Canon*.[21] Sanders is particularly interested in the origins and function of the canon, questions which are closely related to

and continuous with form criticism, redaction criticism, the
history of traditions and comparative midrash. Canon is the
form in which ancient tradition is presented as authoritative.
But linked with authority there is also the question of identity,
since in the process of its formation the canon reflects the
sense of identity and self-understanding of the community. To
study the shape of the canon is to be led back to the hermeneutics of the successive ages in which it was formed. Thus
the Torah-canon takes its shape from the experience of dis-
continuity forced upon Israel during its exiles. This accounts
for the fact that all the laws are pressed into the pre-state
period and explains why the Pentateuch ends not with the
conquest of Canaan but with the death of Moses. At its
center, therefore, stands not a national triumph but a service
of thanksgiving for the promised future restoration (referring
to Deut. 26, the "wandering Aramean passage" so much emphasized by von Rad). In this way Torah preserves for all time
its character of living hope for an exiled people.[22]

Sanders is less concerned with and less clear on the formation of the prophetic collection. His view seems to be that it
was formed, in essence, at the same time as the Torah-canon
though it was not complete until the second century B.C.E.
He does not, however, discuss the problematic relation between Law and Prophecy, apart from saying that the prophets
were tradents and interpreters of the Torah-story for their own
time.

Particularly useful is Sanders' emphasis on the function of
canon in relation to its structure. The major instance, mentioned a moment ago, is the present shape of Torah shorn of
the conquest story as dictated by the experience of destitution
and   exile.   Sanders   realizes,   of   course,   that   the
Deuteronomists, who also decisively influenced the shape of
the tradition, began their work before the destruction of
Jerusalem in 587 B.C.E. He meets a possible objection on this
score by noting that these people were anxious to incorporate
into their work the lessons of the fall of the sister kingdom to
the north 134 years earlier. It remains doubtful, notwithstanding, that either the prospect or the experience of political
destitution was a decisive factor in the publication of a written

law and foundation myth. The fact that religious reform (of the kind presupposed by Deuteronomy) and national revival went together, especially during Josiah's reign, renders this view rather unlikely. And we shall see in more detail in a later chapter that the exilic Priestly work (P) which gave final form to the Pentateuch had a distinct and sustained interest in return to the land.

Renewed attention to the canon opens up the study of the Hebrew Bible to broader perspectives than those shared by most contemporary exegetes. It will tend, for example, to shift attention from original meanings and the prehistory of texts to their function within broad contexts of meaning which are themselves part of what Peter Berger calls the social construction of reality.[23] It will make it less easy for us to speak of the "religion of Israel" and force us to ask whose religion finds expression in the texts we are interpreting. It will raise questions concerning a wide variety of related matters: the role in traditional societies of intellectual and cultic elites, the sociological function of writing, access to and deprivation of power which in the religious context means control of the redemptive media,[24] and the conflict between different claims to authority where what is at stake is the self-understanding of the group within which the claims are staked. And if these questions are considered to fall within the theologian's range of interest, a study of the formation of the canon which takes them into account may even eventually suggest a new way of writing a biblical theology. Study of the canon is not a panacea for Biblical Studies nor can it explain everything. But no historical or theological explanation will be adequate which neglects it.

III. Wellhausen and the Origins of Judaism

The subtitle of this book suggests that the formation of the Hebrew canon is an integral aspect of the origins of Judaism. According to the standard account, the history of Israel came to an end with the loss of national independence in the sixth century B.C.E., and the foundations for a new form of life were laid in Palestine and Babylon, but especially Babylon, during the sixty years from the first deportation under Nebuchadrezzar (598) to the edict of Cyrus permitting the captive peoples to return home (538). After the return at the beginning of the Persian period (the first of several returns), the general trend was in the direction of segregation and isolation which also included rejection of Samaritan claims to participate in the reconstruction. While the Samaritan secession took place definitively only much later, it can be traced back to the rejection of their offer to help rebuild the Jerusalem temple.[25] Judaism is therefore in its earliest phase the religion which took shape among those inhabitants of Judah who resisted assimilation in the *gôlāh* and formed a community apart on their return to Palestine.[26] In this transition from nation to ecclesiastical community organized around the rebuilt temple the dominant role was played by the priesthood. There were still prophets, but prophecy would never be the same again.

Any discussion of the respective roles of priest and prophet in the emergence of Judaism must fall under the long shadow of Wellhausen. As we saw earlier, for Wellhausen the law was subsequent to prophecy. Indeed, his principal thesis in the *Prolegomena* is that since P is the latest rather than the earliest of the Pentateuchal sources the law is the starting point not of Israel but of Judaism (p. v). Judaism resulted from the resolution of the conflict or tension between prophecy and institution. Prophecy, for which Wellhausen had a high regard, gave birth to religious individualism. Judaism preserved it for posterity in spite of itself by encasing its message in the hard shell of a religious institution. The prophets were the religious individualists *par excellence* (pp. 398–399), implying that they approached God without the mediation of religious institutions like the priesthood. Their aim was to transform the state, but when the state collapsed prophecy lost its roots in history, thus preparing the way for apocalyptic in which "hope was released from all obligation to conform to historical conditions" (p. 507). But even before the end of national independence the elaboration of law codes had made its fatal impact on the free exercize of prophecy:

> With the appearance of the law came to an end the old freedom, not only in the sphere of worship, now restricted to Jerusalem, but in the sphere of the religious spirit as well. There was now in existence an authority as objective as could be; and this was the death of prophecy. (p. 402)

According to Wellhausen, then, the forces which, though deeply indebted to prophecy, were fatal to its expression were precisely those which came to constitute the early Jewish ecclesiastical theocracy. They were embedded in Ezra's priestly Pentateuch "canonized" in 444 B.C.E., which became the Magna Carta of Judaism (pp. 404, 408). In its origins, then, Judaism was antithetic to prophecy.

Wellhausen assumed, as did practically all Old Testament scholars, that the priesthood occupied the vacuum created by the collapse of the monarchy. It would be an understatement to say that he did not think highly of this institution and its *chef d'oeuvre*, the Priestly corpus (P). P reconstructed Israel's past in its own image, which means that it judaized it. In the process it transformed early Israel with its natural and spontaneous religious life into an arid ecclesiastical institution. For the living realities of popular religion it substituted dead dogmas (p. 337). The difference between early Israel and early Judaism is the difference between a green tree and dry wood, a fountain and a cistern, the spirit and the letter (pp. 347, 361, 410, 412, etc.). For the priests who elaborated this "petty scheme of salvation" (p. 509) through legal and cultic observance, he has nothing but scorn. "What sort of creative power is that," he asks, "which brings forth nothing but numbers and names?" (p. 361). It seems fair to say, then, that his purpose in writing this work was to drive a wedge between Israel and Judaism, to show that from the former the latter evolved as an entirely different phenomenon.

We cannot evade the question whether this starkly negative evaluation of early Judaism was not just one expression of the anti-semitism which pervaded and poisoned so much of German academic thought throughout the nineteenth century. Under the influence of racial ideology, public expression of anti-Jewish sentiment reached a new high at precisely the time when Wellhausen was publishing his reconstruction of Israel's religious history (1878, 1883). In 1879, for example, Adolf Stöcker, founder of the Christian Social Workers' Party, described Orthodox Judaism in one of his speeches as a "form of religion which is dead at its very core" and in the same year Heinrich von Treitschke, professor of history at the University of Berlin, spoke of the Jews as Germany's misfortune (*"Die Juden sind unser Unglück"*).[27] In one sense, Wellhausen evades the charge since he held identical views about the Christian church which inherited the Jewish ecclesiastical model and was therefore subject to the same strictures. But it must be acknowledged that his presentation of early Judaism stands within a long tradition of denigration which, greatly reinforced by the clarity and persuasiveness of his own work, made its modest contribution in due course to the "final solution" of the Jewish problem under the Third Reich.

In view of the enormous influence of Wellhausen's reconstruction of the religious history of Israel and early Judaism it is of some importance to understand what were its inspirational origins. We saw earlier that the influence of Romanticism, though far less often acknowledged than that of Hegel, must be taken into account. It is the Romantic glorification of natural man living a spontaneous existence close to the soil and to the cycles of nature which lies beneath Wellhausen's admiration for both the religion of ancient Israel and the untrammeled individualism of the prophets. It was the same influence, we may add, which contributed not a little to the emergence of the Teutonic *Volk* theories during the Napoleonic wars, which were to reach their furthest and most bizarre expression in the pseudo-philosophizing of Alfred Rosenberg. It is an open question whether Wellhausen's representation of ancient Israel as a *Volk* which expressed itself in a religion of nature was directly indebted to such ideas. But his debt to the kind of Romanticism represented by Herder is unmistakably clear and at least as significant as his debt to Hegel.[28]

Towards the beginning of the *Prolegomena* Wellhausen tells us that he learned the most and the best from Wilhelm Vatke, a student of Hegel's whose *Biblische Theologie*, published in

1835, applied Hegel's philosophy of history to the history of the religion of Israel. The way this worked out enabled Vatke, and the many who followed his lead, to demonstrate the superiority of Christianity and the concomitant fact that Judaism, together with all other religions, was now completely superseded. But Judaism stood on a higher level than paganism since it represented the passage from the natural to the ideal in the evolution of the Absolute Spirit towards the concrete spirituality of the New Testament. There was for Vatke, therefore, an intrinsic link between Judaism and Christianity, if of a kind decidedly disadvantageous to the former. For Wellhausen, however, the religious history of Israel does not follow the classical Hegelian model. The thesis of the early naturalistic phase is followed by the antithesis of the priestly hierocracy but there is no synthesis; for Israel's religious life ended in *Erstarrung*, the torpidity and rigor mortis of a legalistic and ritualistic institution.[29] In this respect the Christian church was the heir of Judaism and stood in relation to the message of Jesus in much the same way as Judaism did to the message of the prophets.

While there were perhaps few major Old Testament scholars of the nineteenth century who were explicitly and openly anti-Jewish (Friedrich Delitzsch comes to mind as a particularly flagrant example of these few), it is sadly necessary to acknowledge that the discipline was carried on to a considerable extent under presuppositions decidedly unfavorable to a positive theological evaluation of Judaism. This was true whether the dominant influence was the rationalism of the Enlightenment, which dictated a cultured despisal of the miracles and miscellaneous crudities of the Hebrew Scriptures, or a humanism which devalued the Semitic Old Testament in favor of the Greek New Testament (consonant with the Semitic-Aryan dichotomy of the racial theorists), or a Hegelianism which at the very best relegated Judaism to a superseded stage of evolution.[30] Perhaps on the whole the most straightforward and honest view was that of the modern-day Marcionites (including such distinguished names as Schleiermacher at the beginning and Harnack at the end of the century) who believed that the Old Testament was an unnecessary and expendable burden for the Christian. At any rate, the intellectual climate of that long period which saw the consolidation of the critical study of the Hebrew Scriptures goes a long way toward explaining why there was practically no collaboration between Jewish and Christian scholars and why, consequently, the theological problem posed by the on-going existence of Israel was never faced by Christian scholars. Needless to say, the problem is still there today.

It is perhaps fortunate that Wellhausen's bias against religious institutions, especially ritual and law, is so obvious as not to require exposure. We now know better than to regard popular or "natural" religions as unstructured and unin-stitutionalized, and the work of anthropologists—Mary Douglas and Victor Turner, for example—has made it impossible to think of ritual as an artificial exercise divorced from the real life of human communities. More to our point, it is no longer possible to set prophecy over against institution in the way Wellhausen did. A closer reading of the texts has shown that the prophets were not the kind of individualists Wellhausen took them to be. Closer acquaintance with the culture of the ancient Near East (to which Wellhausen was singularly indif-ferent) has confirmed the view that institutions such as the monarchy and the priesthood were thought of as vehicles of salvation, and that in Israel as well, salvation was through institutions, not in spite of them. And, finally, a deeper and more sympathetic study of the Priestly work has brought to light the more positive and expansive aspects of its *Welt-anschauung.*

In spite of all this, the problem posed by Wellhausen in his *Prolegomena* remains; and while we feel obliged to discard his bias we are in his debt for having posed the problem so clearly. Judaism did emerge as a religion based on a normative order, a *tôrāh* written and interpreted authoritatively by priests and scribes. An important concomitant of this circumstance was the relegation of prophecy to an epoch in the past, though the words of the prophets remained as a threat to any "definitive" interpretation of the tradition. We cannot understand this situation simply by taking certain statements in the Talmud at face value. We have to traverse once again much of the ground covered by Wellhausen giving close attention to the formation of the canon and the historical and theological problems which it raises. This may open up ways into the meaning and essence of Judaism which are not apparent in orthodox statements.

2: Deuteronomy: The First Stage

I. The Emergence of Legal Scribalism

"THE CONNECTING LINK BETWEEN OLD AND NEW, BE-
tween Israel and Judaism, is everywhere Deuteronomy." If this
view of Wellhausen is correct,[1] it means that the authors of
this book have better claim than anyone else to be considered
the founders of Judaism. Deuteronomy[2] stands at the beginning of the process which led Judaism, and afterwards Christianity and Islam, to be regarded as a religion of the book. It
speaks consistently, for the first time, not of laws but *the* law, a
law written down and publicly available which could not be
altered.[3] To be sure, the earlier tradents known to modern
scholarship as J and E spoke either of Yahweh or Moses writing
the laws at Sinai,[4] and Deuteronomy is itself presented as the
legacy of Moses handed over to Israel on the day of his death.
Moreover, the "canonical formula" forbidding alterations
or additions to (and therefore conferring special authority on)
an official document has venerable precedent in law codes
and treaties of high antiquity in the Near East.[5] This, however, does not alter the fact that Deuteronomy represents a
decisive turning point with respect to conflicting authority-
claims during the period of the monarchy. Since, moreover,
such claims had to be staked in writing, it is at least clear that
scribal activity played an important role in the production of
such canonical documents. It would then be reasonable to
explore the hypothesis that the scribes contributed in some
way to the production of the Deuteronomic law book.

24

A class of professional scribes or sages (for the moment the terms may be taken as practically interchangeable) is first attested in Israel with the passage to monarchy and the creation of a state system towards the beginning of the first millenium B.C.E. The reason for its emergence at this time was clearly the need for trained personnel in the various branches of government. Since the skill basic to all others—especially for the career diplomat—was writing, it is no surprise to find both David and Solomon served by scribes (2 Sam. 8:17; 20:25; 1 Kings 4:2–3). The function of these people was certainly not restricted to writing. On the probable assumption that both kings borrowed from the Egyptian model of statecraft, scribes should rather be thought of as high-ranking officials with important executive functions.[6] Closely associated with the scribes (*sop*e*rîm*) must have been the royal counselors (*yo*ᵉ*ṣîm*)[7] of whom the best known from this early period is Ahithophel the Gilonite. But in this context *the* depository of sagacity was the king himself. In judicial matters David's wisdom was like that of the angel of God (2 Sam. 14:17, 20; 19:27) while that of Solomon became proverbial (1 Kings 3:6ff.). It will be recalled that one of the titles of the idealized king in Isaiah is "Wonderful Counsellor" while another poem in the same collection, probably from the exilic age, attributes to him the spirit of wisdom, understanding and counsel.[8] It is clear that this kind of language derived from the theology of sacral kingship originating in the great riverine civilizations of the ancient Near East.

It has often been noted that at this early stage "wisdom" was not intrinsically and essentially concerned with religious and ethical values. At its best it was humanistic and enlightened and laid the basis for what there was of higher education in ancient Israel. Often enough, however, it appears far removed from a religious vision of life and somewhat laconic in ethical matters—witness the last words of the dying David to his son Solomon (1 Kings 2:6, 9). The case of Ahithophel, mentioned a moment ago, is instructive in showing how the seeds of conflict between this kind of "secular" wisdom and the traditional Yahvistic faith were already being sown. We are told that the counsel which he gave was as if one consulted the oracle of God (2 Sam. 16:23), which may be taken to indicate that the counsel ('*ēṣāh*) of the professional sage was now in competition with the traditional appeal to priestly or prophetic oracles. David prayed against this counsel (2 Sam. 15:31), and the conclusion of the narrative shows that the prayer was answered. Thus it seems right to speak of an uneasy co-existence of the sage's counsel with the priestly and prophetic word of revelation.[9] In the course of time it was to develop into an open confrontation on such basic issues as the real source of power in the community and the criteria for political and religious action.

Our sources are explicit that the reign of Hezekiah (715–687) was marked by a great deal of scribal activity. The first king to complete his reign without a counterpart in the sister kingdom to the north, he seems to have modelled himself on Solomon as patron of the cultured classes, builder of imposing monuments and probably also founder of scribal schools.[10] A section of the Book of Proverbs is attributed to "the men of Hezekiah" (25:1ff.) and the Babylonian Talmud attributes the whole of Proverbs as well as the Canticle, Qoheleth and Isaiah to him and his men.[11] In addition to collections of didactic and gnomic material, it is also possible that the redaction of the old traditions (JE) took place during his reign. The destruction of the Kingdom of Samaria six years before it began would in all likelihood have brought many refugees into Judah including those among the official custodians of the traditions who had survived. About the same time, incidentally, the great library of Nineveh was established to receive copies of ancient texts prepared by Assyrian scribes, and further afield the Homeric poems were being redacted into their present form.

It is probably not coincidental that the first references to the writing down of prophetic utterances date from the same period. The command given Isaiah to seal the prophetic instruction (*tôrāh*) and testimony (*te'ûdāh*) among his disciples very probably implies writing (Is. 8:16–22), especially when taken together with the reference elsewhere in the book to a vision which is like a sealed book in that no one can read and understand it (29:11–12). It appears, further, that the writing of a prophetic oracle was certified by a solemn act of witnessing, the most likely purpose of which was to authenticate the prophetic word at the time of future fulfillment.[12] This last point is particularly clear at 30:8ff. where Isaiah is commanded to write an oracle on a clay tablet and in a book that it may stand as an eternal witness against faithless Israel. Later prophets receive similar commands,[13] the point being to establish the authenticity of the saying and therefore the authority of its source.

It is important to note that the claim to a hearing staked by a prophet like Isaiah would have had significant political repercussions. Whatever his situation in life previous to his calling,[14] Isaiah played a notable political role during the reigns of Ahaz and Hezekiah. Hence the frequent criticism of the sages (including high officials of the kind referred to earlier) which we find in Isaiah involved more than just strictly religious issues. Put simply, the question concerned the real source of power and how to tap it. Should the king act on the basis of plans drawn up by his statesmen or follow the advice of his prophet? In Is. 5:18–25 Isaiah condemns those who say, in effect, if Yahweh has a plan we can use, let him produce it! It is these same people who, wise in their own eyes, reject the word of God revealed by the prophet (vv. 21, 24).[15] The prophet was certain that his calling gave him privileged access to the divine world and that the messages which came to him from it had to take effect in the political sphere. We must suppose that the sages and counsellors continued, not without reason, to view things differently.

There are no doubt other reasons which led to the publication in writing of prophetic admonitions and comminations about this time. The constant threat posed by Assyrian imperial designs certainly had something to do with it. More specifically, the new Assyrian policy of treating with the entire population of a vassal state rather than with its ruler alone, a policy well illustrated in the parleying before Jerusalem recorded in 2 Kings 18, may help to explain the novel element in prophetic sayings attested in Amos and thereafter.[16] It remains nonetheless clear that the prophet's claim to a hearing involved him increasingly in conflict with state officials, especially those charged with responsibility in the religious sphere.

The Deuteronomic historian informs us that Hezekiah removed the "high places" and carried through reforms in the Jerusalem cultus (2 Kings 18:4 cf. v. 22). The Chronicler goes even further and speaks of repairs carried out on the temple, a thorough clean-up followed by rededication, the renewal of the covenant and a great festive Passover celebrated in Jerusalem. These and other reforms were also extended to the territory formerly constituting the Kingdom of Samaria (2 Chron. 29–31). As was the case later on during the reign of Josiah, these actions must be connected with the expectation of political emancipation. Very likely Hezekiah profited by the death of Sargon II in 705 to assert his independence. This brought on him the anger of Sargon's successor Sennacherib, and while Jerusalem managed to survive the attack of the latter in 702-701 most of the rest of the country remained under Assyrian or Philistine control. But Hezekiah seems to have stayed close to the anti-Assyrian forces which were gathering their strength (witness the delegation he received from the king of Babylon, 2 Kings 20:12–13), so that his attempts to purify Yahvism of foreign influences were hardly confined to one period in his reign.

Hezekiah's proscription of foreign cults and abolition of the local Judean cult-centers (the "high places"), which correspond to major points in Deuteronomic law, have led several scholars to place the origins of the movement which led to the production of Deuteronomy in this reign. Others, however, point out that the record of Hezekiah's religious reforms makes no mention of a book;[17] but this observation is hardly decisive one way or the other. It should not be overlooked that there had been sporadic religious reforms in the Kingdom of Judah from the time of Asa in the late tenth century. These aimed at the removal of Canaanite abuses (fertility symbols, cultic prostitution and the like) and the purification of the temple cultus. After the overthrow of the baalist queen Athaliah (ca. 837) dispositions were also made for the regular upkeep of the temple fabric and its appointments, and in this and other instances we hear of a solemn covenant being made, the purpose

of which was clearly to repristinate the ancient Yahvistic traditions.[18] Thus there was little specifically new in Josiah's
reforms—which were also no less ephemeral than those which
preceded them—with the exception of the discovery of the
law book during repairs on the temple (2 Kings 22:3ff.).
Rather than argue, then, for either the reign of Hezekiah or
the reign of Manasseh as the starting point for the
Deuteronomic movement, it would seem better to view it
within the context of the entire history of cultic and
nationalistic reform in the Kingdom of Judah.

For our present purpose the important question concerns
the identity of the people who made up what we have called
"the Deuteronomic movement" and who therefore were responsible for the book of Deuteronomy. Here, if anywhere,
the adage *tot capita quot sententiae* applies, and it would be
foolhardy to imagine that this situation will easily change. But
while much is uncertain, some things are less uncertain than
others, and these should first be stated before opting for one
category to the exclusion of others.

On the basis of evidence in the book for the impact of
prophetic thinking (which has never been denied) scholars
have from time to time argued for prophetic authorship.[19]
One of the most obvious difficulties here consists in interpreting the diverse phenomenon of prophecy prior to
Deuteronomy and the different ways in which the book itself
speaks of it. One suspects also that if this hypothesis were
correct we would be entitled to look for a rather more sympathetic treatment of prophecy than we actually find (13:1–5;
18:20–22). There is, moreover, the question of Jeremiah's
attitude to the Deuteronomic reform to which we shall return
later.

What then of the priesthood? It seems that we must exclude
the Jerusalem temple priesthood since the book lacks any distinct reference to the cultic and dynastic traditions cherished
in temple and court. The traditions which it does contain are,
on the contrary, of Ephraimite origin and hark back to the old
Shechem federation. Yet priests, generally referred to as
"levitical priests," are very prominent in the book. They serve
at the "place which the LORD will choose" (12:14, etc.),

namely Jerusalem, are entrusted with the law book, preach it, apply it in the form of judicial decisions, and are responsible for seeing that the king also obeys it.[20] This is in keeping with attestations throughout the pre-exilic period that one of the primary responsibilities of the priesthood was to maintain and expound the laws.

But who are these "levitical priests" with whom the book is so much concerned? It emerges clearly from one of the laws that both the Jerusalem clergy and those scattered throughout the country may be described as Levites:

> When a Levite comes from any settlement in Israel where he may be lodging to the place which the LORD will choose, if he comes in the eagerness of his heart and ministers in the name of the LORD his God, like all his fellow-Levites who attend on the LORD there, he shall have an equal share of food with them, besides what he may inherit from his father's family. (18:6–8)

There were therefore two classes of Levites: those in the country who are classed with aliens and fatherless as in need of welfare,[21] and the clergy actually in office in Jerusalem who are variously described as "the tribe of Levi" (10:8; 18:1), "Levi" (10:9), "the priests, the sons of Levi" (10:8; 18:1), "levitical priests" or simply "the priests" (17:12; 18:3; 19:17; 26:3–4). Only in the recital of the curses in chapter 27, generally taken to be a later addition stemming from the Deuteronomic school in the exilic period, do we find a distinction unknown to the original book between levitical priests who conduct the ceremony (v. 9) and Levites who pronounce the curses (v. 14)—with, for good measure, the secular tribe of Levi lined up with five other tribes on Mount Gerizim to represent the blessing (v. 12).[22] We may conclude, therefore, that there is no *essential* distinction in the book between Levites living in various cities and settlements throughout the land and the temple clergy in Jerusalem in that the former enjoyed in principle the rights and prerogatives of the priesthood.[23] The authors of the book, whoever they were, were in no way opposed to the institution of the priesthood so understood. Use of the term "levitical priests" suggests, however, that they had in mind the ancient order of Levites as ideally constituting the priestly class. While the Levites present one of the most obscure and baffling problems in Israelite history, it seems at least clear that they were intimately associated with the institutions and laws of the ancient tribal federation, especially with its judicial and military operations, and that they had close connections with prophecy in its early stages. It also seems likely that their specifically priestly prerogatives did not exclude preaching and instruction.[24] This being the case, much of the material in the book could perhaps be explained quite plausibly on the hypothesis of Levitical authorship.

At this point we should probably suspend judgment while we return for a moment to the scribes, part of whose history was outlined at the beginning of the chapter. In the lists of royal officials from the time of the United Monarchy, scribes are invariably named alongside priests (2 Sam. 8:17; 20:25; 1 Kings 4:2–3). That this is not a chance juxtaposition is suggested by the fact that at a later time scribes share responsibility with priests for the maintenance of the temple fabric and of worship in general (2 Kings 12:11ff.; 22:3ff.; cf. Neh. 13:13). In the reign of Josiah the scribe Shaphan was commissioned to supervise repair work in the temple and it was to him that the scroll found during that work was consigned. He read it to the king and, together with his son Ahikam and others, was sent to consult with the prophetess Huldah in much the same way that an earlier scribe, Shebnah, consulted with Isaiah (2 Kings 19:2; 22:14). The scribal family of Shaphan continued to play an important role in political and religious life well into the exilic period. Their influence was responsible for saving Jeremiah's life in the year 609 (Jer. 26:24) and it was in the temple apartment of another member of the family that Baruch read the prophet's oracles (Jer. 36:10). Yet another Shaphanite was among those commissioned to carry a letter from Jeremiah to the exiles (Jer. 29:3)[25] and, not least important, the first governor of the province conquered by the Babylonians was Gedaliah, grandson of Shaphan (2 Kings 25:22). He, too, seems to have been favorably disposed towards Jeremiah.

We cannot, of course, assume that scribes had a hand in the production of the law book simply because one of them was present at its discovery and his colleagues were involved in its promulgation.[26] For the clear emergence of the figure of the legal scribe we have to wait until well into the post-exilic period. Ezra is both priest and scribe and learned in the law.[27] Just over a century later Jesus ben Sirach paints a portrait of the typical member of his class as forming the intellectual elite, taking part in public affairs, teaching, instructing, handing down decisions in matters of law (Sir. 38:24–39:11). A useful if imperfect analogy might be the medieval schoolman who often played an important role in public affairs without surrendering his religious functions. As for the Chronicler, if we leave aside references to scribes paralleled in his principal source, he seems to restrict scribalism almost entirely to Levites.[28] The almost total absence of hard data makes it extremely hazardous to work back from these (and other) sources from the period of the Second Temple to that of the monarchy. Legal scribalism presupposes a written and authoritative law and this is not clearly attested before the time of Josiah. It is possible, therefore, but for the moment no more than possible, that it originated with those who were responsible for the production of the book of Deuteronomy.

Confirmation for this hypothesis is often sought in the book itself. The distinctive form of Israel's wisdom is observance of the (Deuteronomic) law, and to the extent that she observes it Israel will be regarded by her neighbors as wise and understanding (4:6), a truth which itself can be understood only by the wise (32:6, 29). In keeping with ancient and well-attested beliefs, the judiciary system requires wisdom in order to avoid the temptation of corruption to which it always lies open (1:13; 16:19). The statement that a bribe blinds the eyes of the wise (16:19) is a typically Deuteronomic reformulation of an ancient law (cf. Ex. 23:8), and the more general insistence on wisdom as an attribute of rulers is also in keeping with Deuteronomic formulations.[29] What we find in the book, then, is not just law but expressions of legal piety formulated after the manner of the scribal schools and, therefore—not surprisingly—quite close at several points to material in Proverbs and other scribal productions in the Hebrew Scriptures. Quite apart from the question of authorship, this legal piety of Deuteronomy must be seen as a distinct and original contribution and, indeed, as a turning point in the religious history of Israel. For from it stemmed not only the distinctive Jewish concern for the regulation of human activity by law but also what might be termed the first attempts at a speculative theology in Judaism. Without the work of the Deuteronomists, whoever they were, the wisdom theology which finds expression in such passages as Prov. 8, Job 28 and Sir. 24 is hardly conceivable.

It is of course possible to go beyond this point into questions of rhetorical criticism, genre study and *Weltanschauung,* but only at risk of mistaking possibilities for probabilities and probabilities for certainties. There is also the widespread tendency to find "wisdom influences" lurking in every text. Yet there are undoubtedly some impressive parallels between the legal and paranetic material in the book and didactic material in overtly sapiential collections like Proverbs. The clear educational intent of the authors of Deuteronomy, the abundant provision of motivation, the insistence on retribution—one of the most familiar themes of old Israelite, Mesopotamian and Egyptian scribes—and the wide variety of rhetorical techniques and paranetic formulations used[30] would not *prove* that scribal sages had a hand in the composition of the book. They would, however, enable one to make out a *prima facie* case for such a hypothesis assuming it was not ruled out on other grounds.

It will be clear by now that the greatest single obstacle to our arriving at anything like a consensus on the authorship of Deuteronomy is the defective state of our knowledge of both scribes and Levites during the late monarchic period. We may, however, be sure of one thing, that the real situation was rather less simple and clear-cut than the historians and exegetes represent it. It is likely, for example, that scribalism was not a uniform and unidimensional thing. In the Greco-Roman period, and probably also much earlier, there were scribes belonging to the laity, Levites and priests and claiming allegiance to different parties. There were scribes too who had a

wide variety of competences. The Chronicler tends, as we
have seen, to concentrate almost exclusively on levitical
scribalism for his own good reasons. The levitical scribalism to
which he attests and to which he himself probably belonged
must have been well-established by the time he wrote, since
we can think of no good reason why he should have invented
it lock, stock and barrel. Indeed, his belief that it had behind
it a long history stretching back into the time of the monarchy
should not be too quickly discounted. We have to bear in
mind, of course, that the term "Levite" did not designate a
lower order of temple clergy before the time of Deuteronomy.
But when he tells us that Levites who were excluded from the
cult in the Northern Kingdom began to come south during the
reign of Rehoboam (2 Chron. 11:14, cf. 1 Kings 12:31; 13:33)
we have no good reason to disbelieve him; and this notice may
in fact be a neglected but important factor in explaining the
presence of northern traditions in Deuteronomy. Nor does it
seem to be intrinsicially improbable that the same class of
people played a prominent part in the sporadic reforms carried
out by Judahite kings, imparting religious instruction and at
times attaining to high status in the scribal hierarchy.[31] The
least we can say, at any rate, is that this information is on the
whole consistent with other arguments urged by those scholars
who defend levitical authorship of Deuteronomy.[32] This cannot be the whole story since levitical authorship does not by
itself explain how the book won official recognition in circles
closest to the king so as to become, in effect, the law of the
land. It would, in particular, be reasonable to assume (though
impossible to prove) that it passed through the hands of
scribes who enjoyed a higher status in the political hierarchy,
given the fact that the Deuteronomic law book, whatever its
origins, emerged in the reign of Josiah as a powerful instrument of national policy.[33]

There will obviously be much in the preceding attempt to
describe the situation which will be open to criticism and
revision. Arguments over Deuteronomy which go back to de
Wette's pioneer study of 1805 will go on and there will be no
consensus. It has been shown that scribalism in Israel and
early Judaism has a long and complex history which is only

very imperfectly known. The same is true of leviticism, which, however, certainly overlaps with scribalism. At some point scribes assumed the task of writing and interpreting law. This could not easily have antedated Deuteronomy and it is a reasonable assumption that it accompanied the official recognition and promulgation of the book in the late preexilic period. This event, of decisive importance for the understanding of nascent Judaism, can only be grasped in the context of conflicting claims to authority in the religious sphere, claims which involved on the one hand intellectual and ecclesiastical *literati* and on the other prophets like Isaiah and Jeremiah.

II. The Deuteronomic Law and Jeremiah

In order to understand what "law" means in Deuteronomy, a word must first be said about meanings attached to it before the composition of the book.[34] It will fortunately not be necessary to delve into the question of an "original" meaning or the even more treacherous area of etymology on which a great deal beside the point has been written. A more useful point of departure for our purpose is the assumption that *tôrāh* is best defined in function of the office or institution which dispenses it. Jeremiah puts a fairly clear statement on the subject into the mouths of his opponents. In plotting against him, they insist that "law (*tôrāh*) must not perish from the priest, nor counsel (*'ēṣāh*) from the sage, nor the word (*dābār*) from the prophet" (Jer. 18:18, cf. Ezek. 7:26). In this context *tôrāh* would most naturally refer to legal decisions handed down by the priest, especially in cultic matters, or perhaps instruction in a more general sense, again with special but not exclusive reference to the cult. At all events, competence in *tôrāh* could be expected of the priest, though it was not always forthcoming, and this situation is presupposed for the whole of the biblical period.[35] But the word can also refer to prophetic teaching, the characteristically prophetic "word of the LORD" being attested in parallelism with *tôrāh*.[36] In the broader sense of instruction, including religious instruction, one could also speak of a parent's *tôrāh*,[37] though the dispenser *par excellence* of such instruction was the sage or professional teacher.[38] This, then, is the situation in the earlier period which must be borne in mind as we go on to consider the emerging conflict of jurisdictional claims during the late monarchy.

It will be clear on reading Deuteronomy and other Deuteronomic compositions that a rather far-reaching change has taken place in the understanding of law which is reflected in the way *tôrāh* is used in these writings. In Pentateuchal sources which modern scholarship dates to an earlier period, *tôrāh* generally stands for an individual stipulation of law and there is no unequivocal case where it refers to a legal corpus.[39] The same is true of pre-Deuteronomic historical narrative,[40] and in the earliest prophetic collections the occurrences of the word are few and far between and their precise meaning hardly ever possible to establish with certainty.[41] However, in Deuteronomy, the Deuteronomic history and other writings edited by these people, the individual stipulations are no longer called *tôrôt* (laws) but *dibrē hattôrāh* (words of the law).[42] Numerous references to "the Torah" or "the book of the Torah"[43] point unmistakably to an authoritative written corpus of law, legal interpretation and instruction; in other words, to what we find in the book of Deuteronomy itself. The meaning of this shift is clear: there is now available an authoritative *tôrāh* which takes precedence over all other claims to provide guidance to the community.

In view of the far-reaching nature of the prophet's claim to authority as messenger of the divine overlord, it was predictable if not inevitable that a *tôrāh* fixed in writing would sooner or later provoke conflict. As it happened, one of the major prophetic figures of Israel was active at the time of the Josian reform and the promulgation of Deuteronomy as the law of the land. No one doubts that the attitude of Jeremiah to the Josian reform and the Deuteronomic Torah is both very important and very difficult to determine. We can conclude little from the good relations which seem to have existed, as noted earlier, between him and the family of the scribe Shaphan. Quite apart from doubts as to how extensive their role was in the reform, their attitude to the holy man may have been dictated by nothing more than prudent respect—a respect, we may add, which appears quite justified in view of what happened to the prophet Hananiah and the priest Pash-hur.[44] We do know that Jeremiah found himself in frequent opposition to priests, sages and state prophets and spared no words in denouncing them. At one point he mentions a class of "handlers of *tôrāh,*" who appear from the context to be distinct from priests (2:8), and it would obviously be of inter-est to know who these people were. Analogous phrases else-where in the Hebrew Scriptures (handlers of weapons and musical instruments, for example) suggest the meaning of a special skill in *tôrāh,* and presumably not just in writing it.[45] While we must be careful not to make too hard and fast a distinction between scribes and ecclesiastics, that the em-phasis here is on *scribal* activity appears highly probable. Later on we find a similar accusation:

> How can you say, 'We are wise,
>   we have the law of the LORD,'
> when scribes with their lying pens
>   have falsified it?
> The wise men are put to shame, they are
>   dismayed and have lost their wits.
> They have spurned the word of the LORD,
>   and what sort of wisdom is theirs? (8:8–9)

From the sarcastic allusions which he often makes to foreign sages,[46] and even more so from the admonitions he addresses to those of his own people (e.g., 9:23), it is clear that Jeremiah was in general deeply suspicious of the claims of the sages as Isaiah was before him. In this instance, the claim to wisdom is based on possession of the Torah of the LORD, and the context makes it clear that he is speaking of a *written* Torah. Moreover, the close association in that book between *torah* and wisdom makes the claim to be wise, advanced here, more readily intelligible. There is also more than a suggestion that possession of the written law brings not only wisdom but political security; and we are reminded of the political impli-cations of the rediscovered law book and the unpopular politi-

cal stance of Jeremiah in the years following the death of
Josiah.

What is important to note here is that misplaced confidence in the possession of a written law goes with rejection of
the word of Yahweh as delivered by the prophet. It is this word
which establishes the legitimacy of the prophet's teaching
which, in Jeremiah and other prophetic books, can also go
under the name of *tôrāh*.[47] What is at stake, then, is the
identification and location of that *tôrāh* which must provide
the authoritative basis for the life of the community. So on
the one side we have the authors of Deuteronomy attempting
to cope with the fundamentally ambiguous phenomenon of
prophecy (13:1–5; 18:15–22) and on the other prophets like
Jeremiah struggling to assert their claim to a hearing over
against the ecclesiastical *literati* who have donned the mantle
of Moses. As Max Weber pointed out, this is a situation likely
to occur at a certain point of any religious organization's development.[48]

To avoid misunderstanding it must be emphasized that
Jeremiah is not asking his contemporaries to choose between
revealed law and the prophetic word; for the prophet also—
and he in particular—proclaims the covenant law and
threatens with the curse those who transgress it. His attack is
aimed rather at a misplaced confidence arising out of possession of a law written down, edited and authoritatively interpreted. This confidence, he is saying, blinds the official political and religious leadership, including priests, scribes and
stipended prophets, to what is actually taking place or, to put
it more prophetically, to what God is doing in the world. It is
not surprising, therefore, that by the time of the Josian reform
and its aftermath the writing down of prophetic oracles and
discourses is a much more overtly polemical act than it was in
the time of Hezekiah and Isaiah.[49] Here especially the act of
writing is *the* way of making a claim stick, even though in the
circumstances it could only be vindicated in the future.

There is no easy way, and perhaps no way at all, of attaining
certainty on the relation between Jeremiah and the
Deuteronomic reform and law.[50] What is, rather, of decisive
importance here is the advancing of a claim to final and exclu-

sive authority *by means of writing* with which the prophetic claim was irreconcilable. To put it more clearly, Deuteronomy produced a situation in which prophecy could not continue to exist without undergoing profound transformations, and the Deuteronomic history put its seal on this achievement (as we shall see shortly) by "canonizing" the prophets as belonging to a past dispensation. It might be considered misleading or flippant to say that for them, as for rabbinic orthodoxy, the only good prophet is a dead prophet. But in point of fact the Deuteronomic scribes, despite their evident debt to and respect for the prophets, contributed decisively to the eclipse of the kind of historically oriented prophecy (*Geschichtsprophetie*) represented by Jeremiah and the emergence in due course of quite different forms of scribal prophecy.

III. Prophecy in Deuteronomy

If this view of the matter is correct, we would expect it to be supported by what is said or implied about prophecy in Deuteronomy and other Deuteronomic writings. Before going on to test this hypothesis, one or two preliminary remarks about this substantial corpus are in order:

(i) The accumulated evidence from stylistic, rhetorical and source analysis has suggested that it is just as appropriate to speak of a "Deuteronomic school" as it is for historians of Christianity to speak of an Antiochean or Alexandrian school. By this term we mean a theological and exegetical tradition extending over several lifetimes in the hands of people sharing more or less the same presuppositions and methods. So understood, the Deuteronomic school, whose origins date back well before the Josian reform, survived the destruction of the state in 587 and continued on throughout the exilic period, whether in Palestine or Babylon need not for the moment be discussed. Post-exilic writings assume at several points familiarity with the Deuteronomic law, and the reforming activity of Nehemiah presupposes Deuteronomic rather than Priestly legislation.[51] This may mean no more than that Deuteronomy was in force as the law of the land

down to the mission of Ezra. At all events, the influence of
the book remained very great, and no one will need to be
reminded how important it was for both early Christianity and
the Qumran community.

(ii) The position has been taken that the work of the
Deuteronomists is best understood as resulting from the confluence of the ancient scribal tradition and the legal-
covenantal piety of clergy outside of the state sanctuary.

(iii) Any assessment of the Deuteronomic view of prophecy
must rest on a prior assessment of the character of the corpus
as a whole. Thus it is important to note that Deuteronomy,
which is cast in the form of a farewell discourse or valedictory
of Moses delivered on the day of his death, is essentially a
pseudepigraphal work, a genre which was to become so popular in the Greco-Syrian and Greco-Roman periods. This
means that where it speaks of historical realities it assumes a
prophetic and predictive view which is, however, really retrospective; and where it speaks of the future its vision will tend
to be controlled by theoretical and utopian considerations
drawn from its understanding of the past. The character of the
Deuteronomic history is different since it is determined by an
etiological imperative—the need to explain the catastrophes
of 721 and 587 and in so doing give an answer to the problem
of theodicy which they raised. This called for a forceful reinterpretation of Israel's history in which prophecy played a
crucial role.

(iv) It is assumed in what follows, as the best explanation
offered to date, that Deuteronomy was expanded and incorporated into the Deuteronomic history during the exilic
period.[52] The process by which the book was again separated
from the history and joined with the Priestly Tetrateuch will
be taken up in a later chapter.

How, then, does the law book understand prophecy? We
have seen that the perspective adopted is that of Moses on the
day of his death in Moab. This allowed the division of the
history into a before and after: the normative period from
Sinai to the promulgation of the law in Moab; that of infidelity and lost opportunity following on the death of Moses.[53] In
the normative period the only prophetic figure is that of Moses

himself. As such, his ministry recapitulates every aspect of prophecy including denunciation, intercession and the prediction of the future.[54] Since Moses is the prophet *par excellence*, and since this prophetic portrait draws on the historical experience of prophecy, we may expect that the description in the book of his person and ministry will betray something of the Deuteronomic understanding of prophecy.[55]

To state first what is most obvious, Moses is above all concerned with the law. He does not originate it but receives it at Horeb on behalf of the people. His communication of the law is expressed in a great variety of ways: he speaks, announces, expounds, teaches and gives instruction in it.[56] As with the canonical prophets, his discourse is both exhortatory and comminatory (e.g., Deut. 8:19–20) and is concerned above all with the prohibition of idolatry (e.g., 4:15-16). When, as frequently happens, the people disregard the law, he prays and intercedes for them, and his intercession is accompanied by ascetical practices and the voluntary acceptance of suffering.[57] In all of this the Deuteronomic Moses mediates between the LORD and his people in the covenant bond; not unexpectedly, since this is the principal function of the prophet as attested explicitly in the book.[58]

The preceding are inferences drawn from the Mosaic addresses which form the framework to the law code in chapters 12–26. The latter, however, contains two passages which deal explicitly with prophecy; one, we may say, negative and the other positive. Deut. 13:2–6 is the first of three ordinances drawn up in the familiar casuistic form and having the purpose of eliminating the contagious disease of apostasy. The three possible sources of contagion are: prophets and dreamers, relatives and friends, a city infiltrated by unbelievers. They all follow more or less the same pattern: protasis, apodosis in the form of apodictic command, paranetic expansion using familiar Deuteronomic clichés, pronouncement of death penalty and appropriate conclusion.[59] Read in this form-critical context it becomes clear that the first of the three is not concerned to say anything about prophecy as such. The prophet (*nābî*) is bracketed with the dreamer (*ḥolem ḥᵃlôm*) and it is expected of him that he produce, like a magician, some extraordinary sign assuring the truth of his prediction. In this he may or may not be successful.[60] The imposition of the death penalty on prophets urging the service of foreign deities (as on individuals and cities doing the same) probably reflects Josiah's anti-Assyrian policy. But the passage as a whole tells us little about the Deuteronomic understanding of prophecy as such.

It is quite different with the positive and explicit statement in 18:9–22, and here, too, the first task is to grasp the function of the passage in its context. To begin with what is most obvious, it occurs in the law code (12–26), and this is strange because it does not look much like a law. It does indeed contain a command to obey the prophet like Moses raised up by Yahweh, but we are reminded nonetheless that chapters 12–26 contain not so much a law code as "a collection of material for the public proclamation of law."[61] And since the far-reaching consequences of obedience and disobedience to the prophetic word is one of the major themes of the Deuteronomic history, we have reason to suspect that the passage in question belongs to the exilic stage of the book's editorial history. For the moment, however, this is not a major issue.

The immediate context of the passage shows that it is one of several dispositions concerning offices or functions within the community: judges and officers (16:18–20), levitical priests and the judge who together form a central judiciary (17:8–13), the king (17:14–20), the levitical priesthood (18:1–8) and the prophet (18:9–22).[62] This suggests at once that an attempt is being made to fit the problematic phenomenon of prophecy into a structure of legitimate office and that the law book is essentially a program for the future. We know, in fact, from the outset that it is a law for living in a land not yet occupied.[63] It is understandable, therefore, that this whole section (unlike those where the casuistic form predominates) does not legislate in detail on how the responsibilities associated with the various offices are to be discharged. It deals rather with general principles such as the need for impartiality in the judicial system (16:18–20), limiting the scope of the monarchy (17:16–20) and establishing the economic independence of the clergy (18:1–5).

The conclusion may be drawn, then, that this is an ideal portrait of the prophet and his place within the community to be established in the land after Moses' death. The principal concern is to trace the group's organization to Moses and thus legitimate its offices and ministries. It begins with the prohibition of debased Gentile forms of revelation such as soothsaying and necromancy. Israel must avoid such things since she has been given her own unique mode of revelation:

These nations whose place you are taking listen to soothsayers and augurs, but the LORD your God does not permit you to do this. The LORD your God will raise up a prophet from among you like myself, and you shall listen to him. All this follows from your request to the LORD your God on Horeb on the day of the assembly. There you said, 'Let us not hear again the voice of the LORD our God, nor see this great fire again, or we shall die.' Then the LORD said to me, 'What they have said is right. I will raise up for them a prophet like you, one of their own race, and I will put my words into his mouth. He shall convey all my commands to them, and if anyone does not listen to the words which he will speak in my name I will require satisfaction from him. But the prophet who presumes to utter in my name what I have not commanded him or who speaks in the name of other gods—that prophet shall die.' (18:14–20)

It is understandable that Israel should be contrasted with the nations on this point since its uniqueness by reason of divine election is one of the major themes of the book.[64] Moses tells the people that they will not have to have recourse to soothsayers and the like for Yahweh will raise up a prophet to whom they must have recourse. Use of the singular has proved troublesome here, and from an early time interpreters, both Jewish and Christian, have found in it the promise of an eschatological prophet.[65] In the modern period this interpretation has for the most part been accepted only by more ecclesiastically conservative exegetes, though even such a gifted and critical interpreter as von Rad does not seem to want to exclude it.[66] But in view of the context as described a moment ago (which also, incidentally, refers to "a king" in the singular) it must be considered precarious. For what we must look to find here is the description of a real institution comparable to the priesthood or the judiciary which will fulfil in the future, beginning with the immediate future following on Moses' death, the role played by Moses himself during his lifetime.[67]

If this is granted, it will be reasonable to conclude, as most commentators now do,[68] that the passage refers to the prophetic succession as a whole. But even this *sententia communis* calls for an important qualification. For if this institution must be present from the moment of Moses' death, and if, according to the Deuteronomic schema, prophecy in the strict sense is co-extensive with the monarchy, it follows that the "prophet like Moses" must take in more than those ordinarily designated as prophets. It must, in other words, take in Joshua, the charismatic leaders including the so-called "minor judges" and those who are called prophets in the history. We are not for the moment concerned to ask whether this schema corresponds with "real history" but rather with the understanding of prophecy in this book. The implications would seem to be the following. First, by placing prophecy within a programmatic and schematic plan for the Israel of the future it was given a specific institutional character and to that extent deprived of its power to challenge and disrupt.[69] Second, the redefinition of prophecy as "Mosaic" and its insertion into a divinely revealed pattern of order brought about a shift from concentration on historical realities in the direction of covenant and law; in other words, from *Geschichtsprophetie* to *Rechtsprophetie.*[70]

We should add that this move corresponds with a historical schematization which the perspective adopted in the book imposes. The death of Moses is, in other words, the great divide between the paradigmatic prophetic age represented by Moses himself and the age following his death which belongs to all those who carry on his work and ministry. As elsewhere in the book (e.g., 16:19, cf. Ex. 23:8) this point is supported by what might be called a scriptural argument, the people's request for a mediator at Sinai-Horeb (18:16, cf. Ex. 20:18–19).

The implication seems quite clear. Prophecy is God's an-

swer to Israel's request for mediation, and it is in this respect
that the prophet is like Moses. Hence the prophet's essential
function, whatever else he does, is to mediate the covenant
between the LORD and his people and "speak" the laws
which guarantee its survival.[71]

The further question arises whether to represent prophecy
as God's answer to Israel's request for mediation implies that it
was understood to be a cultic phenomenon. In a well-known
essay written many years ago on "The Origins of Israelite Law"
Albrecht Alt argued that in ancient Israel the laws were
promulgated within the amphictyonic cult.[72] Since, according to Deuteronomy, prophetic mediation is granted during the act of covenant-making, after the proclamation of the
Ten Words but before the promulgation of the detailed stipulations, it might seem logical to speak of the prophet's cultic
role or even of prophecy as essentially a cultic activity.[73]
Whether this was historically the case has been endlessly discussed and does not concern us for the moment. It certainly
does not oblige us to conclude that the Deuteronomist author
understood prophecy to be essentially cultic. Indeed, we have
just seen that it must include functions which are clearly not
cultic.

The final section of the paragraph (vv. 21–22) provides a
rule of thumb for dealing with the ambiguities of prophecy:

> If you ask yourselves, 'How shall we recognize a word that
> the LORD has not uttered?', this is the answer: When the
> word spoken by the prophet in the name of the LORD is
> not fulfilled and does not come true, it is not a word spoken
> by the LORD. The prophet has spoken presumptuously; do
> not hold him in awe.

The first criterion for evaluating prophecy is fidelity to the
Yahwistic tradition (13:1–5; 18:20). A further test is that the
prophet speak only what Yahweh commands (18:20). Now
we have the criterion of historical verification (cf. Jer. 28:8–9
where it is valid only for prophets of well-being), which is
hardly of much use to the prophet's contemporaries except for
short-range predictions. Such a retrospective view of prophecy
which   emphasizes   successful   prediction—as   in   the

Deuteronomic history—must have been prevalent during the
exile which saw so many prophetic reputations made and broken. That the passage quoted above has nothing to do with its
preceding context, introducing as it does the totally different
element of prediction, strongly suggests that it belongs to the
exilic edition of the book.

IV. Prophecy in the Deuteronomic History

The publication of Deuteronomy was by any reckoning a
decisive event in the religious history of Israel. The tendency,
still widespread, to think of *one* religion of Israel with everything more or less in place from the beginning can make it
difficult to appreciate how profound was the change brought
about by the centralization of worship and the promulgation of
an official law code. As Robert Pfeiffer put it, Deuteronomy
"marks substantially the end of the old religion of Israel and
the beginning of Judaism, the death of a national religion and
the birth of an ethical religion of salvation for all men."[74]
It was practically inevitable that the Mosaic, covenantal
theology of the authors of the book should lead sooner or later
to a rewriting of the history. This, at any rate, is what generally happens when a movement of revolution or renewal is
successfully established. The rewriting and re-editing was already underway before the death of Josiah in 609 but received
its decisive imprint from the experience of total disaster after
the destruction of Jerusalem twenty-two years later. If we use
the term "Deuteronomic (or Deuteronomistic) History"—
following the widely accepted hypothesis of Martin Noth[75]—
this is not meant to imply a work comparable to, say,
Herodotus or Thucydides with a definite structure, beginning
and end and consistent method of reporting and using sources.
Thus, we know where the story ends—with the paroling of the
exiled king Jehoiachin in 561 (2 Kings 25:27–30)—but not
where it begins. Anyone who has read Deuteronomy atten-
tively would have no difficulty identifying the homiletic (von
Rad would say "protestant") and rather prolix style marked by
an almost standardized terminology.[76] Now this style is almost

entirely absent from Genesis and only very rarely in evidence in Exodus through Numbers. It is found often in Joshua and Judges, infrequently in Samuel and is prevalent in Kings. How is one to interpret these data? That we have a consecutive history of the monarchy from at least Solomon to the exile is hardly in doubt. That the Deuteronomic school was not interested in retelling the story from creation to Moses is also reasonably assured. But whether the history actually began with Moses, or whether alternatively we have only an updating of the traditions between Moses and the monarchy to bring them into line with the Deuteronomic perspective, is a more difficult question to answer. All we can say is that we have narrative composed or edited by this school covering very unevenly the following: the Mosaic age from Sinai-Horeb to Moab, the conquest and settlement, the "judges" or charismatic warlords, the monarchy from Saul to the exile.[77]

If this historical and exegetical work follows the theology of Deuteronomy, as is generally supposed, we would expect prophecy to play an important role in it. We would also expect it be viewed somewhat differently, given what had happened between the Josian reform and the time of writing in the mid-sixth century. We shall go on to test this by briefly surveying the Deuteronomic history. Questions of sources, literary analysis and redactional criticism, generally in dispute, will be raised only where they directly affect the issue of prophecy in the work.

The first remarkable thing we notice about the story as told by the Deuteronomists is the chronological gap between the giving of the Ten Words at Horeb and the promulgation of the entire covenant-law in Moab. The reasons for this change are transparent. It allowed the authors to portray Moses as prophetic mediator and the law as a law for life in the land soon to be occupied. The appropriateness of this latter representation would, of course, have been particularly apparent during the exilic age. The prophetic office in all of its aspects is concentrated in the person of Moses. The normative age is that which preceded the establishment of kingship. This, it seems, was the main thrust of the exilic re-editing of the law book, and its intent was to prepare a new generation to seek

inspiration in the archaic period and avoid the mistakes which
had brought about the disaster of exile.

Whatever uncertainties beset the literary analysis of Joshua,
and they are many, it is generally agreed that at least in the
first part of the book the Deuteronomists edited old traditions
into a form consistent with their own point of view.[78] The
link with the preceding age is the commissioning of Joshua by
Moses, the model for which was the succession of Elisha to the
prophetic office of Elijah.[79] Joshua is the first "prophet like
Moses" and therefore plays the same role as his master.
Yahweh will be with him as he was with Moses (Jos. 1:5, etc.);
the Israelites revered him as they had his great predecessor
(4:14); and he, too, is described as "servant of the LORD"
(24:28), a standard synonym for prophet in Deuteronomic
writings. Joshua's crossing of the Jordan is meant to recall the
crossing of the Papyrus Sea (4:23), both are granted
theophanies (5:13–15) and the obituary notices on Joshua and
the priest Eleazar (24:29, 33) parallel those on Moses and
Aaron. Like Moses, Joshua is concerned not just with warfare
but with responsibility for the law and the covenant (e.g.,
1:8). The book ends with a twofold conclusion not unlike
Deuteronomy. Chapter 23 has Joshua's valedictory in which
he exhorts the people in the Deuteronomic style to keep the
law and the covenant. The following chapter recounts the
solemn renewing of the covenant at the end of his life. It
consists in a historical resumé, words of exhortation, allusion
to the actual ceremony and the writing of the terms agreed on
in the book of the Law of God. It presents, in other words, a
sort of précis of the contents of Deuteronomy. Joshua is therefore the first example and embodiment of prophecy as rede-
fined by the Deuteronomic school.

The period between the conquest of Canaan and the
monarchy is bridged by a series of charismatic leaders arranged
according to a very firm theological schema set out clearly at
the beginning.[80] The series ends with the valedictory of
Samuel (1 Sam. 12) in which four such "judges" (*šopᵉṭîm*) are
listed of whom the last (incongruously in the context) is
Samuel himself.[81] Thus, the concern to divide the history up
into discrete dispensations is clearly indicated by the valedic-

tory addresses put into the mouths of Moses, Joshua and Samuel. In this particular dispensation mediation is effected not through the prophetic word (as during the monarchy) but by the charisma of inspired leadership. Yet the difference is not, perhaps, essential, since the "judges" are "raised up" just like the prophets, in a remarkable and literal way in the case of Gideon.[82] In fact, wherever this school speaks of functions and ministries (including the monarchy, Deut. 17:15) we find a characteristic blending of the charismatic and the institutional.

It is now widely accepted that the six who receive only brief notice in Judg. 10:1–5 and 12:7–15, the so-called "minor judges," belong to a different category from the military leaders, their principal function being the enunciation, interpretation and administration of the tribal law.[83] Yet even here there are hints that judicial and military activities could go together. Deborah (not one of the six) engaged in prophetic, judicial and military action, for example. Two of the six, Jair and Abdon, seem to have had their own private armies,[84] and Jephthah, we are told, was both military leader (10:6–12:6) and judge in the ordinary sense (12:7). Samuel also delivered Israel from danger on the battlefield and administered justice around the country (1 Sam. 7:15–17).[85] All of this is hardly surprising since Moses and Joshua are also portrayed in this double role.[86]

The career of Samuel marks the intermediate stage between the judgeship and prophecy since he is described as judge (in both senses) and prophet.[87] In 1 Sam. 1–12, the final stage of this dispensation, there are relatively few indications of the Deuteronomic hand.[88] The account of Samuel's call to a prophetic ministry deserves special mention since it clearly marks a decisive turning point. Before that time prophecy had made only a rare and sporadic appearance, but from then on it was to be a regular feature of Israelite life (3:1; 4:1).

Prophet though he was, Samuel continued in the judgeship not for a limited number of years as had the previous judges but for his entire lifetime (1 Sam. 7:15). He then appointed his sons to succeed him, but their conduct in office is evaluated and found wanting according to the provisions of the Deuteronomic law.[89] The convocation at Mizpah, during which Samuel "judged" Israel (7:2–14), provides valuable clues to the Deuteronomic understanding of the judgeship. For here Samuel presides over a liturgical gathering during which the people pray, confess their sins and fast while Samuel intercedes for them. This liturgy of covenant renewal closes with the miraculous defeat of the Philistines and thereby allows Samuel to exemplify both aspects of the office. His valedictory (1 Sam. 12), similar to that of Joshua (Jos. 24), looks back over the Mosaic age and that of the judges now coming to an end and forward to the monarchy inaugurated with ominous proleptic signs of doom. The historical schema is clearly that of the Deuteronomists.

In covering the period from Saul to the building of the temple, our historian has for the most part kept himself in the background.[90] The pattern of prophecy and fulfillment which punctuates and indeed structures the history of the kingdom is adumbrated in the oracle of Nathan to David (2 Sam. 7:4ff.). It seems that this oracle, which is undoubtedly ancient, originally forbade the building of a temple at all, but that the insertion of a single clause by the Deuteronomic editor (*"he* will build a house for my name," v. 13) radically changed this meaning.[91] Thus, the building of the temple by Solomon and, no less important, the reason for building it,[92] acquire prophetic authorization. Typically, the fulfillment of this oracular prediction is noted at the appropriate point (1 Kings 8:15, 21–24). We will recall in this connection that for the Deuteronomists the temple housed the law book. Temple and Torah, the twin pillars of post-exilic Judaism, rest on foundations laid by the Deuteronomists.

What of prophecy during this period? We have already noted a shift in the direction of prediction and the interpretation of historical events. Since the entire history is written from the perspective of historical catastrophe, the role of the prophet is to warn, recall to fidelity, threaten doom and in general put the blame squarely where it belongs. He is, in short, the apologist of God, and the apologetic note is heard even before the division of the kingdom (1 Kings 8:46–53;

9:3–9). While the author clearly did not see the Babylonian exile as the end of Israel's relation with Yahweh (as many of his contemporaries did), he undoubtedly viewed it as a catastrophe of a quite different order from the many which had preceded it. If prophecy was to continue, it would necessarily have a quite different role, one on which, it seems, the author was not prepared to speculate. Indeed, it is of interest to note that in passages which refer explicitly to the prospect of exile we find exhortations to repentance but no further mention of prophets.[93]

With Solomon securely on the throne and the temple built, the two predictions in the re-edited oracle of Nathan were fulfilled. As another oracle at 1 Kings 9:1–9 makes clear, however, the continued existence of both dynasty and temple was conditional on the king faithfully observing the Deuteronomic law. The historian goes on almost at once to note Solomon's violations of this law: the accumulation of wealth, the "multiplication" of horses and the setting up of an impressive harem.[94] The consequences are clearly spelled out in a further oracle, presumably delivered by a prophet (1 Kings 11:11–13), which marks, we may say, the beginning of the end. From this point on the history moves in a descending spiral from one prophetic oracle to the next,[95] and in each case the predictions of doom are linked with failure to observe the Deuteronomic law. Since, moreover, the predictions correspond to the literal fulfillment of the curses attached to that law, the understanding of prophecy has not really changed. Particularly revealing in this respect is the historian's reflection on the fall of the Kingdom of Samaria:

> Still the LORD solemnly charged Israel and Judah by every prophet and seer, saying, 'Give up your evil ways; keep my commandments and statutes given in the law which I enjoined on your forefathers and delivered to you through my servants the prophets.' (2 Kings 17:13)

The prophet, then, is Yahweh's agent in communicating the law to king and people, appealing for its observance and predicting doom in the event of non-observance. In this sense he

is "the servant of the LORD."[96] The same conclusion is
suggested by the oracle pronounced by the prophetess Huldah
when consulted after the discovery of the law book:

> I am bringing disaster on this place and its inhabitants as
> foretold in the book which the king of Judah has read. . . .
> (2 Kings 22:16)

The reference is clearly not to the stipulations of law but to
the curses contingent on their non-observance; it was this
which caused the fear and consternation of the king and his
entourage. Prediction of the future and concern for covenant
and law go together.

These conclusions are reinforced by a study of those prose
passages in Jeremiah, sometimes called the C source, which
have been edited or in some cases composed by the same
school.[97] That this is the only book of the *Nᵉbîʾîm* which has
been substantially edited by Deuteronomists raises some interesting questions which have surprisingly received little attention. It may be suggested that they saw him as the last in
the prophetic series and his ministry as a kind of recapitulation
and climax of all the prophetic ministries which had gone
before. The frequent occurrence of the phrase "his servants
the prophets" in these passages would, at any rate, be consistent with this view since it suggests that the prophetic witness
is now a matter of past history.

The Deuteronomic Jeremiah is, then, one of "his servants
the prophets" and his ministry illustrates the pattern of disobedience which is a basic theme of the history. He is, moreover, a *Mosaic* prophet. He proclaims the law to his contemporaries and predicts the fulfillment of the curses attached to
that law.[98] In his encounters with rival prophets he applies
the Deuteronomic criteria for the discernment of prophetic
spirits.[99] The portrait of him which emerges from the book in
its final form, including the Deuteronomic editings, is in some
respects remarkably similar to the portrait of Moses sketched,
as we have seen, in Deuteronomy.

Whatever his attitude to Josiah's reform, the effects of
which did not survive the death of the young king at Megiddo
in 609, it seems clear that Jeremiah and the circle of his

disciples were persuaded that a more radical remedy was necessary if Israel was to survive. The death of Josiah, the collapse of his reform and the unprecedented catastrophe of the exile had shown that it was no longer adequate simply to renew the covenant in its original form. Something quite different was called for, a radical *novum* as the theologians would say, which would lead to a juridically less definable understanding of the God-Israel relationship (Jer. 31:31–34).

The covenant had been broken definitively and there was no way back. The Law of God remained as an eternal reality but the instruments by which it was maintained and inculcated had been shown to be inadequate. The passage about a new covenant is not a programmatic statement. It expresses rather a stubborn faith reaffirmed in an age of deep spiritual disorientation. Since there is no compelling reason to deny it to Jeremiah or the circle of his disciples,[100] it may be read as a meditation on God's ways with Israel inspired by the collapse of the reform based on the Deuteronomic law book. Christian scholars have not been slow in grasping its significance for their own faith (it is the only passage in the Hebrew Scriptures which speaks of a new covenant or testament) but have had little to say on its enduring significance for Judaism. In one way or another we will be dealing with this latter question in subsequent chapters.[101]

3: The Priestly Work (P): The Second Stage

I. The Character of the Priestly Work (P)

THE BREAKTHROUGH IN UNDERSTANDING THE FORMA-
tion of the Pentateuch, and therefore also the religious history
of Israel, was the demonstration by Karl Heinrich Graf in
1865 that the Priestly document (which goes by the conven-
tional symbol P) came not at the beginning but at the end of
the process of formation of the Pentateuch. After the publication of Wellhausen's *Prolegomena* thirteen years later, this thesis came to be widely accepted. Wellhausen's achievement
was to show with brilliant clarity that the history of Israel's
worship, traditions and legislation can be adequately explained on the supposition that Deuteronomy (D) follows
chronologically the Yahwistic and Elohistic sources (J and E)
and precedes P, and that it is rendered incomprehensible if the
order is reversed. P was therefore responsible for the final form
of the Pentateuch, identical with the "law of the God of
heaven" promulgated by Ezra with the sanction of the Persian
state. It set down the main lines along which Judaism was to
develop, laying the foundations for a community based on cult
and law, a community which was no longer a nation but a
church.[1]

Wellhausen was equally clear as to how P fitted into the
religious development of Israel as it passed over into early
Judaism. P presupposes Deuteronomy which bridges the gap
between nation state and theocracy. The Deuteronomic law
was in force in Palestine right down to the official promulga-

tion of the Priestly Torah by Ezra. In fact, Ezra himself acted in accord with it in the early part of his mission (p. 406). But Ezra's Torah was no improvised work, for during the exile there had come together in Babylon a group or school of priests who began to set down in writing ritual law in force while the Temple yet stood. This corpus of legislation, now found in Lev. 17–26 and generally referred to as the Holiness Code (H), eventually found its way into P. Numerous affinities between the Holiness Code and the blueprint for the future temple in Ezek. 40–48 lead to the conclusion that this priestly academy drew its inspiration in part from Ezekiel. He played a decisive role in the emergence of the theocracy, and his visionary plan for the future temple provides the key to understanding the religious transformation then going on (pp. 59, 122).

This trajectory traced by Wellhausen, which has proved to be greatly oversimplified, allows us to situate P roughly in relation to prophecy. Wellhausen saw Jeremiah as last of the prophets and Ezekiel as first of the *epigoni*. The latter was both priest and prophet but more priest than prophet. As such, he may be seen as the link between pre-exilic prophecy and post-exilic cultic theology. He started out with prophetic ideas which were not his own and turned them into dogmas. And since he "swallowed a book and gave it up again" (p. 403), he may be taken to signalize the passage from oral to scribal prophecy. It was his "program for the future restoration of the theocracy" (p. 60), a program which was both prophetic and priestly, which reached its furthest elaboration in P.

Wellhausen believed that in the earliest period there was no distinction between prophet and priest (pp. 396–397). Moses himself fulfilled both functions so that prophets and priests throughout the history could claim descent from him, the latter, however, with more justification than the former (p. 397). Numerous references to both categories acting together testify to this original unity. With Ezekiel and his priestly successors we may say that the wheel comes full circle as prophecy is taken over by and absorbed into the priestly office.

We today, with an additional century of discovery and study behind us, will find much to criticize in Wellhausen's

reconstruction of the history. It would be strange if it were
otherwise. Quite apart from his transparent prejudices, discussed earlier, the whole thing seems just too clear, too
schematic and unilinear, too "documentary." More specifically, we have learned the importance of distinguishing the age
of rituals and laws from that of their collection and redaction.
We have also learned to distrust explanations of similarities in
terms of causal relationship. Similarities between Ezekiel and
P, for example, may perhaps be better explained on the
hypothesis that both draw on ancient cultic and priestly traditions. With all that, Wellhausen's exegetical work has stood
the test of time remarkably well and is still very much with us
despite repeated obituary notices.[2] For our present purposes it
provides us with a necessary point of departure in our attempt
to relate the Priestly Work to the fate of prophecy in the exilic
and post-exilic periods.

Despite the formulaic character of its language and the
many numbers and names which so offended Wellhausen, P
has proved to be in several respects very elusive. As generally
understood, it is a narrative source containing a great mass of
legislative and cultic material (making up about a third of the
entire Pentateuch), much of which is clearly of high antiquity. It is not an independent narrative since literary
analysis reveals that it was intended as a framework for the old
JE epos, supplementing and re-editing to bring it into line
with its own perspective and the needs of a later generation.
Hence, it would make sense to speak of P as a *tradent* rather
than an author in the modern sense.[3] P, nevertheless, does
offer new interpretations, and these have to be disengaged
from the narrative as we have it, by the way earlier sources
are re-edited, re-presented and restructured.

While we are in no danger of forgetting that P is a priestly
work, it may need to be said that it is equally scribal in character. We might even say that this is what we would expect in
view of the close association between priests and scribes noted
in the previous chapter. If, moreover, P came into existence
in Babylon (as most scholars believe), it is not unlikely that it
was more directly influenced by the ancient Mesopotamian
scribal tradition which was still very much alive. Comparison

with the *Babyloniaka* of the priest-scribe Berossus, written towards the beginning of the third century B.C.E. in Babylon, is instructive in this regard. Both contain the history of a people inserted into a cosmic history beginning with creation and moving rapidly on to catastrophe. While P does not share the astral determination of Berossus, it, too, gives great importance to the computation of times and seasons, conformity with heavenly paradigms and the like. Both works also contain motifs which will appear regularly and even monotonously in Jewish apocalyptic writings: a point which is worth noting in view of the strongly scribal character of apocalyptic. Specifically, the importance which P attributes to revelation in the primeval age of world history (following the pattern of Sumero-Akkadian myth[4]) paved the way for the apocalypticists. The annoyingly brief reference to the taking up of Enoch (Gen. 5:24 P), for example, drew on an ancient Mesopotamian mythologoumenon and provided a starting point for the circles to whom we owe the extensive Enoch literature in circulation from the second century B.C.E. and perhaps much earlier.[5]

At the risk of appearing to labor the point, some further aspects of this scribalism in P ought to be mentioned. It is not just the care with which the early history of mankind is told but the fact that the entire subsequent course of the history is linked structurally and thematically with this earliest phase. All of Israel's cultic institutions and ordinances, the establishment of which is the *raison d'être* of the history, are taken up into the cosmic order. Sabbath is reflected in the initial act of creation (Gen. 2:1–3), the sanctuary is made according to a heavenly archetype (Ex. 25:9, 40), and the account of its construction is (as we shall see shortly) rounded off in such a way as to suggest that it is the climax of the work of creation and the fulfillment of the purpose implicit in it (Ex. 39:43, cf. Gen. 1:31; 2:3). There is dominant concern to present the history in discrete periods marking a succession of covenants, ritual institutions and the progressive revelation of the deity's name. From end to end it breathes an atmosphere of reflection, learning and scholarship which brings it within the ambit of the scribal tradition and its conventions.[6] In particu-

lar, the finely structured creation recital with which the work
opens is, as Wellhausen noted,[7] a product as much of cosmological as it is of theological reflection, and finds its closest
thematic parallels in the work of the sages.[8]

One of the major arguments for Wellhausen's hypothesis,
repeated many times in the *Prolegomena,* is that no pre-exilic
writing betrays the slightest acquaintance with P. He therefore felt entitled to conclude that P was a product not of Israel
but of early Judaism. After the return, the prophets Haggai
and Zechariah do not refer to it either, while Malachi, from a
somewhat later period, appears to be familiar with legislation
in the Holiness Code but not with P itself.[9] The Chronicler,
writing probably in the fourth century, refers to both
Deuteronomic and Priestly legislation,[10] which would be consistent with the view that the Priestly code first came into
force during the mission of Ezra less than a century earlier.
Priest of the line of Aaron and Zadok and scribe learned in the
Law of Moses, he had prepared for his mission by study and
brought with him Levites skilled in Torah who were put to
work instructing the laity.[11] It would be a reasonable deduc-
tion that such study and learning had been going on in the
gôlāh for some time prior to Ezra's mission, and that, therefore,
P is to be dated somewhere between 587 and 444, the latter
date being the one Wellhausen assigned to Ezra's mission.[12]

In the century since Wellhausen wrote there have been
numerous attempts to refine (and, indeed, also to refute) these
conclusions which it would be pointless to evaluate individually. It will have to suffice for the moment to note that P
probably had a long editorial history which eventuated in the
Pentateuch as we know it. Since (as will be shown) it was
written with the reoccupation of the land and the re-
establishment of temple worship in mind, the first stage of the
work must be dated prior to 515 when the rebuilt temple was
consecrated. This would seem to put it practically at the same
time as the Deuteronomic history. The process by which
Deuteronomy was incorporated into the Priestly Hexateuch
should be taken as a distinct issue. It is probably connected
with the mission of Ezra and the objectives which it had in
view. As to the actual circumstances under which P was pro-

duced we are unfortunately almost totally in the dark. We know that the *gôlāh* communities continued to worship together at designated places—Casiphia certainly, perhaps also Tell Abib and others[13]—and we may surmise that where the faithful gathered for prayer and worship there would also be a kind of *bēt hammidrāš* (house of study) where Scripture study and interpretation went on. At such distant ancestors of the rabbinic academies of Sura and Pumbedita, it seems, the work of scholarship and piety which we call P came into existence.

II. Some Major Themes in P

Since Gunkel, Old Testament scholars have been aware of the importance of determining genre or type in their work of interpretation. More recently, the emphasis has shifted somewhat to the structure of texts, the internal relation between the parts (narremes, mythemes, motifs) as revealing the meaning of the whole. Much of this is being done under the influence of structuralist theoreticians such as Lévi-Strauss, Barthes and Greimas. Some of it is potentially quite important, but for our present purpose too little concerned with the overt structures of texts. No doubt a deep-structural analysis of P will appear sooner or later, but in the meantime we might be better advised to look for inspiration to the Russian formalists best known to English readers in Vladimir Propp's *Morphology of the Folktale* (1928). The advantage of the latter method is that it relates structure and theme without hypostasizing the former or permitting a purely desultory and uncontrolled disengagement of particular themes. In other words, the significance of themes can be established only as functioning within the structure of the text as a whole.

We have seen that P is a continuous if uneven narrative with a definite beginning and an as yet undetermined ending. It has obviously undergone editorial expansions and revisions but for the moment we can ignore distinctions between narrative framework (P^G) and legal-ritual insertions (P^S), two strand theories and the like.[14] It is, as we have seen, a highly formulaic and structured work, which in some respects makes

it easier to analyze. Historical detail does not abound, probably because P was never meant to be read apart from the
earlier sources.[15] The history is, in fact, largely a framework
for the progressive establishment of the cultic institutions of
Israel. It is no doubt this characteristic which explains the
prevalence of two types of formulaic expression: one indicating the execution of a command given directly or indirectly by
God, and the other the successful completion of a task. These
deserve our attention since they lead directly into some of the
major structures and themes of the Priestly work as a whole.

What we may call the "execution formula" runs as follows:
"X did according to all that the LORD (God) commanded
him" or, since most of the commands come through Moses,
"X did according to all that the LORD (God) commanded
Moses." A more elaborate and solemn form, used only on
special occasions, is as follows: "X did according to all that the
LORD (God) commanded him / according to all that the
LORD (God) commanded Moses; thus did he." This formula,
with only minor variations of detail,[16] occurs regularly
throughout the history, the first occurrence being the construction of the ark by Noah (Gen. 6:22) and the last the
allotment of Levitical cities (Jos. 21:8). The "conclusion formula" is much less frequent, being restricted to three points in
the history:

(i) creation of the world (Gen. 2:1, 2): "Thus heaven and
earth were completed with all their mighty throng... God
completed all the work he had been doing."

(ii) construction of the wilderness sanctuary and its appointments (Ex. 39:32; 40:33): "Thus all the work of the
Tabernacle of the Tent of the Presence was completed...
thus Moses completed the work."

(iii) dividing of the land among the tribes after the setting
up of the wilderness sanctuary at Shiloh (Jos. 19:51): "Thus
they completed the distribution of the land."

A glance at the incidence of these formulaic expressions
shows the importance which P attaches to the exact fulfillment throughout the history of a pre-established plan. The
same is true of the spatial axis of the work since the physical
constructs—Noah's ark, the sanctuary, the altar and

menorah—are built according to divine specifications.[17] There are, of course, incidents recorded in P which do not consist explicitly in the obedient fulfillment of a divine command (for example, Abraham's purchase of the cave at Machpelah, Gen. 23), and there are recurrent formulaic expressions which indicate other levels of intentionality.[18] But if we are trying to get at the structure of the work, we could do no better than start with those formulae which indicate more explicitly the *completion* of successive stages in the history. Thus, if we put together our conclusion-formulae with the expanded form of the execution-formula (and bear in mind that the creation of the world could not, in the nature of things, end with an execution formula), we are led to give prominence to the following points in the narrative:

(i) creation of the world,

(ii) construction of the sanctuary,

(iii) establishment of the sanctuary in the land and distribution of the land among the tribes.

Before this triadic structure is examined more in detail, a disquieting problem must be faced. Everyone who has worked on P in the modern period has assumed that the covenant plays a major role in it both as a theological datum and as a structuring factor in the narrative. In particular, the covenant with Abraham (Gen. 17) is considered to be of decisive importance, and yet according to this reading it does not seem to emerge as structurally very significant. That Abraham fulfilled the command to circumcise Ishmael, Isaac and all his household is indeed explicitly noted in the P formulaic manner (Gen. 17:23; 21:4), but that is all. The reason, it seems, is to be sought in the *promissory* nature of this covenant in P. To the promise of land in the earlier sources P adds that of the divine presence ("I will be their God," Gen. 17:8), and this is fulfilled in the construction of the sanctuary and the establishment of its cult in the wilderness.[19] Where our structural analysis helps us at this point is in drawing our attention to the thematic association in P between the land and the divine presence in the cult as objects of the promise. Further, the promissory nature of the Abrahamic covenant explains why no independent P version of the Sinaitic covenant can be

62

Prophecy and Canon

arrived in the Sinaitic wilderness (19:1), Moses went up the
mountain (24:15–18) and received from God the specifications for the sanctuary, ark and related matters (25–31),
after forty days he came down again (34:29–35),[21] and executed the commands which he had received (35–40).[22] The
entire focus is on the establishment of the cult as the precondition for the presence of God with his people, which is
what the covenant is all about. What happened at Sinai is
therefore explicable only in the light of what happened in the
archaic period, what passed between God and those just men
Noah and Abraham. The triadic structure of P, therefore,
subsumes the promissory covenant in the setting up of the
sanctuary and the occupation of the land. These are crucial
aspects of P's message. And they are perhaps still not without
significance for contemporary Judaism.

Our examination of formulaic expressions up to this point
has highlighted the structural significance of the creation of
the world and the construction of the wilderness sanctuary. A
synoptic reading of these two passages in P reveals their close
parallelism, as follows (literal translation):

Creation of the world	*Construction of the sanctuary*
And God saw all that he had made, and behold, it was very good (Gen. 1:31)	And Moses saw all the work and behold, they had done it as the LORD commanded; so they had done it (Ex. 39:43)
Thus heaven and earth were completed (Gen. 2:1)	Thus all the work of the Tabernacle of the Tent of the Presence was completed (Ex. 39:32)
God completed all the work he had been doing (Gen. 2:2)	So Moses completed the work (Ex. 40:33)
So God blessed the seventh day (Gen. 2:3)	So Moses blessed them (Ex. 39:43)

These linguistic parallels are, however, only worth noting if
we go on to discover the thematic association between these

two points in the narrative. Part of this will be taken up when we pass on to consider the deluge story, but for the moment two thematic parallels ought to be mentioned:

(i) The Sinaitic stipulations concerning the sanctuary and its appointments end with the injunction to observe sabbath as a perpetual covenant and a sign of creation which ended with the sabbath of God (Ex. 31:12–17). It is thereby implied that just as God rested after making the world so should Israel after the construction of the sanctuary. We are not thereby obliged to conclude, with Wellhausen[23] and others after him, that for P creation implies a covenant. If P had wished to say that, he would have found a way of doing so. In any case, sabbath was not instituted at creation but in the wilderness of Sinai.[24] Its significative value has therefore to be understood within the priestly-scribal reinterpretation of what the older sources had to say about Sinai. These last recognized only two covenants, one made with the fathers (Gen. 15), the other with all Israel at Sinai (Ex. 19–24). P also has two covenants, one made with Noah in the archaic period, the other with the fathers. This temporal shift represents a profound reinterpretation of the covenant idea. It sets alongside the dispensation of grace to Israel another offered to the nations which is chronologically and logically anterior. It seems to imply the conviction that the old dispensation, conditional on Israel's observance of the covenant law, a dispensation which is central to the theology of Deuteronomy, is no longer viable; in which respect P is perhaps to be seen as the heir of Ezekiel. Thus in P the perpetual (and therefore unconditional and unrenewable) covenants made in the archaic period (Gen. 9:16; 17:7, 13) lead up to the moment when God has ordained to be indefectibly present to Israel through its cultic, institutional life.[25]

(ii) The construction of the sanctuary requires the Spirit of God with which Bezalel and his colleagues are endowed (Ex. 31:3, cf. 35:31). While *rûaḥ 'elohîm* at Gen. 1:2 *may* be translated "a mighty wind" or something of the sort, it is difficult to exclude the more theological meaning in the context of the entire work.[26] This being the case, the divine spirit occurs only three times in P, all at crucial points of the history: the

creation of the world (Gen. 1:2), the construction of the
sanctuary (Ex. 31:3; 35:31), and the commissioning of Joshua
(Num. 27:18; Deut. 34:9).[27] Since Joshua is commissioned
precisely to occupy the land and distribute it among the tribes,
it will be seen that this also corresponds with the triadic structure mentioned above. In other words, we have here another
confirmation of the structural interdependence within P of
creation, construction of the sanctuary and occupation of the
land.

After the creation recital, P moves on to reshape the story
of the great deluge with a view to bringing it within its own
theological perspective. Here the formulaic correspondence is
between the construction of the ark and of the sanctuary:

Construction of the ark	*Construction of the sanctuary*
Noah did according to all that God had commanded him; thus did he (Gen. 6:22)	According to all that the LORD had commanded Moses, thus did the Israelites all the work (Ex. 39:42)

As was suggested earlier, these correspondences in P can
generally be traced along both the temporal and spatial axes of
the work. Like the sanctuary, Noah's ark is constructed according to divine specifications, though there is no mention of
a heavenly model (*tabnît*). According to the P chronology,
the new world emerged from the flood waters on the first day
of the liturgical year, which is precisely the day on which the
sanctuary was set up and dedicated in the wilderness (Gen.
8:13; Ex. 40:2). It will be recalled that the first temple was
also dedicated during Sukkot, the autumnal New Year Festival
(1 Kings 8:2, 65). We are told that it took seven years to build
(1 Kings 6:38), which in view of probable Near Eastern parallels may be related to the seven days of creation. The same
dating system requires that the week of creation in the first
chapter of Genesis be the first week of the liturgical year, the
primordial New Year Festival. While we know nothing of a
cultic use of the creation story during the biblical period, we
do know that "the book of the Law of Moses" or, more simply,
"the Torah" (Neh. 8:1–2), presumably the Pentateuch, was

read at least once—during the ministry of Ezra—and the occasion was Sukkot, the Feast of Tabernacles (Neh. 7:73; 8:14–18). In view of the probable Babylonian origins of P, it is worth recalling that the creation myth *enuma elish* was recited in the course of the *akitu* or New Year Festival.[28]

Given the dependence of P's archaic history on ancient Sumero-Akkadian myth, the relation between creation and deluge in this source cannot be viewed exclusively in chronological terms. P does of course speak of an ostensibly chronological sequence, a primitive *historia mundi:* creation, multiplication of mankind, sin and violence, punishment by deluge. This, however, serves a theological purpose, to give expression to the belief that judgment lies essentially in the past and that God is now offering his people a new dispensation of grace. Hence we are justified in reading the P-edited deluge story as a kind of parable of the inundation of Israel by the nations resulting in exile from the land (read also, earth).[29] This is, very likely, the way P was designed to be read throughout. It is noticeable, for example, that the P version of the plagues has some interesting linguistic and thematic parallels with Ezekiel's oracles against Egypt.[30]

Moreover, P was doubtless aware of the fact that the old Mesopotamian deluge myth functioned as a creation myth in its own right. In *enuma elish* (I 69–79) Ea overcomes Apsu (who stands for the watery deep) and establishes his sanctuary on him (it). The outcome of Marduk's victory over Tiamat, the female monster of watery chaos, was the building of the sanctuary Esagila for him. Its foundations, we are told, reached down as far as the *apsu;* therefore, it too was built over the deluge waters (*enuma elish* VI 62–64).[31] Something of the same representation is found in the ancient Canaanite texts from Ugarit.[32] Similarly, Lucian of Samosata reports, with thinly veiled scepticism, that the temple of Hierapolis on the Euphrates was founded over the flood waters by Deukalion, the Greek counterpart of Ziusudra, Utnapishtim and Noah.[33] We are reminded of the symbolism of the temple-ziggurat, which stood for the mound of creation, the first heap of dry land to appear over the flood waters.[34] As for Israel, one of the temple hymns speaks of the LORD enthroned over the abyss of flood waters.[35] This powerful mythic representation, which for obvious reasons is not given free play in biblical literature, is however fully exploited by later Jewish midrashists.[36]

For P, then, the deluge serves a double function. It is a parable of judgment and salvation for those who had come through the flood waters of the exile (cf. Ps. 124:4–5). It is also the celebration of the Israelite God's victory resulting in the building of a sanctuary infinitely greater than that of Marduk in the Babylon that had been left behind.[37] In this latter respect, P comes quite close to the author of Is. 40–55 who uses the creation as conquest theme to such telling effect.[38] For obvious historical reasons the element of royal ideology present in the myth is not stressed by P, from which, however, it does not follow that P is opposed to the monarchy.[39] We may assume that P emphasizes the building of the sanctuary rather than accession to the throne as the climax of the myth, thus providing Israel with a highly unique and appropriate version of creation as a foundation or charter myth for the rebuilt sanctuary and the cult which was to be carried out in it.

It does not seem possible to draw any significant conclusions from a comparison of the dimensions of Noah's ark with those of the wilderness sanctuary. Like the Temple of Solomon, the latter reflects in its appointments and probably also in its architecture a cosmic symbolism which has been recognized at least as early as Josephus.[40] It is also noteworthy that both Noah's ark and the Temple reflect the three-decker world of ancient Near Eastern cosmogonies. For obvious reasons, this feature could not be reproduced in the wilderness sanctuary.[41]

The presence of the P formulae in Joshua raises the question alluded to earlier of the extent of this narrative source. Nowadays the tendency to deny to P any substantial hand in the book seems to be on the increase, but that this tendency needs to be reversed can be argued on several grounds. First, some passages of undisputed P vintage in the Pentateuch—the promise of land to the fathers, the purchase of a parcel of land by Abraham as a kind of down-payment, the mission of the spies, the census, the order of the camp—are unintelligible on the assumption that P had no interest in the occupation of the land. This does not, of course, prove that P had a conquest and occupation narrative, but it at least puts the onus of proving otherwise on those who deny it. The assumption that the work ended with the death of Moses generally stems from failure to distinguish between P and the P-edited Pentateuch. It is recognized that the P version of the last days of Moses and appointment of Joshua as successor (Num. 27:12–23) has been repeated with modifications towards the end of Deuteronomy (32:48–52 and 34:7–9). This piece of editing gives us a valuable clue to the final stages in the production of the Pentateuch (as we shall see in the following chapter) but tells us nothing about the original ending of P. We are therefore left with the task of applying the same stylistic and thematic criteria to Joshua as have been applied successfully to the Pentateuch over the last 150 years. The results will not be certain (they rarely are), but the incidence of the formulaic expressions listed earlier already shows that a reasonable case can be established.[42] More specifically, the structural correspondence between creation-deluge, construction of the sanctuary and its establishment in the land strongly suggests that P originally ended at much the same point as the old JE epos, namely, with the conquest and occupation.

This point about *the land,* a central issue in the Dispersion of the sixth century B.C.E. as it still is today, requires more careful formulation. Nothing like a coherent and consecutive P account of the conquest can be identified in the first half of Joshua and it is probable that no such account ever existed. The reason would seem to be that (for theological reasons) this source was not interested in the conquest. If the dispersed "remnant" would ever return to the land, it would be God's doing, not man's; and therefore (as Robert Pfeiffer put it), P simply wiped the Canaanites off the map with a stroke of the pen.[43] It was different, however, with the lists of tribal territories and descriptions of boundaries (chapters 13–21). These had to be included since P, like Ezekiel, was interested in laying down a program for the future. But it is important to note that P's interest in the land is dictated by cultic concerns. The sanctuary is the center of the land or, conversely, the land is the hinterland of the sanctuary. It corresponds to the camp in the wilderness which constitutes an area of secondary holiness around the sanctuary, itself surrounding the Holy of Holies.[44] It is the property of the deity who inhabits the sanctuary and is held in fief from him, tenure depending on observance of the laws of holiness. It is this *cultic* view of land tenure which explains, for example, the sabbatical law as stated in the Holiness Code (Lev. 25:18–24) taken over by P. Ritual purity is attainable only in Yahweh's land (*'ereṣ 'ᵃḥuzzat YHWH*), where his sanctuary is (Jos. 22:19); all other lands are impure.[45] If P associates possession of the land and the divine presence within the covenant context, it is because of this intrinsic theological relation between sanctuary and land. It is this new idea, or rather new appropriation of an ancient theologoumenon, which provides the key to understanding P's version of the occupation and distribution of the land.

According to P, the concluding stage of land distribution was carried out at Shiloh under the supervision of Joshua, successor of Moses, and Eleazar, successor of Aaron, with the latter apparently playing the dominant role. It begins with the setting up of the sanctuary (Jos. 18:1) and ends with the conclusion formula as described earlier (19:51). Affinity with the P creation narrative is slighter at this point but still unmistakable:

Creation of the world	*Distribution of the land*
Be fruitful and multiply, and fill the earth (*'ereṣ*) and subdue it (*kibšuhā*) (Gen. 1:28)	And the land (*'ereṣ*) was subdued (*nikbᵉšāh*) before them (Jos. 18:1)
God completed his work which he had done (Gen. 2:2)	So they finished dividing the land (*'ereṣ*) (Jos. 19:51)

Use of the same verb (*kbš*) suggests that with the allotment of land the command given at creation to fill the earth and subdue it has now been fulfilled. It is also noteworthy that in P the word *'ereṣ* stands for both the created world and the land of promise, the usage strongly suggesting symbolic association between the two meanings. It is also possible that there is a conscious parallelism between the work of dividing in creation and the dividing of the land, even though different verbs are employed. Assuming that the Priestly corpus ended at this point,[46] we would then have an example of the literary device of inclusion used so frequently in ancient Near Eastern compositions.

An important passage in the Holiness Code (H) also makes an association between the occupation of the land and the observance of the purity laws (Lev. 20:22–26). If Israel does not observe these laws, it says, the land will vomit them out. It then goes on, "I am the LORD your God who has *divided you off* from the nations; you shall therefore *divide* (make a distinction) between the clean and the unclean. . ." This may seem surprising and even perplexing, for P is generally thought to reflect the needs and speak to the situation of the diaspora in Babylon.[47] In point of fact we have no idea how representative P was or whether it was representative of anyone except the learned clerics who wrote it. If the interpretation presented above is correct, the closest affinities would be with the author of Ezek. 40–48 or those "Zionist" prophets who returned with the *aliyah* led by *Zerubbabel* (one of them speaks of "Zion dwelling in Babylon," Zech. 2:11). Our conclusion, then, is that the P history probably ended at much the same point as the earlier sources which it incorporated, but that its interpretation of the ancient promise of land was very different from theirs.

III. P and Ezekiel

The brief description of P just presented suggests that the time is ripe for a re-evaluation, not to say a rehabilitation of this work. It is no secret that a century after Wellhausen it is still regarded as one of the least attractive parts of the Bible. Most of it is never read even by the devout Bible-reading public, very little of it has found its way into Christian worship and even professional (Christian) exegetes find little good to say about it. Worse still, this negative evaluation has contributed not a little to the still common misrepresentation of Judaism as an arid system of ritual and legal observance, a religion of the letter that kills rather than the spirit that quickens. What I have tried to show, on the contrary, is that beneath the surface of this work one can still make out the contours of an encompassing mythic pattern. As for the ritualism (with which we have not dealt), it is not too much to view it as embodying a concern for man's concrete existence in relation to the cosmos, his corporeality, the significance of bodily states, his entire existence on the temporal and spatial axis. Nor is it far-fetched to suggest that this product of ancient Jewish piety and learning may act as a corrective to some of our own unexamined suppositions: the vague assumption, for example, that only "internal" acts are significant. Lack of interest on the part of the modern reader may simply reflect lack of concern for how he relates to the world, or for the body as that part of the world for which he is more directly responsible. It goes without saying that a theology of P incorporating such insights still remains to be written.

One of the standard ways since Wellhausen of downgrading P has been to contrast it with prophecy. One can see the point of such a contrast, but prophecy has turned out to be a much more complex and multidimensional reality than scholars took it to be a century or even a few decades ago. Thus it is not otiose to point out that priests and prophets are often found in close association and collaboration during the monarchy and on into the exilic period. Jeremiah addressed a letter to elders, priests and prophets in the *gôlāh* in which two prophets executed by the Babylonians are mentioned by name (Jer. 29). Another *gôlāh*-prophet, Shemaiah, in his turn wrote to the temple clergy in Jerusalem urging them to exercise control over deranged prophets like Jeremiah who were causing trouble (Jer. 29:24ff). The "false prophets" denounced so often by Jeremiah and Ezekiel were much concerned with temple worship and some of them belonged to the temple staff. Haggai and Zechariah appear to stand in the same line of development as the "false" prophecy represented by Jeremiah's opponent, Hananiah of Gibeon, and the "Zionist" prophecy which sustained those in Babylon who never gave up hope of going home. It is a striking fact that oracles attributed to such

"false" prophets in Jeremiah and Ezekiel often resemble sayings of Haggai and Zechariah.[48] We are given no clue as to the
origins of the former (unless it be his name), but the latter
appears to belong to an exiled priestly family.[49] Thus there are
good grounds for believing that close ties continued to exist
during the exile between priests and prophets, and this may
well bear on our understanding of the context of P.

Contrasting P with "classical" prophecy is misleading in a
more basic sense in that it ignores the very different historical
situation in which the former came into existence. Much had
happened between the time of Amos, or even of Jeremiah,
and that of the exiled communities in Babylon. Not just the
obvious political changes but some deeper shifts which accompanied these changes; and, in particular, the displace-
ment of the idea of collective responsibility and guilt by a new
emphasis on the individual. Thus, if we wish to understand
why "classical" prophecy disappeared about this time, it will
not help to speak vaguely (as many do) of the drying up of
inspiration. We have to deal in the first place with the
emergence of a different situation in which it could no longer
function.[50]

One aspect of the change might be described inelegantly as
the scribalization of prophecy. Jeremiah is still very definitely
an oral prophet, collections of whose sayings were, however,
written down not long after they were spoken. While Ezekiel
was also clearly a speaker, he is a *literary* figure in a way in
which Jeremiah was not. The visionary feat of swallowing a
book (whether or not he "gave it up again," as Wellhausen
added) was therefore an appropriate symbol of the change that
prophecy was undergoing. Known to his contemporaries as
"the parable monger" (the reason for which is apparent even
after a superficial reading of the book), he is commanded to
use sapiential forms such as the parable and riddle and does so
frequently.[51] An exponent of *halakah* addressed to the needs of
the individual, he stands much closer to subsequent than to
preceding prophetic figures.[52] If he is not the first of the
epigoni, as Wellhausen characterized him, he is the first to
exhibit clearly in his work the collapse of propheticism into
priestly and scribal forms.

Granted this reading of Ezekiel, he will be readily seen as the bridge between prophecy under the monarchy and ecclesiastical scribalism such as is found in P. The closest affinity is between P's cultic theology and the "law of the temple" in the last section of Ezekiel (chapters 40–48). Both Ezekiel's temple and the priestly sanctuary derive from visionary experiences in which the architectural model is revealed. In both works the cosmic temple set on a high mountain is described in mythic language and presented as the climax of creation.[53] Together with other thematic similarities this will suggest the possibility that P stands in some way within the ambit of Ezekiel's disciples. For even if the "law of the temple" is denied to Ezekiel (for which a convincing case has yet to be made), it still has to be explained why it was placed where it is. And in fact the similarities are not confined to these last chapters. In both works the modality of the divine appearance is the mysterious "glory" (*kābôd*) which manifests itself to Israel in the wilderness according to P and to the exiled community in Ezekiel.[54] The revelatory form "I am the LORD" is also characteristic of both works, suggesting that they draw on the same ancient theophanic tradition to describe how God may be present in the midst of a sinful people.[55] One could also compare the learned use of mythological themes in Ezekiel and P.[56] The case is less clear with the ethical and ritual legislation and instruction in these two works, but there are interesting affinities which call for an explanation.[57] A detailed comparison could also be made on the basis of vocabulary and style, the results of which would also indicate a fairly close affinity. Allowing full recognition to the fact that both P and Ezekiel would have drawn on ancient priestly traditions, formulations and even vocabulary,[58] one could still make out a reasonable case that in some important respects P represents a systematic presentation of Ezekiel's theology, with particular emphasis on his teaching on the "remnant."[59]

Such conclusions, however, remain speculative and subject to revision in the absence of hard data from the period in question. The fact is that we have no definite information on the "circles" responsible for P who were laboring over the old traditions and laws in the *gôlāh*. Nor do we hear anything definite about a group of disciples which gathered around Ezekiel. The closest we come to a clue is the repeated reference to elders who gathered in his house and, on one occasion at least, witnessed his prophetic ecstasy (Ezek. 8:1ff.; 14:1ff.; 20:1ff.). The elders, we know, retained their association with the priesthood during the exilic period and during the difficult days following the first return.[60] In the older sources and in P they are frequently associated with Aaron. Together with him they witness the revelation of the *kābôd* at Sinai and are seized ecstastically when Moses calls them to the Tent of Meeting for their commissioning.[61] If in the absence of hard information we may offer a suggestion, it would be that the elders are the "missing link" between Ezekiel and the priestly-scribal circles from which P comes. It is no more than a guess that they came to Ezekiel's house to discuss with him the feasibility of building a temple for the exiled communities, but we do find them active in the work of rebuilding after the return. Their association with the scribes is also attested for the same period.[62]

IV. The Overcoming of Time in the Priestly Work

It would probably be agreed that the priestly world-view as it comes to expression in P is dominated by the sacred. There is a sacred time, which is in the remote past, a sacred place which is the temple, and sacred people who are the priests who serve there. It would also be widely agreed that the great prophets of judgment do not confine God's activity to the remote past, nor to the cult, nor to officially designated persons responsible for it. Without necessarily claiming that the prophets of Israel were the first to confer theological significance on history,[63] it would seem proper to emphasize the importance for them of contemporary events as the arena of God's activity and to conclude that this is a fundamental characteristic of prophecy under the monarchy. In Ezekiel this rootedness in present historical realities is already much less apparent; and, as we would expect, the mythological coloring is correspondingly higher. With P, however, the attempt to

overcome time (to use a favorite phrase of Eliade) is carried
out in a thoroughgoing and systematic way. How this leaves P
in relation to prophecy may be seen if we consider briefly the
time, the place and the recipient of revelation in this work.

In keeping with the work of the Deuteronomists, but not
necessarily dependent on it, the exodus and wilderness periods
down to the occupation of the land constitute Israel's normative time.[64] The account of the deaths of Aaron and Moses
(Num. 20:22–29; 27:12–23), while they did not stand at the
end of the P narrative, were clearly of great structural importance in it and became even more important when the book of
Deuteronomy was joined with the priestly Tetrateuch. One
very significant difference was the role of Aaron, ancestor of
the priesthood, who was a figure of no particular importance
for the Deuteronomists.[65] But P also differs from the work of
this school in another very noteworthy respect, in that its
authors showed no interest in interpreting the history of the
monarchy. This, in its turn, implies that they did not feel
called upon to deal explicitly with the historical phenomenon
of prophecy even if, in the nature of the case, they could not
have ignored it. What P did instead was present the wilderness
period as a paradigm of the ideal Israel of the future. Decisions, judgments and evaluations affecting that generation
refer cryptically to the time of the monarchy and pass judgment implicitly on that later history as one of spiritual failure.[66] It is no surprise, then, that during that paradigmatic
generation the Aaronite priesthood takes precedence over all
other offices. Earlier traditions are reworked and sometimes
radically modified to fit into the priestly institutional pattern.
Num. 16–18, for example, deals with the respective competences of priests and levites. In the first incident recorded here
(Num. 16) P seems to have grafted on to an old tradition
about the rebellion of two Reubenites an etiological narrative
dealing with the attempt of Kohathite Levites to break the
Aaronite monopoly of the priesthood. The offenders are
brought before the Tent of Meeting and disposed of by a
precisely engineered earthquake. The lesson, spelled out
clearly for all to read (v. 40), is that the Aaronite priests share
their duties and prerequisites with no one. But it is noticeable

that Moses presents himself as the divinely appointed emissary
or prophet (vv. 28–29) and that in atoning for the survivors
Aaron fulfils in a somewhat different way the traditional prophetic role of intercessor.[67] This is just one indication that in
P the prophetic has been absorbed into a comprehensive pattern of theocratic government.

It goes without saying that in P major decisions are not
made with prophetic help. Important and disputed legal
points—the punishment appropriate for sabbath violation
(Num. 15:32–36) or inheritance claims (Num. 27:1–11), for
example—are decided by appeal to the cultic oracle, in
agreement with evidence that the ancient Urim and Thummim was revived in the post-exilic period.[68] From a modern
critical viewpoint we may say that P undercut the entire history of prophecy under the monarchy to return to its distant
origins in the cultic and oracular.

Compared with the work of the Deuteronomists, one of the
most salient characteristics of the P narrative is its extension
back into the archaic history of mankind. If, as suggested
earlier, the P-edited story of the great deluge functions as a
parable of Israel's inundation by the *gôyîm*, the history of
spiritual decline which led up to it (with the emphasis in P on
violence) corresponds with the history of Israel's failure under
the monarchy. The message is then one of hope, for judgment
is seen to lie in the past and, in a sense, the end of the world
has already taken place.[69] This interpretation is strengthened
by the fact that only in P does God make a perpetual covenant
(*bᵉrît 'ôlām*) with humanity after the deluge (Gen. 9:16), one,
that is, which does not have to be renewed from time to time
in order to remain in effect.[70] In this respect also, then, the
learned appropriation of mythological themes serves the purpose of de-emphasizing the importance of present historical
realities in favor of a distant and paradigmatic past. It will be
clear that this involved a radical reassessment of the historical
phenomenon of prophecy.

A similar "remythologizing" is also at work in regard to the
place of revelation as conceived by the priestly-scribal school.
The thematic link between creation and cult, cosmos and
temple, detectable in the very structure of the work, points

clearly in this direction. We recall that Gudea, the ruler of the
Sumerian city of Lagash, was given a plan by the gods for
building the temple of Ningirsu, and that the temple Esagila
in Babylon was not only planned but built by divine beings.[71]
Moses received the heavenly model (*tabnît*) of the sanctuary
together with its furnishings on the mountain, just as Ezekiel
was given the design (*toknît*) of the new temple, also on a
mountain, with the command to pass it on to the people of
Israel.[72] That the sanctuary owed its existence to a visionary
experience comparable to those of the prophets is a point of
some importance for understanding P. It fits in with the de-
mand that the master craftsman Bezalel be filled with the
divine spirit (Ex. 31:3) before he can undertake work on the
sanctuary. In later Judaism this association between the temple and the Holy Spirit—which is pre-eminently the spirit of
prophecy—is explicitly attested. Josephus, for example, informs us that the temple owed its existence to a divine oracle
and received at its dedication a portion of the Holy Spirit.[73]
Within it were carried on activities which could be properly
designated prophetic, and after its destruction by the Babylonians the Holy Spirit left Israel.[74] This concentration of the
prophetic within the cultic sphere, first consistently attested
in P, implied a very definite interpretation of prophecy which
was to leave its mark on Judaism thereafter in a variety of
ways.

In P, then, the wilderness sanctuary—variously described as
the Tent of Meeting (*'ohel mô'ēd*), Tent of Witness (*'ohel
ha'ēdût*), sanctuary (*miškān*) or sanctuary of witness (*miškan
ha'ēdût*)—is *the* place of revelation. It was there that Moses
was summoned to hear God speaking to him from above the
cover of the ark (e.g., Ex. 25:22), it was there that guidance
was available in the crises which developed during the wilderness sojourn, and it was the cloud and fire above the sanctuary
which dictated the pace and direction of the journey from
Sinai to Canaan.[75] Since the wilderness period is the
paradigm time for Israel, what the P source is in fact saying
with all this is that for Israel there is no other access to the
divine world except through the cult and its ministers.

The point will be made more forcibly if we recall that the

priestly tent-sanctuary, like so much else in this work, is a product of the reinterpretation of ancient tradition. This tradition also knows of a tent in the wilderness, and it has been pointed out that wherever it is mentioned in the ancient (i.e., pre-Deuteronomic) form of the story it is associated in one way or another with prophecy.[76] When it was set up outside the camp (not in the center as in P), anyone who needed oracular guidance went out to it (e.g., Ex. 33:7). It was therefore an oracle-tent, perhaps serviced by a cultic ecstatic.[77] It was there that the seventy elders received their commission and were endowed with the prophetic spirit (Num. 11:16ff.), and it was there, too, that the oracle was given which brought to an end the "prophetic" rebellion of Miriam and Aaron (Num. 12:4ff.). Here too, then, we see how the historical development of prophecy has been undercut by a return to the archaic period, in this case by the simple expedient of combining the oracle tent of the old traditions with the central camp sanctuary controlled by the priesthood. For a generation anticipating a new start in the homeland the message was unmistakable: the essential decisions affecting legitimacy and authority had all been made in the canonical epoch and remained unaffected by later developments. The way was clear for a new start.

A final instance of the rewriting of ancient tradition remains to be considered. The early version of the call of Moses (Ex. 3:1–4:17), attributed to JE, is guided by a profound acquaintance with and appreciation for the prophetic calling. Given the fact that Moses was recognized as a prophet at least as early as Hosea, it is hardly surprising that an ancient shrine-theophany of a kind popular throughout the ancient Near East should have been written to resemble the numinous experiences which generally accompanied the call of a prophet. The pattern is particularly clear in Jeremiah's call: the commission to speak to an unreceptive public, the prophet's expostulations, the assurance of ultimate success, the role of the prophet as the mouthpiece of the deity.[78] When we turn to the P version, which in this case has not supplanted the earlier one, we note that Aaron is now explicitly designated as prophet (*nābîʾ*); "see," the LORD says to Moses, "I have made

you God to Pharaoh, and Aaron your brother will be your
prophet" (7:1). This would suggest that the prophetic office
has now devolved on the priesthood in the person of its
eponym and ancestor, and that therefore the passage is to be
read as an etiology (and therefore legitimation) of the exercise
of prophecy by the priesthood.

The apologists for priestly supremacy in the new situation
created by the collapse of the monarchy had clearly given
much thought to the refashioning of these ancient traditions.
The position of Moses as charismatic founder, ultimate source
of legitimacy, a figure both priestly and prophetic,[79] was
well-established before the time of P. Aaron, therefore, remains subordinate to him in the latter work but his role is
greatly expanded. It is P, for example, who stresses the seniority of Aaron and effects the transfer of the magical staff from
Moses to him.[80] Whereas in the earlier traditions Aaron is
involved in unsuccessful rebellion against Moses (Ex. 32 and
Num. 12), in P he saves the mission to Pharaoh from failure
by assuming the prophetic role at the critical moment. After
the death of Moses and Aaron, the successor of the latter,
Eleazar, plays a more decisive part beginning with the investi-
ture of Joshua as Moses' successor (Num. 27:15–23). This is
even more significant since it provided a pattern for leadership
in the theocratic commonwealth the design for which it was
P's intention to provide.[81]

The situation, then, begins to look something like the following. Before the loss of national independence religious
authority, which meant control of the redemptive media,
resided in the monarchy and the state institutions, including
the cult. During and after the exile, the temple priesthood
filled the vacuum created by the disappearance of the
monarchy, their goal being to create "a kingdom of priests, a
holy people." It is of interest to note that several items of
priestly attire give symbolic expression to this assumption of
royal prerogative: the breastpiece appears to derive from the
royal pectoral, the turban from the crown and the rosette from
a badge of some sort worn either by the king himself or those
in his service.[82] Armed with this power the priesthood set out
to forge anew the links with Israel's past before the monarchy

and, therefore, also before the emergence of prophecy as a recognizable historical phenomenon. The intent was transparently clear: to establish their own claim to authority beyond challenge and on this basis to set up an institution as immune as possible to the vicissitudes of history. The measure of success attending this enterprise is to be gauged by the fact that that institution still survives 2,500 years later. The price that had to be paid was the encapsulation of the charismatic (and, therefore, potentially disruptive) within the bounds of the institution.[83] In the present chapter we have verified these conclusions to the extent of showing that P not only reflects the transformation which prophecy was undergoing but also decisively furthered that transformation. By providing its own answer to the issue of authority, it effectively neutralized the claim of the free prophets under the monarchy. Once that answer was incorporated into the priestly-scribal Torah-canon it became a decisive force in shaping Judaism in the post-exilic period.

4: No Prophet like Moses

I. The Final Stage of Redaction

THE LAST STAGE IN THE FORMATION OF THE PENTA-
teuch was the incorporation of the Deuteronomic law book,
detached from the history of the post-Mosaic era, into the
expanded P version of the Israelite epos. We have no direct
information on when this final combination took place. It
could not have happened after the secession of the Samaritan
cultic community, since the Samaritans based themselves on
the Pentateuch, regarding any additions to it as unwarranted.
Since, however, the Samaritans probably did not achieve a
separate identity at one precise point in time, we can do no
better on that score than establish a *terminus ad quem* in the
late fourth or early third century B.C.E. Perhaps all we can say
is that the Pentateuch was a product of the Persian period. We
note that it ends not with the exile, as did the Deuteronomic
history, nor with the occupation of the land, as did the early
sources and P, but with the death of Moses. This will remind
us that the reforms of Nehemiah and Ezra, unlike those carried
out under Assyrian domination, must have presupposed re-
nunciation of claims to independent possession of the land. If
the "law of the God of heaven" brought by Ezra to Jerusalem
was in fact our Pentateuch, the omission of the conquest
narrative—the logical conclusion of the story from Abraham
onwards—is readily intelligible.

It has, moreover, already been pointed out that whereas
Nehemiah's reforms were based for the most part on the

Deuteronomic law Ezra moved in the world of the Priestly
Work. Ezra's book could then be viewed as a compromise
between the Palestinian Deuteronomy and the Babylonian
Priestly Work. As such, it served as an instrument of Persian
imperial policy in a particularly sensitive part of their empire
and at the same time as an instrument of reconciliation between *golah*-Jews and Palestinians including Samaritans.

As we follow the successive steps in the production of the
Torah-canon the question of the kind of authorization or
legitimation required to take them will naturally call for discussion. Deuteronomy, we have seen, is presented as a prophetic book since its author was a prophet.[1] In studying P, we
have noted evidence for the assimilation of the prophetic
function to the priesthood which claimed descent from Moses'
family. The ascription of the entire Pentateuch to Moses, held
almost universally down into the early modern period, was the
logical outcome of this need for legitimation, expressing as it
does the conviction that this first canon was prophetically
inspired. According to the creed of Maimonides, Moses was
the father of all prophets before and after him.[2] Everything
essential for Israel's life was revealed at Sinai including therefore not only the Prophets and Writings but the Mishnah and
Gemarah.[3] Ezra, too, as the one who re-established Torah
after the disasters of the monarchy and the exile, had to be not
only priest and sage but also prophet. In the Ezra Apocalypse
(2 Esdras), an anonymous composition from the last decades
of the first century of the era, he is explicitly designated as
such (1:1; 12:42) and is granted a series of seven apocalyptic
visions. In the last of these he is ordered to write out again all
the books which had been destroyed consisting of twenty-four
for the worthy and unworthy and seventy reserved to the wise
among the people (chapter 14). These correspond to the canonical books and the esoteric, apocalyptic writings, all of
which were revealed to Moses at Sinai (14:4–5). While it is
understandable that an apocalypticist should transform the
revelation at Sinai into an apocalyptic vision, this move
would hardly have been possible had not prophetic inspiration
of the highest kind been attributed already to Moses.

Thus we can say that the entire canon is prophetic, but only if we add that in the meantime prophecy has undergone a profound transformation.

The final stage of editing the Torah-canon can be deduced with some assurance from the conclusion of the work, namely, the last four chapters of the last book in it (Deut. 31–34), which deal with the final dispositions and death of Moses. This section is not organically part of Deuteronomy but was appended to it as the finale to the Pentateuch as a whole. That it was not composed at one writing is apparent from the fact that almost everything recorded in it is repeated at least once.[4] Moreover, the critics, despite the usual disagreement in detail, are generally at one in finding evidence here of the early traditions (JE), the Deuteronomic school and the priestly-scribal tradent. It represents, then, a deposit of tradition accumulated over several centuries which testifies to the abiding significance of the death of Moses as the "great divide" in the history of Israel. The following brief analysis of the section would be fairly representative of the modern critical position:

(1) An account of the last dispositions of Moses, predictions concerning the future, the all-important matter of a successor (31:1–13, 24–29; 32:45–47); from the Deuteronomic school.

(2) A psalm recorded as a witness against Israel (31:16–22, 30; 32:1–44); probably from one of the older literary strands, though inserted here when the Pentateuch had reached more or less its present shape.

(3) The commissioning of Joshua at the Tent of Meeting (31:14–15, 23), the command given Moses to die (32:48–52), his actual death and the succession of Joshua (34:1, 7–9); the first of these passages betrays some affinity with the priestly tradent while the others are unequivocally P.

(4) A psalm incorporating oracles or blessings on ten of the tribes (33); while we need not doubt the antiquity of much of this composition, it was inserted here at a mature stage in the formation of the Pentateuch.

(5) An account of the actual death of Moses (34:1–6); probably already part of JE, it has been elaborated by the

Deuteronomists and furnished with an introduction in the P style.

(6) An *excipit* extolling Moses and the age which passed with his death (34:10–12); presumably the last touch, later than either D or P but using language borrowed from the former.[5]

Once we have our bearings in this section it should be possible to gain some insight into the editorially crucial process of conflation which resulted in the Pentateuch. And here it is of the greatest importance to note that the P version of the last days of Moses and commissioning of Joshua is a revised edition of Num. 27:12–23, indubitably from the main body of the Priestly Work. The incorporation of the book of Deuteronomy into the P-edited narrative was achieved elegantly and economically by the simple expedient of inserting a date near the beginning (Deut. 1:3) which brought the book firmly within the P chronology. The ensuing disadvantage, however, was that an intolerable gap was thus created between the announcement of Moses' death in Num. 27 and its actual occurrence.[6] It was in order to mitigate this awkward situation that the P version of the command given Moses to die and the commissioning of Joshua was repeated. In order to grasp the implications of this piece of editing the two passages (Num. 27:12–23; Deut. 32:48–52; 34:7–9) should be read synoptically.[7] It will be noted that there are some relatively minor adjustments which are explained by the necessity of aligning the new conclusion with the law book immediately preceding it. Such, for example, is the statement that Moses may see the land from a distance but not enter it, a point often made in Deuteronomy.[8] The introductory phrase "that same day" (Deut. 32:48) puts the death of Moses on the same day as the promulgation of the law in Moab, and thereby redefines the book as a valedictory rather than a law book. The new version of the succession of Joshua is telegrammatically brief in comparison with the earlier version in Numbers. Unlike the Deuteronomic version of the same event,[9] the *semikah* or laying on of hands is involved. Joshua is therefore ordained to office in an institutionally valid way. While such an official act clearly limits the operation of the charismatic principle, which Max Weber has shown to be particularly important in succession to office,[10] there is a significant difference between the two versions at this point. Whereas in Num. 27:18 Joshua is *antecedently* spirit-endowed, in the later version this condition is attributed to an efficacious, valid act, one which appears to derive from the sacrificial cultus.[11] Charisma is therefore not the reason for but the result of the act of commissioning, making it look rather like what some Christian theologians call "the grace of state." Moreover, the spirit with which Joshua is endowed is now more carefully described as "the spirit of wisdom," wisdom signifying here and elsewhere skill in governing. It would therefore seem possible to conclude that one reason for ending the story in this way was to lay a firm foundation for law, order and obedience in the new era about to begin. There is no authority apart from legitimately established office standing in the valid line of succession. Rule, teaching and guidance cannot be left to the vagaries of personal inspiration and revelation.

It will be noticed, too, that in the original P version the political leader represented by Joshua must be guided by the priesthood in the person of Aaron's successor, Eleazar. Moses did not need a priestly mediator since he recapitulated in his own person the office of both prophet and priest. This, however, was a unique occurrence and the situation would be quite different beginning with Joshua. Unlike the actual situation under the monarchy, when the ruler sought guidance from the prophet, it is now the priest who takes over this function with the help of the archaic Urim and Thummim. We are, again, reminded of the role of the *nāśî'* in Ezek. 40–48, the relation between the political ruler Zerubbabel and the high priest Joshua after the Restoration and the political function of the priesthood in the post-exilic period in general. P, therefore, anticipated the problems created by dyarchic rule and provided an answer by a clear affirmation of the theocratic principle.

This etiology of legitimate succession to office affords a fascinating glimpse into the situation of tension between charisma and institution (to use Weber's terms) in the Second

Temple period. The standard model for charismatic succession was that of the prophet and his disciple, and the paradigmatic instance was the endowment of Elisha with a double share of Elijah's spirit.[12] So powerful was this paradigm that the tradition of the seventy elders sharing leadership with Moses (Num. 11:16–25) had to conclude with their ecstatic prophesying even though we hear nowhere of this happening to elders. This last is thematically very close to Joshua's succession to Moses where it is also a question of government and the perseverance of the charismatic principle. Indeed, it seems likely that the P versions of Joshua's succession depend in some way on the tradition about the seventy elders—in which, incidentally, Joshua also plays a part. Both are solemn cultic acts initiated by a command to Moses to *take* (*lāqaḥ*) the designated persons. The key phrase in both passages is also similar: "I will take some of the spirit which is on you and put it on them" (Num. 11:17); "You will put some of your authority (*hôd*) on him" (Num. 27:20). This suggests that the P tradition has superimposed on a prophetic-charismatic model what Max Weber called the hereditary charisma of the priesthood.[13] The spirit no longer blows where it wills; its flow is purposefully controlled to serve designated ends. The charisma which was once the prerogative of the prophet is now embodied in legitimate institutional forms and procedures. On this showing, then, the implications for the free exercise of prophecy are hardly in doubt.

II. The Last Paragraph of the Pentateuch

The revised P version of the succession of Joshua was intended as the final incident in the official account of the community's origins. The few remarks which follow bringing the Pentateuch to a close (Deut. 34:10–12), do not in fact have anything in common with P. Whatever affinities may be detectable would rather be with the Deuteronomists, referring back quite deliberately to those parts of the law book which speak of prophecy. That the opening verse of the Former Prophets (Jos. 1:1) follows on more naturally after Deut. 34:6

or 34:9 confirms our impression that it is a relatively late
statement, the purpose of which was to round off the Pentateuch after the combination of Deuteronomy with the
Priestly Tetrateuch.

The heart of the matter lies in v. 10: "there has never since
arisen in Israel a prophet like Moses whom the LORD knew
face to face." Here at once we have a problem with the translation. It might seem possible to render the sentence "There
has not yet arisen in Israel a prophet like Moses" with the
implication that such a prophet will arise in the future. This
would be in accord with the promise of a prophet like Moses in
Deut. 18:15–18 which we discussed earlier. It might even
seem possible to take this a little further and interpret it as the
first eschatological exegesis of that passage, in line with later
use of this important text in the Qumran and early Christian
communities. Attractive as this option may sound, we would
be well advised to put it aside from the start. For one thing, in
all instances where this particular construction occurs in the
Hebrew Bible (*lo'* . . . *'ôd* with the past tense) it never means
"not yet" with the implication "it hasn't happened yet but it
will later." Following attested usage it must on the contrary be
translated "never again," "never since" or "no longer" with no
limitation of time unless expressly stated.[14] The phrase in
Deut. 34:10, therefore, implies an all-inclusive retrospective
evaluation of the period from the death of Moses to the time
of writing.[15] It denies parity between Moses and the prophets
and therefore puts the entire history of prophecy on a decisively lower level than the Mosaic epoch.

It seems quite clear, to begin with, that the scholiast who is
here extolling Moses over the prophets wished to refer
explicitly to the promise of a "Mosaic" prophet occurring earlier in the book.[16] This being the case, it will be of interest to
know what the point of the reference is. We are not obliged to
conclude that he wanted simply to negate the promise for in
the one case it is a question of similarity and in the other of
equality.[17] It is conceivable that his intention was to elimi-
nate the identification of Joshua with the promised prophet.
The statement, in fact, follows immediately after the account
of Joshua's endowment with the spirit, and it was noted earlier

that Joshua is actually so identified in later Jewish tradition.[18] It seems more likely, however, that the sense is more generalized, a warning against reading Deut. 18:15–18 in such a way as to put Moses and the prophets who followed him on the same level.

The promise of a prophet like Moses leads directly into what we shall identify as the central issue in the religious history of Second Temple Judaism: the tension between theocracy and eschatology. While we are in no position to reconstruct the history of the interpretation of this text, we know from its importance in early Christian and Essene *testimonia* that it served to keep alive the eschatological hope at that time. How much further we can go back is uncertain. The Maccabees, we are told, decided to store away the stones of the desecrated altar "until a prophet should arise who could be consulted about them."[19] The prophetic collection ends with two programmatic statements, one enjoining observance of the law of "my servant Moses," the other promising that Elijah the prophet will be sent before the day of Yahweh (Mal. 3:22–24). Given the close thematic links between the Moses and Elijah of Jewish tradition, it is not impossible that the eschatological messenger identified in Mal. 3:23–24 with Elijah was thought to be the Mosaic prophet,[20] though this cannot be proved. At any rate, the conclusions of the Pentateuch and the Prophets provide an interesting contrast and testify indirectly to the tension which developed during the post-exilic period between theocratic order and eschatological thinking.[21] While the gaps in our knowledge of developments during the Persian and early Greek periods throw us back much more than we would wish on speculation, it begins to look as if the promise of a prophet like Moses in the Pentateuch played an important role not only for the official representatives of the theocracy but also for the Samaritans[22] and the eschatological groups.

After this summary statement the last two verses (Deut. 34:11–12) can hardly fail to appear anti-climactic. Introducing as they do a different and distracting idea of prophecy, they must derive from a different source, and this is also apparent in the awkward syntax resulting from the combination.

Since practically every phrase in this last addition can be found in the sermons in the book,[23] it would be reasonable to follow S. R. Driver in assigning them to a later and lesser member of the Deuteronomic school or a writer imitating the Deuteronomic style.[24] The intent was clearly to expand the words of praise for Moses as the prophet without equal:

> (Remember) all the signs and portents which the LORD sent him to show in Egypt to Pharaoh and all his servants and the whole land; (remember) the strong hand of Moses and the terrible deeds which he did in the sight of all Israel.

The regularity with which these clichés keep on appearing in the sermon passages in the book—including the well-known recital to be made at the offering of first-fruits (26:5–10)— suggests that the glossator is drawing on familiar language from the cult. The closest parallels, in fact, can be found in liturgical hymns which review Israel's past in the style and spirit of the Deuteronomists. Two of them, literally translated, are particularly close:

> He sent Moses his servant, Aaron whom he had chosen,
> He put in them the words of his signs (*dibrē 'otôtâv*) and his
>   wonders in the land of Ham (Ps. 105:26f.)
> He sent signs and wonders
> Against Pharaoh and all his servants (Ps. 135:9)

It is noteworthy, though, that not even here are the signs and wonders, much less the strong hand and terrible deeds, attributed to Moses. These belong invariably and routinely only to Yahweh. While it is more than likely that our glossator allowed himself to be carried away with enthusiasm for his subject, it also appears likely that he had in mind the ruling about prophets at Deut. 13:2–4 which speaks of them performing signs and wonders which may or may not come true. This has led to a rather unfortunate combination of the signs and wonders which even false prophets are capable of producing with those wrought by Yahweh in Egypt—brought about, to be sure, by means of Moses. Hence, the emphasis is moved from the central issue of how God reveals himself to his people (v. 10) to the peripheral working of miracles and prediction of the

future. This, however, must not be allowed to obscure the
force of the statement to which this comment is appended; the
statement, that is, about the direct face-to-face communication which existed between God and Moses against which
every subsequent claim to prophetic revelation must be
evaluated and, inevitably, found wanting.

III. Face-to-Face Knowledge

We may take it, then, that Deut. 34:10 affirms a quantitative difference between the epoch of Moses and that of the
prophets. Its position at the end of the Pentateuch gives it a
structurally privileged status as recapitulating the sense of the
entire work and providing a heuristic tool for its interpretation. What then of the "face-to-face" knowledge of Moses
which is implicitly set in contrast to the well-known modes of
communication familiar to the prophets? We have seen that
Deut. 34:10 refers back to the promise of a prophet like
Moses. In the passage in question we find a classical description
of the prophetic mode of communication: Yahweh will put his
words into the prophet's mouth and the prophet will then
speak these words to the people (18:18–19). Understandably,
this formulation draws on the actual experience of prophets as
they themselves articulated it. Jeremiah, for example, tells us
that this is precisely what happened to him (Jer. 1:9). It is an
extraordinary and very privileged mode of communication but
it cannot compare (we are now told) with the unique face-to-
face relationship between God and Moses.

What, then, is this face-to-face knowledge of which the
text speaks? At this point the writer has inherited a great
depth of reflection accumulated from early times on the
unique standing of Moses. According to one early tradition,
probably Elohistic, this was the habitual way in which God
communicated with him: "thus the LORD used to speak to
Moses face to face, as a man speaks to his friend" (Ex. 33:11).
Such a way of speaking would seem to indicate simply the easy
and unstinted familiarity existing between friends. The context, however, does not allow us to leave it at that since it

shows that the exchange used to take place in the old oracle-
tent of the wilderness—a quite extraordinary means of communication since in all other cases the sight of the deity's face
was deemed fatal.[25] In another old tradition, which may be
related, Yahweh spoke to Moses "mouth to mouth" rather
than in visions, dreams and riddles by means of which revelation came habitually to the prophets (Num. 12:6–8). To this
passage an interesting gloss has been appended,[26] to the effect
that Moses contemplated the form (*tᵉmûnāh*) of Yahweh. This
way of speaking of the *face* or the *form* of God is known to us
from the psalms where it betrays its origin in the experience of
worship. One of the complaint psalms, for example, ends with
the following expression of trust (literally translated):

> Since my cause is just I shall see thy face,
> I shall be sated with thy form when I awake (Ps. 17:15)

It was this form of Yahweh which the Israelites did not see
during the covenant-making at Horeb; they only heard a
voice. It is not stated, but is surely implied, that Moses himself
did see it.[27] If this is meant to provide an etiology—and therefore legitimation—of the office of mediator in the cultic re-
enactment of the covenant, an office which recent
scholarship tends to assign to the cultic prophet,[28] it is clear
that Deut. 34:10 has something quite different in mind. For its
purpose is, as we have seen, to contrast the revelation proper
to Moses with that of the prophets.

Much closer thematically would be the tradition dealing
with the "prophetic" rebellion of Miriam and Aaron against
the authority of Moses (Num. 11:35–12:8). It begins with the
questioning of Moses' unique standing as the recipient of divine communications to which the answer comes through an
oracle from the Tent of Meeting:

> Listen to my words:
> If he were your prophet and nothing more,
> I would make myself known to him in a vision,
> I would speak with him in a dream.
> But my servant Moses is not such a prophet;
> He alone is faithful of all my household,

With him I speak mouth to mouth
Openly, and not in riddles
(He shall see the very form of the LORD)
How then do you dare speak against my servant Moses?

There are many uncertainties of interpretation here, but it is at least clear that a distinction is being made between prophetic communication and the form peculiar to Moses. The one is characterized by visions, dreams and riddles—all well-attested in the prophetic writings—while the other is "mouth to mouth" and "open."[29] We have seen that this is precisely the contrast intended in Deut. 34:10. Whatever the origins of the tradition in the passage quoted, which we are not concerned to investigate here, its intent seems to be to place limits on the claims which some prophets or prophetic groups were making at some point in the history. It is, in other words, difficult to imagine why it would have been preserved unless some elements in the community claiming descent from Moses felt themselves to be threatened by the contemporary phenomenon of prophecy. It shows close familiarity with the usual modes of prophetic communication and betrays anxiety that Israel not be drawn away from the cultic center of its existence.[30] The contrast by means of which this critique of prophecy is stated has surely contributed to Deut. 34:10 which recapitulates the Pentateuch and at the same time defines an important aspect of Israel's life for the future.

The same problematic relationship between Moses and the prophets underlies the tradition about the seventy elders referred to earlier in this chapter (Num. 11:16–30). While much about this passage is of uncertain interpretation, it is widely accepted that it contains an attempt to legitimate ecstatic prophecy by attaching it to Moses.[31] This is not, to be sure, what the text says. The seventy men chosen from among the elders and officers are commissioned to share in the government of the community, and to this end they are endowed with a part of Moses' spirit. Since to speak of the spirit is to bring prophecy to mind, the fact that they engaged in some form of prophetic activity once the spirit rested on them may simply be a way of legitimating the succession after the manner of Elijah and Elisha. However that may be, the final part of the narrative, dealing with Eldad and Medad who prophesied without being commissioned at the Tent of Meeting, would most naturally refer to the exercise of prophecy outside the cultic sphere. If this conclusion is warranted, it would serve to remind us that those whom we identify as *the* prophets constituted only a small and anomalous minority among the prophets in Israel at any given point in the history.

The curious passage in which Moses is allowed to see not the face but only the back of the LORD (Ex. 33:18–23) appears to contradict what had been said a little earlier about Yahweh speaking with him face to face. As the preceding conversation between Moses and Yahweh shows, the question at issue was how Yahweh, whose domain was at Sinai, could be present with Israel during its journey through the wilderness. The first request of Moses, that he and the people may know the ways of Yahweh, is answered by the promise that the divine presence (literally, face) will go with them, a probable allusion to the mobile ark-sanctuary. The second request, that he see the glory (*kābôd*) of Yahweh, receives its answer when Moses, hiding like Elijah in the cleft of the rock, his face covered by God's hand as Elijah's was with his mantle, does indeed see the *kābôd* described as the "back" of Yahweh.[32] No one, not even Moses, it is emphasized, can see the face of God. In view of the failure of the source critics to assign this passage to any of the standard Pentateuchal documents, it should perhaps be read as a relatively late midrash on the "face-to-face" theologoumenon; a midrash the purpose of which was to clarify a theological point by distinguishing between the face as the recto and the "glory" as the verso of the divine image. In making this distinction the midrashist may well have had in mind Ezekiel's vision of the "glory" in which he saw only "the likeness as it were of a human form" (Ezek. 1:26).

No discussion of this "face-to-face" tradition would be complete without mention of the transfiguration of Moses on the mountain of revelation (Ex. 34:29–35). The critics generally agree that this passage is late and assign it to either the Priestly Work or a later tradent close in spirit and style to P.[33]

Later Jewish discussions of this text—in the Babylonian Talmud and Midrash Rabbah—associate it with the theophany in
the cleft of the rock, the transfiguration being the reward for
his having hidden his face when the *Shekinah* passed by.[34] In
the text itself, however, the skin of his face shone because he
had spoken with Yahweh on the mountain. It is, therefore,
the result of the unmediated (that is, face-to-face) communication enjoyed only by Moses. In some mysterious way the
pure light of the divine "glory" rubs off on Moses so that he
has to wear a veil when he once again enters the world of
men. It is unfortunate that this word for veil (*masveh*) occurs
only here and is therefore of uncertain meaning. Allusion to
seers or shamans covering their faces during trance[35] is not
helpful since Moses *uncovers* his when he speaks with God.
The analogy of priests wearing masks of their deities is also out
of place in this context, quite apart from the fact that this
custom is unattested in Israel. Given the affinity of this tradition with P, however, it would be worthwhile recalling the
high priest's entry into the Holy of Holies once a year at Yom
Kippur and the visions allegedly accorded to priests in the
sanctuary from the time of the Hasmoneans.[36] Though much
later, these are in line with P's concentration of all divine
communications in the sanctuary. We do not know when this
transfiguration tradition emerged. It is, however, entirely possible that here, too, we have a narrative midrash on the phrase
pānîm 'el pānîm making oblique reference to the mediatorial
function of the high priest.[37]

   This brief examination of the concluding statement in the
Pentateuch had the purpose of providing us with a fresh
perspective on the old question of the relation between law
and prophecy. Our starting point was not with the historical
data on law and prophecy in Israel but solely with their juxtaposition in the Hebrew canon as itself an important datum
in the religious history of Israel and early Judaism. I have
assumed from the beginning that canonicity has to do with
claims to religious authority and legitimation; that the most
direct and basic of such claims was that staked by the
prophets; and that the prophetic claim concerns essentially
the mediation and interpretation of the shared tradition in the

light of contemporary reality. While prophetic influence on
the official version of the founding events and laws (that is,
the Pentateuch) is unmistakable, profound and pervasive, the
emergence of a written Torah-canon contributed, paradoxically, to the eclipse of prophecy. To put it more forcibly, the
Torah-canon, to which no addition was contemplated, represented a very definite solution to the problem of conflicting
authority-claims created by free prophecy.

In point of historical fact, however, prophecy of this kind
did not so much disappear as undergo a metamorphosis. In the
course of the history of the Second Commonwealth it was
reabsorbed into the institutional framework of the theocracy,
and therefore also into the cult. During the same period,
however, the process which led to the authoritative edition of
the prophetic sayings was also going on and, concomitantly
with it, a movement guided by the prophetic eschatology
which was to lead to new and unanticipated conclusions. The
result was that Law and Prophets taken together came to
represent a kind of unresolved tension between different hermeneutics of the tradition. The coda at the end of the Pentateuch is already indicative of this tension, as we have seen in
the present chapter. The paragraph with which both Law and
Prophets are brought to a close (Mal. 3:22–24), consisting as
it does in an appeal to observe Torah without abandoning the
eschatological hope, points even more clearly in the same
direction.[38]

That those responsible for the editing of the biblical material did not on the whole expunge views in conflict with their
own, but rather allowed them to exist side by side in a state of
unresolved tension or unstable equilibrium, is clearly a fact of
significance for the understanding of Judaism—and, *mutatis
mutandis*, of Christianity also. It suggests that one may appeal
to a fixed tradition with absolute seriousness and still affirm its
"infinite interpretability."[39] Given the formative influence of
different interpretations of the tradition on the shape and
self-understanding of the community at different times, it also
suggests that the community must be prepared to accept creative tension as a permanent feature of its life. And if Law and
Prophecy are at opposite poles of the tension, it will be seen

that the fundamental problem is that of keeping alive the charismatic impulse within the founding events without succumbing either to bureaucratic paralysis or to division and sectarianism. We will now go on to test this assumption by a closer consideration of the formation of the prophetic collection during the Second Temple period.

5: The Making of
the Prophetic Canon

I. The Formation of the Latter Prophets

THE LAST PARAGRAPH OF THE PENTATEUCH GIVES AN
impression of finality. By denying parity between the age of
Moses and that of the prophets, it in effect defines a period of
Israel's history as normative, and does so in such a way as to
exclude the likelihood of any addition to this canonical narrative. This intention notwithstanding, the Hebrew canon was
extended to include prophetic writings comprising a history
attributed to prophetic authorship and collections of sayings
attributed to individual prophets. According to the standard
rabbinic view, to be discussed later, these last formed in essence a kind of commentary on Torah. In some respects
modern scholarship has reaffirmed this view, but redactional
study of prophetic material has also rediscovered an alternative view which gives the prophetic corpus a distinctive status
over against Torah. To understand this divergence in
viewpoint we have to go back to the process of formation
which eventuated in the corpus of fifteen books. More specifically, we have to identify the point of reference within Second
Temple Judaism which will explain how the collection came
to be accepted. I believe that in doing so we shall see, once
again, that what we call "canon" is intelligible only in the
context of conflicting claims to control the redemptive media
and, in particular, to mediate and interpret authoritatively the
common tradition.

Modern critical scholarship on the prophetic books, which

entered a new phase with the publication of Bernhard Duhm's commentary on Isaiah in 1892, shifted the emphasis from the predictive and oracular to questions of ethics and social justice. The cumulative effect of this work was to displace the center of gravity within the canon from Torah to $N^eb\hat{\imath}'\hat{\imath}m$. As the "religious genius" *par excellence,* the prophet represented the apex of religious development in the Old Testament. Inevitably, therefore, the subsequent history of early Judaism could only be considered as a progressive falling away from the high standards of prophetic religion. The principal reason for this misleading assumption is to be sought in the methods by which critical scholarship sought, with a good degree of success, to reconstruct the *ipsissima verba* of the prophets. What one had to do was elaborate criteria for distinguishing between the authentic and inauthentic parts of a prophetic book. After discarding the so-called secondary material, the original prophetic message could then be allowed to emerge. The predictable outcome of this approach was neglect of the editorial history of the prophetic books and the historical and theological problems to which it gives rise. While the task of reconstructing the original message of the prophets is obviously of prime importance, it remains unclear on what theological grounds the "secondary " material should be relegated to a lower level of significance. Even in the most conservative circles anonymity has never served to disqualify any part of the Bible from the privilege of divine inspiration. At any rate, the task of assessing historically and theologically the editorial history of the Latter Prophets for the most part still remains to be done.

In the Babylonian Talmud[1] the books belonging to $N^eb\hat{\imath}'\hat{\imath}m$ are listed as follows: Joshua, Judges, Samuel, Kings, Jeremiah, Ezekiel, Isaiah and the Twelve. The chronological order is disturbed to bring Jeremiah and Kings together since the latter ends with the disasters foretold by the former. Hosea had to be first among the Twelve since "the LORD first spoke through Hosea" (1:2). Joshua was written by Joshua who was himself a prophet (he is also so described by Sirach, 46:1), though it had to be rounded off after his death by Eleazar and Phineas. Samuel was written partly by Samuel and partly by

Gad and Nathan. Kings was written by Jeremiah. Since the
Three and the Twelve are all named, the determination of
authorship posed no problem. Isaiah was, however, put together by Hezekiah and his men and Ezekiel by the men of
Ezra's Great Assembly.

The concern to attribute all of the historical books to prophetic authorship is of course a way of commending them as
authoritative on account of their inspired origin. Most of the
sources named by the Chronicler were written by seers and
prophets. In reviewing the history of Israel from the death of
Moses, Sirach makes no distinction between Former and Latter Prophets. Josephus also emphasizes the prophetic nature of
historiography among his fellow Jews. Only prophets, he says,
could write history since only they had access to information
about the past through divine inspiration.[2] It is hardly surprising, then, that the historical books came to be classified under
the rubric of prophecy.

From the more strictly historical point of view it is entirely
possible, as we shall see, that the author or authors of the
Deuteronomic History during the exilic period put together a
first collection of prophetic sayings as a sort of supplement to
their work. This corpus must have enjoyed prestige from the
time it first appeared due to its association with the
Deuteronomic law. The Deuteronomic History was well
enough established to survive the challenge of the Chronicler's work, one of the main intentions of which was to de-
emphasize Ephraimite-Samaritan traditions. The compiler of
2 Maccabees, or his source, Jason of Cyrene, says that
Nehemiah founded a library to house books about the kings
and prophets (2:13). If this information is correct, and if these
works correspond more or less to our historical books, the
Former Prophets may have achieved definitive and official
status about the same time as the priestly-scribal Pentateuch.
In the same author (2 Macc. 15:9) we find the first attestation
of the term "the Law and the Prophets" for the canonical
collection of writings, and it is well-known that it continued
in use down into the first century of the era.[3]

What may be described as the standard critical position is
that Law and Prophets (much later to be divided into Former

and Latter) were in existence as an authoritative corpus by about the beginning of the second century B.C.E. The reasons for this judgment are well-known. Writing a litttle after that time, Sirach knew of an Isaian book including both 1–39 and 40–55 as well as a collection of twelve shorter prophetic books (the *Dodekapropheton*).[4] A little over thirty years later, the author of Daniel describes how the youthful sage came upon Jeremiah's prophecy of seventy years' desolation while perusing "the books" (9:2). That this book did not gain admittance into the Latter Prophets does not necessarily imply that the corpus was already closed.[5] This conclusion may, however, be drawn on other grounds.[6] It will not escape us that by this time we have heard the last mention in the canonical writings of prophets actually engaged in prophetic activity—not a very flattering reference, as it happens (Zech. 13:2–6). The reason is not far to seek, given the tendency for dead prophets to displace the living. In other words, the eclipse of prophecy as an observable reality and the canonization of prophetic writings are related events which cannot be understood apart.

The conclusion, therefore, may be drawn that the Latter Prophets were in existence as an authoritative collection by about the beginning of the second century B.C.E. So far we are on firm ground, the only problem arising when we go on to ask whether we can date it much before that time. We are not, of course, to think of a precise point in time when *N^ebî'îm* was promulgated as an authoritative corpus. This is possible with a law code but rather unlikely with a miscellaneous collection of prophetic utterances. The main problem here arises with the dating of anonymous additions to the name prophets. Thus, David Noel Freedman argues for a date in the mid-sixth century when a prophetic collection was put together as a supplement to the history. Such a view obliges him to postulate a supplement containing post-exilic prophetic writings, and this he dates in the first half of the fifth century.[7] He does not, apparently, think it necessary to deal with arguments for a rather later date for some well-known passages in Isaiah, especially the so-called Isaian apocalypse (24–27). On Zech. 9–14, which proves particularly recalcitrant to this hypothesis, he wisely suggests suspending judg-

ment, but then goes on to make the problematic judgment
that the reference to Greeks at Zech. 9:13 must fit into the
sixth or fifth century but no later. While concurring with his
view that the sixth century was decisive in the formation of
the prophetic collection, we must insist that the Latter
Prophets contain material from a much later time and this,
too, must be taken into account.

It would be widely agreed that the process of which we are
speaking began with the activity of disciples individually or in
groups who either committed to memory or wrote down the
words of the master as the occasion warranted. This seems to
have happened with Isaiah (see especially 8:16) Jeremiah
gathered together his own sayings with the help of the scribe
Baruch around the year 605, amplifying the collection on
subsequent occasions (36:1–4; 36:32, cf. 45:1), and the same
was no doubt the case with others even where their disciples
are not explicitly mentioned (e.g., Hab. 2:2). It is quite a
different question, however, with the claim that prophetic
"schools" continued in existence over a period of several generations or even centuries. With respect to the Isaian corpus,
where something of the sort is widely assumed, it seems highly
unlikely that such a school was in existence continually for a
period of not much less than half a millenium. But there can
be no doubt that in many instances the "sons" of a particular
prophet provided the initial impetus towards a written corpus
of the master's sayings.

We must add, however, that even at this stage the picture is
by no means uniformly clear. As long as we remain uncertain
as to who the "classical prophets" really were, and in particular how they stood in relation to institutions including the
cult, we will be involved to a large extent in guesswork. Is it
not possible, for example, that even at an early stage propheticism and scribalism were quite closely related? Baruch, we
know, was a *soper,* and the colophon to Hosea (14:9) suggests
sopheric handling of, or at least interest in, the book. Or,
again, is it possible to suppose that Amos was as well-informed
as the book reveals him to have been unless he was something
more than a herdsman and dresser of sycamore-figs? Or, to
take another example, does not the designation *nābî'* in the

superscription to Habakkuk, taken with other indications in the book, suggest the possibility of the Jerusalem cult as a traditioning medium? Probably no explanation designed to account for all the books in the collection is likely to prove satisfactory.

While we have no explicit evidence, it seems reasonable to conclude that those who expanded Deuteronomy and wrote the final version of the Deuteronomic history in the decades following the deportations to Babylon also began making collections of prophetic sayings suitably edited in view of the new situation.[8] While considerable caution is needed in identifying material in prophetic books as Deuteronomic,[9] stylistic and rhetorical analysis does appear to point in that direction. That such indications are much more in evidence in Jeremiah than elsewhere (the so-called C source) is perhaps of special significance. The phrase "his servants the prophets," which occurs with some regularity in Deuteronomic material of the exilic age and especially in the Jeremian C source, suggests that for the first time the prophets were being viewed as a series, and that therefore, by implication, prophecy was beginning to be seen as essentially a past phenomenon. In this respect the sense is not very different from "the former prophets," a phrase which we find for the first time in Zechariah (1:4; 7:7, 12). The aim of these exilic editors, then, would be to present Jeremiah as a paradigm of prophecy as they understood it, as the last in the series and therefore appropriately recapitulating the history of prophecy as a whole. The parallelism between the Deuteronomic Moses, the prophetic "servant of the LORD" at the beginning of the history, and the Deuteronomic Jeremiah at the end, has often been noted and confirms the impression of a deliberate attempt to give a theological account of the historical phenomenon of prophecy as a closed epoch of Israel's history.[10]

It is also worth noting that the prophets who play a significant role in the Deuteronomic history—those, that is, the fulfillment of whose prophecies is explicitly noted—include only one of the canonical prophets, namely, Isaiah. It is quite a question why Amos, for example, is passed over in silence. It is not impossible that the Deuteronomic author found this prophet's absolute condemnation of Israel unacceptable,[11] and there is also the fact that Amos' prediction of the violent end of Jeroboam II (7:11) remained unfulfilled. In general, though, the almost complete lack of overlap between the Deuteronomic list and the Latter Prophets would tend to confirm the impression that a first collection of pre-exilic prophecies had been put together as a supplement to the history. This in itself would be an adequate explanation of an otherwise almost inexplicable state of affairs.

I would therefore have no hesitation in accepting the view of Elias Auerbach, and others, that a *grosse Uberarbeitung der biblischen Bücher* did take place at this time and that such redactional activity did include prophetic material.[12] Consonant with this hypothesis is the fact that, beginning about this time, we begin to hear increasingly frequent allusions to earlier prophets and their sayings. At his trial for sedition in 609 Jeremiah was saved by timely appeal to the eighth-century prophet, Micah of Moresheth (Jer. 26:17–19; Mic. 3:12). This incident, by the way, provides one of the firmest pieces of evidence for the expansion of prophetic books in the direction of eschatology and the millenarian expectation. For if Micah's prediction of the destruction of Jerusalem were to have any force when quoted at the trial it could not have been followed then, as it is now, by the prospect of a glorious future. About half a century later the exilic Isaiah ascribed great importance to the fulfillment of predictions by his prophetic predecessors. Shortly after the return, Haggai berated his contemporaries in language borrowed from Amos. He also made use of Jeremiah's metaphor of the king as Yahweh's signet ring (2:23, cf. Jer. 22:24), while Zechariah used the other Jeremian figure of the Branch (3:8; 6:12, cf. Jer. 23:5; 33:15). The prediction of seventy years' exile in Jeremiah (25:11; 29:10) is also taken up by Zechariah (1:12; 7:5) and perhaps also in Haggai's reference to the right time ('*ēt*) for rebuilding the temple (1:2). With this process of appropriation and reinterpretation a decisive step has been taken towards the "recycling" of prophetic texts in apocalyptic writings of the Greco-Syrian and Greco-Roman periods.

II. The Editorial History of the Prophetic Books

It is now generally agreed that Isaiah, the first and longest book in the corpus, is the product of centuries of collecting, arranging and editing. That chapters 40–66 were not authored by the eighth-century prophet has been recognized since the late eighteenth century, but it is also clear that a good part of 1–39 is also of later origin. That the collection was substantially as we have it by the early second century B.C.E. may be deduced from Sirach (48:22, 24–5). We do not know the dates of Greek Isaiah and the Qumran copy (1QIs^a), but they were probably no more than half a century after Sirach wrote. One or two sentences absent from Greek Isaiah (e.g., 2:22) may have been added to the text later, but in general the beginning of the second century marks the *terminus ad quem* of the formation of the book. We therefore have a time span of about half a millenium during which the expansion and arrangement of the original collection of Isian oracles could have been taking place. If it were possible to reconstruct this process in detail, we would clearly be in a good position to grasp the significance for Second Temple history of the formation of the Latter Prophets as a whole. We would, in particular, be better able to answer the questions how and why the pre-exilic judgment-prophets were progressively transformed into witnesses to the millenarian hope which reached its furthest expression in the idiom of apocalyptic. Such a possibility, however, depends on our coming up with sound criteria for dating individual passages in the book which, judging by the experience of the last century, rarely succeed in commanding a consensus.

There are some questions here which, however obvious, have received surprisingly little attention. Why were these sayings of anonymous prophets (comprising perhaps three quarters of the entire book) included in this particular scroll and thus attributed to Isaiah ben Amoz? Why, especially, were the sayings of the so-called Deutero-Isaiah placed here? No doubt a great name from the past was needed for these people to claim a hearing. But why Isaiah? As suggested earlier, there is little justification for speaking of an "Isaian school" in continuous existence from the eighth to the sixth century and beyond. The three main sections of the book have certain features in common, but the differences are just as noteworthy. Perhaps the political situation at the time of First and Second Isaiah, the eighth and sixth century respectively, may suggest a better explanation. The anti-Assyrian oracles of Jerusalemite Isaiah held out hopes which were focused on dynasty and temple. Salvation prophets during the late neo-Babylonian period could hardly have failed to see themselves playing a similar role. It would have been natural, in other words, for them to have read their great predecessor as an ardent "Zionist." In something of the same way Haggai and Zechariah drew on previous prophets to proclaim, cryptically to be sure, the downfall of the Persian empire during the troubled times following the death of Cambyses.[13]

If this is granted, it will not be surprising that the anonymous author of Is. 40–55 is so much concerned with the fulfillment of prophecy, a theme which is also central in the contemporary Deuteronomic history.[14] His argument seems to be that events prophetically announced in the past are now being fulfilled,[15] and that Yahweh's role in the catastrophe of exile is thereby vindicated. In the historical context of the time this can hardly refer to anything else but the collapse of the Babylonian empire. It would, therefore, be logical to conclude that the "former things" of which he speaks include reference to the anti-Babylonian passages in First Isaiah (13:1–22; 14:3–23; 21:1–10) which cannot very well be earlier than the sixth century. This, too, would have to be borne in mind in attempting to explain the appending of chapters 40–55 to 1–39.

It would be reasonable to conclude that the first draft of the original Isaian book (1–35) was part of the "great redaction" of the exilic period. It was then, took very likely, that the historical supplement (36–39) was borrowed from the Deuteronomic history and appended to this collection. Then, a few years later, the prophecies of the exilic "Isaiah" (40–55) were added. We have seen that it was becoming common at that time to speak of the prophet as "servant of Yahweh," so

that it is not surprising to find this anonymous prophet describing not just the prophet but Israel as a whole in terms of
service, ambassadorship and mission.[16] At much the same
time occurred the Deuteronomic expansion of Jeremiah discussed earlier, while Ezekiel was handed on, and possibly also
compiled and edited, by those priests and elders who were the
official custodians of worship.[17] It is unlikely, however, that
Isaiah, Jeremiah and Ezekiel already constituted a sort of prophetic trilogy by that time.

Criteria for dating passages or whole sections of prophetic
books based on content, style and vocabulary are notoriously
subjective. Only in very few cases (e.g., Is. 40–55) is anything
approaching a critical consensus attained. In other instances
(e.g., Is. 24–27 and other apocalyptic-like passages in 1–39)
agreement on the "secondary" status of the material does not
exclude considerable dispute about dating. In this area a great
deal of careful work is required before we can go beyond mere
possibilities. In the rare cases where we have parallels (e.g., Is.
2:2–4 and Mic. 4:1–3) we are obviously much better off. The
juxtaposition of prose and verse also opens up possibilities
which can be prudently exploited. We would want to explore
the hypothesis, for example, that the many short prose passages in Is. 1–39 beginning or ending with "in that day"
(bayyôm hahû') represent a special kind of addition in which
certain common features can be identified. We would want to
take seriously the proposition that the first stages of exegesis of
the text are often part of the text as we now have it. Many
instances of this are well-known, but their full significance is
not seen so long as they are considered under the rubric of text
criticism.[18] A further area of study would be the titles and
superscriptions scattered throughout the book. On this point
it is perhaps necessary to note that chronological indications
at the beginning of narrative passages (6:1; 7:1; 20:1; 36:1) are
not superscriptions in the strict sense. We are therefore left
with the oracles against foreign nations,[19] the section beginning with 2:1 introduced as a saying (dābār) communicated in
a vision, and the more solemn and inclusive title at the beginning of the work as a whole introducing it as a vision (ḥazôn).
The likelihood that this was added at a very late editorial

stage is increased by the Chronicler's reference to Isaiah as author of a *ḥazôn* (2 Chron. 32:32).

To repeat, the ideal point of convergence of these and similar detailed exegetical studies would be the reconstruction of the editorial history of Isaiah and, ultimately, of the Latter Prophets as a whole. We would then be in a better position to test certain assumptions about what was happening during the exilic and restoration periods, about tensions which were allegedly developing during the period of the Second Commonwealth (as set out, somewhat intuitively, by Otto Plöger, for example[20]) and on the hotly contended question of the origins of apocalyptic. At that point—if we could ever reach it—the results of our work would emerge as an important chapter in the religious and social history of nascent Judaism.

So far we have spoken only of Isaiah, but the hypothesis that the editing of this book moves progressively in the direction of millenarianism and apocalyptic would appear to be borne out when we turn to the Twelve. As is clear from the titles, the first nine of these were thought to come from the period of Assyrian and neo-Babylonian supremacy. With the exceptions of Joel and Jonah, critical scholarship would concur with this judgment, but would also allow that most of them have been expanded by the inclusion of later anonymous material. Such editorial activity is, however, more apparent in some books than in others, no doubt because some were seen to lend themselves more readily to readaptation than others. Hosea was probably edited for use in Judah after 721 B.C. but shows little signs of exilic or post-exilic reworking.[21] Nahum would probably have been read as referring to Babylon during the exilic period. Its relevance to the new situation would have been sufficiently clear without extensive rewriting; in fact, the only addition which can be clearly identified is the reference to the messenger bringing good news (2:1, cf. Is. 40:9; 52:7) which would have sufficed to make the poem serviceable in the changed conditions of the *gôlāh*. It may be for the same reason that the enigmatic Habbakuk has been left virtually untouched. Its heightened sense of historical crisis and its highly colored language would have made it unnecessary to add an explicitly eschatological dimension. It is no surprise that, furnished with its *pešer*-commentary (IQ-pHab), it played such an important part in the self-understanding of the apocalyptic Qumran community. Jonah, attributed to one of Jeroboam II's prebendary prophets (2 Kings 14:25), is a prophetic *Legende* similar to stories about Elijah and Elisha in Kings, but with a marked didactic and polemical intent. Its inclusion in the Twelve constitutes an intriguing problem in its own right and warns us against over-simplistic explanations.

If Hosea, Nahum and Habbakuk have been left more or less to speak for themselves, the situation is very different with other books in the *Dodekapropheton*. Since the timer of Wellhausen it has been widely agreed that the promise of return from exile, rebuilding of the ruined cities and restoration of the Davidic dynasty at the end of Amos (9:11–15) are quite out of character with the rest of the book and must come from a later time, probably the late exilic or early post-exilic period. As in Hosea, there are also clear indications of an earlier Judahite redaction. Micah also ends with the assurance that Israel's enemies will be humbled, the walls of Jerusalem rebuilt and the covenant between Yahweh and the people re-established (7:8–20). Chapters 4 and 5, which hold out the promise of universal peace, the supremacy of Jerusalem and the humiliation of the hostile *gôyîm*, also suggest that eschatological prophets from the same period or later have turned the original scroll into a palimpsest. In this instance confirmation is at hand, as we have seen, in the reference to Micah at the trial of Jeremiah. In general, the fortunes of the Micah scroll seem to have been closely associated with Isaiah. Both prophets stand within the Jerusalemite cultic tradition and their books appear to have been preserved and expanded within the same traditioning circles.[22]

The two remaining books among the first nine of the *Dodekapropheton* are Zephaniah, dated to the reign of Josiah, and Obadiah, undated, but probably from the early exilic period. In the former the vehement description of the Day of Yahweh serves first to highlight the sins of Israel, as in Amos, but is then turned against the nations (3:8). The prediction which follows, that the nations will be endowed with "pure

speech" to qualify them for genuine worship, is strongly reminiscent of the pure offering of the nations at Mal. 1:11 and
can hardly have been written before the end of the exilic
period. The oracle against Edom in Obadiah, which fits very
well with the early exilic period when the Edomites profited
by the deportations from Judah, has likewise been developed
in the direction of a more universal eschatological sense. It
ends with the prediction that Yahweh's kingdom will one day
be finally established on Mount Zion.

In contrast to the manner in which most pre-exilic prophetic books have been expanded by editorial additions, those
which date from the Second Temple evidence little
editorializing in the body of the work, receiving instead fairly
clear-cut anonymous supplements. This is the case with
Zechariah in which 9–11 and 12–14, each introduced as an
oracle (*maśśā'*), have been appended to chapters 1–8. Despite
its attribution to a name prophet, Malachi really constitutes a
third supplement introduced in exactly the same way. Much
the same can be said of Joel in which 3–4 are best read as an
apocalyptic supplement to 1–2. Haggai, closely related
chronologically and thematically with Zechariah 1–8, comes
to us in much the same form as it circulated shortly after the
death of Cambyses.

It will be obvious that the preceding remarks have barely
scratched the surface. The task of reconstructing the editorial
history of the Latter Prophets, and of relating that history to
the social and ecclesiastical realities of Second Temple
Judaism, will require a great deal of detailed work. Much has
been done, of course, but we know that in exegesis results
depend to a great extent on the expectations we bring to the
task and the kinds of questions we put to the texts under
consideration. We have seen that modern critical scholarship
set itself the task of getting at the original message of the
prophets, and did this by stripping away "secondary" material.
In the process it isolated a type of *homo religiosus* with a highly
individual ethical consciousness which in some ways, one can
say without undue cynicism, betrayed suspiciously close affinity with the denominational ethos of the commentator in
question. When it was not simply ignored, the material at-

tributed to later editors was considered to be quite distinct from the residual genuine parts of the book. The question as to its function within the totality of the text, and in particular the ways in which its presence there could profoundly alter the meaning of the text, was for the most part left unmasked. What, however, our surface exploration is beginning to suggest is that these anonymous additions transform the message from one of judgment on Israel to eschatological salvation for the transformed Israel of the future. To assume this position does not involve denial of the possibility that judgment and salvation stand together both in prophetic writings and hymns containing prophetic oracles (e.g., Ps. 50). The point is rather that the cumulative evidence from redactional study indicates a profound shift in the understanding of both the man and his message.

If this view of the matter is granted, it would be natural to go on to ask the question: which interpretation of prophecy is correct? Modern critical orthodoxy has tended, at least by implication, to impose its own canonical meaning on prophetic texts. Now, however, we see that this is only one of two, or perhaps more than two, canonical meanings. Perhaps the hermeneutical issue at stake, then, is whether we are to accept one fixed meaning as canonical or appeal to what, following Gershom Scholem, we can call the "infinite interpretability" of the texts.[23] That the Hebrew Bible accommodates a wide variety of re-interpretations without expunging the original texts suggests that different interpretations may be allowed to co-exist in a state of tension. That the text is still there after everyone has interpreted it inevitably poses a problem for any supposedly definitive interpretation.

III. Theocratic and Eschatological Prophecy

What do we know of the ongoing history of prophecy in the post-exilic period?[24] At first sight, the prediction of Ezekiel that prophets would no longer be enrolled in the register of Israel (13:9) seems to have been fulfilled, for no prophets appear on any list of returned exiles. Yet prophets did survive

the catastrophe and were active in the *gôlāh*, and in some cases
their names have come down to us. Haggai, Zechariah and no
doubt others[25] urged the re-establishment of the temple cult
without abandoning hopes for a spectacular reversal of for-
tune. Indeed, it seems that for them observance of Torah and
the temple cultus were necessary preconditions for the coming
of God's kingdom on earth. While prophetic opposition to the
rebuilding of the temple was not lacking,[26] most of the
prophets during the early Persian period seem to have worked
closely with the temple clergy and were much concerned with
cult and ritual. Haggai was familiar with the ritual legislation
of the Holiness Code (H), Zechariah was himself of priestly
family, Malachi, about a lifetime later, was much concerned
with the priesthood and correct sacrificial worship, a good part
of the material in Joel is liturgical in origin, and the Chronicler gives pride of place to cultic and levitical prophecy.

Beginning with the exile, we detect a growing tendency to
anonymity by prophets or those responsible for the publication
of their sayings. While this was in part due to the new political
situation caused by loss of independence, increasing polarization between the priestly and scribal classes in power and
prophetic groups deprived of it must also have played a role.[27]
It is to this tendency that we owe the practice of expanding
existing collections of prophetic material which, as we have
seen, were beginning to appear during the exilic period. This
is, in effect, something more than anonymity and something
less than the pseudonymity which was to become the fashion,
in Judaism and elsewhere,[28] during the Greco-Roman period.

That prophecy was, however, still a force to be reckoned
with as late as the fifth century is apparent from the allegation
of Sanballat and his allies that Nehemiah was soliciting prophetic support for his own messianic pretensions (Neh. 6:7).
The opposition to Nehemiah also had its prophetic backing.
We hear of a prophetess, Noadiah, and a certain Shemaiah
who may have been a cultic ecstatic.[29] Scant as they are,
these allusions give the impression that prophecy no longer
stood in high repute. Jonah, perhaps written a few decades
later, does not evince a high regard for prophecy either. By
the early Greek period its stock had sunk so low that it could

be bracketed with idolatry; and in order to avoid being put to death for prophesying falsely—in accord with the Deuteronomic law—the prophet will even be willing to pass for a cult prostitute.[30]

Laments that prophecy is no more are often heard in periods of crisis and disorientation.[31] Beginning with the epoch of Seleucid rule, however, such complaints (e.g., in Dan. 3:38 LXX and I Macc. 9:27) are accompanied by the expectation that the prophetic spirit would be revived some time in the future. We hear, for instance, that the stones of the altar desecrated by Antiochus were to be set aside until a prophet would arise to rule on their disposal (I Macc. 4:46). Simon was to be civic leader and high priest until a faithful prophet should appear and make a final disposition on the question of leadership (I Macc. 14:41). Such hopes, which perhaps were based on the promise of a prophet like Moses (Deut. 18:15–18), also find expression in the last paragraph of the Latter Prophets (Mal. 3:23–24). We have, therefore, the following situation. The actual practice of prophecy during the Second Temple period declines in prestige until it eventually disappears.[32] At the same time the process of collecting and expanding the sayings of earlier prophets is going on apace. Moreover, a closer study of this process reveals an increasing shift in the direction of a more sharply defined eschatology. These incontrovertible data necessarily pose the further question what relation, if any, the fate of prophecy in the period in question had to the related events of the emergence of sects and the production of apocalyptic writings. Here, too, we will have to be content with a brief survey and evaluation of the considerable literature on the subject over the last few decades.

We can say, to begin with, that the prevalent tendency has been to derive apocalyptic from prophecy or wisdom or a combination of both. At one end of the spectrum von Rad ruled out the possibility that prophecy could have been its source.[33] The prophetic understanding of the *Heilsgeschichte*, he maintained, had nothing in common with the pessimistic despair of history evidenced in apocalyptic writings. Correspondingly, the apocalyptic "secret," which stands for the divine revelation of the future course of events, had no basis in the experience of the prophets.[34] The matrix of apocalyptic is rather to be sought in the teaching of the sages, dealing as it does with cosmological speculation, knowledge in the most general sense, and history as a vast panorama with a definite beginning and ending.[35]

Such a view of the matter has not won wide approval, and for good reasons. There are indeed clear points of contact between scribalism and apocalyptic, some of which will be touched on in the present study, but the problem of origins is not well-posed by setting wisdom over against prophecy, quite apart from other problems which critics have not been slow to point out.[36]

Perhaps the best-known representative of the view that apocalyptic is the child (or at least the stepchild) of prophecy was H. H. Rowley.[37] He stressed the prophetic themes of the Day of Yahweh and the holy Remnant as containing the seeds of apocalyptic and noted further developments in post-exilic compositions such as the so-called Isaian apocalypse (24–27), Joel and the additions to Zechariah (9–14). At the same time he warned against confusing prophetic eschatology with apocalyptic and insisted on some rather basic differences.[38] Jewish apocalyptic derived from a situation of crisis quite different from anything experienced during the period of classical prophecy, with the result that it is improper to describe any writing earlier than Daniel as apocalyptic.[39] Yet the links between classical prophecy and apocalyptic are clearly discernible and of basic significance.

A new element was injected into the rather unprofitable prophecy-versus-wisdom debate by Frank Moore Cross, who suggested that the origins of apocalyptic are to be sought in the late exilic and early post-exilic periods, the decisive factor being the need for a radically new answer to the situation created by the loss of the monarchy.[40] In itself, this observation is quite in keeping with the general approach of Rowley and a great many other writers on the subject. Where he goes beyond this familiar position, however, is in the high dating of Job, Is. 24–27, Zech. 9–14 and Is. 56–66, all considered important stages in the development of full-blown apocalyptic. Rather curiously, he took no account of P in describing this stage of development to which he gave the name "proto-apocalyptic."

The general position of Cross has been taken further by Paul D. Hanson, one of his students. He, too, traces it back to the experience of disorientation and *anomie* induced by the exile in the sixth century. One of its salient characteristics is disillusionment with history leading to a purely eschatological perspective articulated with the help of ancient myths. It first came to expression among the disciples of the Second Isaiah whose prophecies are to be found in the third part of the book (56 to 66), as well as in Is. 24–27 and Zech. 9–14, none of which postdates the fifth century.[41] Following Albright and Cross, he assigns a date as early or earlier to Job, which is also presumed to play an important role in the development towards apocalyptic.[42] Like Plöger, whom we will consider in a moment, he associates the development towards apocalyptic with the formation of sects, evidence for which can be found as early as the sixth century.[43]

While this is clearly not the place for a thorough review and critique of Hanson's work, two remarks of a general nature—not unimportant for the development of our argument—may be permitted. The first concerns the elusive matter of dating. New hypotheses which challenge widely accepted positions are always welcome and should be judged by the quality of the arguments which sustain them. In this instance, however, heavy reliance on a certain theory of prosodic development and on the presence or absence of mythic elements does not, in my judgment, lead to a convincing alternative. Moreover, the anxiety to fit so much into the late sixth and early fifth centuries makes it all the more difficult to account for developments during the large gap between that time and the composition of such indubitably apocalyptic works as Enoch and Daniel. This leads to our second point, which is that this "proto-apocalyptic theory"[44] does not give an adequate account of the transition from anonymity to pseudonymity and from direct revelation to revelation obtained by the inspired interpretation of prophetic texts. Such an account would involve a much broader treatment of the editorial history of the Latter Prophets and an attempt to relate that history to the

Jewish apocalyptic writings of the Greco-Syrian and Greco-Roman periods. In his recent book Hanson has made some striking points about the late exilic and restoration periods. But by failing to account for the gap between that time and the Seleucid period (there is no discussion of the "Isaian apocalypse,"⁴⁵ Joel or even Daniel), he makes it impossible to see how the dawn passes into the full light of day.

The same complaint cannot be made against Otto Plöger, whose *Theocracy and Eschatology* marks an important point in the investigation of the most obscure period of Second Temple history, that which begins with the activity of Ezra and Nehemiah and ends with the Maccabee uprising.⁴⁶ His principal argument is that literary analysis of the prophetic books, together with other indications from that time, suggests that they were redacted and brought together by eschatological circles who must be considered the precursors of the *ḥᵃsîdîm* (the Devout) mentioned in I Maccabees (2:42; 7:13). The Second Temple period was in general marked by an increasing tension between the leaders of the theocracy and groups estranged from the center whose faith was nourished on prophetic eschatology. It is their theological perspective which predominates in the additions to the prophetic books which we discussed earlier in this chapter. This tension did not develop overnight. Haggai and Zechariah in the period shortly after the first return represent the theocratic viewpoint and yet announce the coming of the millennium. But as time went on, and especially from about the last century of Persian rule, the question began to emerge as to whether "a theocracy could be based on the eschatological faith and still remain a theocracy, or whether a life *in statu promissionis* must ultimately lead to the dissolution of the theocracy."⁴⁷

The core of opposition to the "final solution" of Antiochus IV came from the *ḥᵃsîdîm* whose forebears were, according to Plöger, responsible for the putting together of the Latter Prophets. These prophetically inspired groups, among whom the book of Daniel originated, held fast to Torah but did so in view of the eschatological hope. Their break with the Maccabees, which resulted (according to the standard view) in the emergence of "hasidic" splinter groups or sects, represents the furthest limits of a tension which had been building up beneath the surface during the preceding centuries.

An important point made by Plöger is that the loss of a "sense of an ending" by the leadership of the theocracy contributed significantly to the secularization and assimilation which, according to our sources, had been going on apace during the early Greek period.[48] Malachi testifies that this was no new problem. The spiritual aimlessness and scepticism castigated in this book must have been due in good measure to the disappointment of the ardent hopes cherished during the early years after the first return.[49] It is probably correct to conclude that this corresponds to a general tendency: the more immune a religious group is to eschatology the more open it leaves itself to assimilation and loss of identity.

A strong point in Plöger's thesis is that the interpretation of prophetic texts and the understanding of prophecy in general were determining factors in the emergence of apocalyptic sects including the Christian sect. The theocratic solution was to assimilate prophecy into the instutional setup and thus deprive it of a future outside of the received theology.[50] The prophets were, so to speak, buried in the foundations of the theocracy.[51] Among those groups alienated from the center of power, however, the interpretation of prophetic texts provided a revolutionary tool for the discovery of truths of overwhelming relevance and transforming power. Thus a definite line of development is established leading from anonymous additions in the prophetic books to overtly apocalyptic writings. Taking Joel 3, Zech. 12–14 and Is. 24–27 as points on this line, Plöger attempts to trace a widening dichotomy between the empirical and the ideal Israel, an increasingly dualistic world-view and a movement of thought which would inevitably lead to the formation of sects. Thus the additions to the Latter Prophets provide the missing link between prophetic eschatology and apocalyptic.

Plöger's brilliant reconstruction is understandably not free of difficulties. The existence of the eschatological conventicles of which he speaks has to be deduced from hints here and there in the literature of the period; as a matter of direct historical knowledge we know nothing of them. He also draws

the lines too cleanly between theocratic and eschatological
elements. Sirach, for example, is eminently theocratic, yet he
speaks of Isaiah seeing the last things and of the Twelve giving
a message of hope and comfort to Israel (48:24–25; 49:10). If
it is true, moreover, that the Latter Prophets was put together
by such groups, the question how it achieved official standing
remains to be answered. We would prefer to say that the
prophetic canon found a place alongside Torah as a compromise or way of maintaining a balance between law and
prophecy, institution and charisma, the claims of the past and
those of the future. Such an inclusive canon, which contained
within itself both the seeds of tension and the means of over-
coming it, corresponds to something important in the make-
up of Judaism and Christianity. Both faiths can test the truth
of the proposition that a theocratic institution which excludes
prophecy and the millenarian hope leaves itself open to assimilation, while prophecy left to itself tends of its nature
towards disunity and sectarianism. It is the fate of prophecy to
be always necessary and never sufficient.

That Torah was already in existence as a norm of faith
before the prophetic corpus was put together suggests that the
latter could itself become authoritative only by association
with the former. If $N^eb\hat{\imath}'\hat{\imath}m$ is then seen as a sort of supplement
to Torah, it would seem natural to conclude that the essential
function of the prophet was to transmit and interpret Torah.
Such a view is suggested by the liturgical practice of reading a
passage from the Prophets (the *haftarah*) after the Torah-
pericope. It is also the view expounded routinely in rabbinic
writings, most compendiously in the well-known opening paragraph of *Pirke Abot.* [52] On this showing, prophetic teaching is
strictly traditional, deriving both its character and content
from the Sinaitic revelation. [53] The prophet cannot be the
vehicle of a new revelation.

The rabbinic leadership was also at pains to emphasize that
prophecy belongs to the past. According to several attestations in the Talmud, it came to an end with the death of the
last prophet, at which time the Holy Spirit also left Israel. [54]
Since rabbinic chronology telescoped the Persian period to
little more than thirty years, the last three prophets could be

represented as contemporaries of Ezra and his Great Assembly and even of Alexander the Great.[55] For reasons of his own, Josephus extended the lifetime of prophecy to the reign of Artaxerxes I (died 424 B.C.E.), and even residually to that of John Hyrcanus (died 105 B.C.E.), holder of the threefold office of priest, king and prophet.[56] According to yet another view, the activity of the Holy Spirit, a term practically synonymous with prophecy,[57] came to an end with the destruction of the First Temple.[58] Whatever the variation, it was agreed that prophecy as a distinct dispensation had come to an end.[59]

The most significant effects of this rabbinic redefinition of prophecy were to sever its links with history and annul the tension created by the claims which it staked. Faithful to Deuteronomy, the rabbis saw Moses as the prototypal prophet. Where even the greatest of them saw but dimly, he looked into a crystal-clear mirror.[60] None of the prophets could equal him to whom were given all save one of the fifty gates of understanding.[61] Everything that God had to say to the House of Israel was contained in the one revelation vouchsafed to Moses at Sinai.[62] It follows that no prophet is authorized to change a word of the commandments, add to the content of the faith or introduce new institutions.[63] Everything was contained, explicitly or implicitly, in the one revelation at Sinai.[64] Not unlike certain Christian theories on the development of doctrine, this was clearly intended to discourage any departures from the tradition controlled by the religious elite. Prophecy was thereby not so much excluded as rendered superfluous.

It is sometimes suggested that this effort to contain prophecy by redefinition and historical schematization derives from reaction to the messianic *Schwärmerei* which led to the revolts under Vespasian and Hadrian. Josephus never tires of denouncing the messianists for perverting the meaning of prophetic sayings, and the same accusation is leveled against the priests in the Testament of Levi and against the opponents of the Righteous Teacher (*môreh haṣṣedeq*) in the Damascus Document.[65] For both Josephus and the rabbis, it was the ambiguous nature of prophetic sayings which left them open to abuse. A passage in the tractate Megillah of the Babylonian Talmud illustrates the problem as they saw it. It purports to tell us what happened when Jonathan ben Uzziel had finished writing the targum on the Prophets. The land of Israel, we are told, quaked, and a *bath qol* came forth and exclaimed, "Who is this that has revealed my secrets to mankind?" It continues:

> Jonathan ben Uzziel thereupon arose and said, "It is I who have revealed thy secrets to mankind . . . He further sought to reveal a targum of the Writings but a *bath qol* went forth and said, "Enough!" What was the reason? Because the date of the Messiah is foretold in it . . . Why did not the land quake because of the (targum on the) Torah? The meaning of the Torah is expressed clearly, but the meaning of the Prophets in some things is expressed clearly and in others enigmatically. (b. Meg. 3a)

Misgivings about $K^e t\hat{u}b\hat{i}m$ were, of course, due to Daniel, which speaks of the coming of God's kingdom in an uncomfortably precise way. It is interesting to note that Josephus also declined to offer an explanation of "the stone not cut by human hand" (Dan. 2:34) and simply omitted the vision of the four beasts (Dan. 7) from his historical survey.[66]

Attitudes towards apocalyptic enthusiasm may well have hardened during the Javnean period. In addition, the need to counter Christian claims that prophecy had passed to them may also have to be taken into account.[67] It is even possible that some formulations found in rabbinic writings may have arisen in such a polemic context. The dictum that prophecy has been taken from the prophets and given to fools and children, for example, is oddly reminiscent of the so-called Johannine logion (Mt. 11:25–27).[68] Yet even if such connections can be made, it remains true that rabbinic views on prophecy have much deeper roots. In other words, both the institutionally acceptable "prophecy" of the sages and priests and the "new prophecy" of apocalyptic are the product of developments which cover the entire period of the Second Temple.

To avoid another source of misunderstanding, it should be added that the eschatological perspective did not disappear from Judaism after the failure of the two revolts against Rome.[69] In targum, midrash and Talmud, texts from both the Law and the Prophets serve to show that in the age to come the Holy Spirit (or the Shekinah) will again descend on Israel. In Tannaitic exegesis the origins of Israel witnessed the great flowering of prophecy. In the midrash *Mekhilta,* for example, the Israelites in Egypt are described as greater than the prophets since they *saw* God (why else would they exclaim, "this is my God and I will glorify him"?) whereas the prophets dealt only in similitudes and visions.[70] They knew prophetically of Pharaoh's designs and sang the Song at the Sea in the Holy Spirit.[71] These primal events presage the age of eschatological redemption when the enemies of Israel, described cryptically as Edom, will be humbled and the tables turned.[72]

While therefore the eschatological and even apocalyptic element by no means disappeared in postbellum Judaism, the problem is to determine to what extent it was operative in shaping the world-view and the orientation to action of those who shared it. The religious leadership, at any rate, saw themselves, and not the apocalypticists and messianists, as the heirs of the prophets; for "since the days when the Temple was destroyed prophecy has been taken from the prophets and given to the wise."[73] Following in the steps of Torah-scribes like Ezra and Sirach, they were not afraid to claim for their teaching an inspiration and authority analogous to that of the prophets.[74] Life had to be based on a firm foundation of law and order. Important decisions affecting the well-being of the community could not be left to the vagaries of personal inspiration. So strong was this conviction that not even a *bath qol* (heavenly voice), the standard surrogate for prophecy, could claim precedence over the authorized biblical interpretation of the schools.[75]

The argument advanced so far may be provisionally summarized as follows. One of the most important impulses towards the creation of a canon was the claim of the free prophets, implicit in all of their activity, to interpret the common tradition in light of their own vision of divine activity in human history and especially the history of their own times. In response to this challenge an authoritative torah was promulgated during the last days of the monarchy, then in a greatly expanded form in the late Persian period. This process of codification, however, remained essentially incomplete until the formation of the Mishnah in the Roman period. The redaction of the prophetic writings covered a long time-span from the Babylonian exile down into the Greek period. It reveals a progressive transformation of the prophets into heralds of a new age, a transformation which laid the groundwork for apocalyptic. At the same time, the fact that the prophetic corpus came to be officially accepted alongside Torah sanctioned the view of prophecy as commentary on Torah. The juxtaposition of Law and Prophets in one authoritative corpus, therefore, gives expression to an unresolved tension which was to be characteristic of Judaism right from the beginning.

IV. The Last Paragraph of *Nᵉbîʾîm*

Sirach's reference to "the bones of the twelve prophets" (49:10) shows that the division of the Latter Prophets into three and twelve was an accomplished fact by about the beginning of the second century B.C.E. Looking below the surface of this division, we note that the book of the Twelve ends with three short sections each of which is introduced under the same title, *maśśāʾ* (oracle), continuing with "the word of the LORD" (Zech. 9:1; 12:1; Mal. 1:1). The first two of these are additions to Zechariah and are anonymous. The third is introduced as the work of a certain Malachi, but the name is clearly fictitious, being taken from the reference to "my messenger" (*malʾākî*) in 3:1. It is, therefore, more pseudonymous than anonymous. Since, however, the ensuing identification of the author with the eschatological messenger of the covenant is clearly inappropriate, we are entitled to look for a reason why in this instance it was thought necessary to have a separate book with a distinct title. Taking account of the organization of the Latter Prophets as a whole, it may be suggested that another book was necessary to make up the number twelve. In that case it is reasonable to ask whether the division into three and twelve is not meant to have a particular significance, whether in fact it is not meant to refer to the three patriarchs and the twelve sons of Jacob—Israel.[76] Such a practice is in any event by no means unattested. At some point in its history the book of Psalms was divided into five books, in all probability with reference to the "five fifths of the Law," and the same may be the case with the Gospel of Matthew and the much later liturgical grouping of the five *megilloth*.

The reason for this arrangement may be found in the last two paragraphs of the Latter Prophets (Mal. 3:22–24). Similar in function to the last paragraph of Deuteronomy examined in an earlier chapter, these are intended to serve as the conclusion to the entire prophetic collection, perhaps even to both Law and Prophets combined. The first (3:22), couched in the Deuteronomic style, is a final recall to the Mosaic law and the unique revelation of Horeb:

> Remember the law of my servant Moses, the statutes and ordinances that I commanded him at Horeb for all Israel.

The second (3:23–24) is clearly intended as an explanatory gloss on Mal. 3:1, the promise (or threat) of a pre-eschatological messenger. It reads as follows:

> Behold, I will send you Elijah the prophet before the great and terrible day of the LORD comes. And he will turn the hearts of fathers to their children and the hearts of children to their fathers, lest I come and smite the land with a curse.

It is related to the first by virtue of the close thematic association between the figures of Moses and Elijah, and especially by the theophany granted to both at Horeb. What it seems to be saying is that reconciliation is necessary in order to avoid the eschatological judgment, and that it will be effected through the prophetic ministry of Elijah returned to earth or a prophetic figure like Elijah. It stands, therefore, in interesting contrast to the final statement in the Pentateuch which denies parity between Moses and the prophets.

But what does this reconciliation between fathers and sons really mean? To interpret it in purely ethical terms, as if it meant reconciliation between members of the family, would be

to miss the point completely. A surer indication of the meaning can be found in Sirach who also refers to *Elias redivivus:*

> You who are ready at the appointed time, it is written,
> To calm the wrath of God before it breaks out in fury,
> To turn the heart of the father to the son,
> And to restore the tribes of Jacob (48:10)

This in its turn refers back quite unmistakably to the Servant
of Yahweh in Second Isaiah whose mission also has as its goal
the ingathering and restoration of the dispersed tribes of Israel:

> And now the LORD says,
> who formed me in the womb to be his servant,
> to bring Jacob back to him . . .
> to raise up the tribes of Jacob
> and to restore the preserved of Israel (Is. 49:5–6)

The mission of the pre-eschatological prophet is therefore to
bring about the final reintegration of Israel represented by the
twelve sons of Jacob and thereby prepare for the Days of the
Messiah.

This view of the matter would be confirmed by the tendency within the prophetic tradition itself to embody the ancient charismatic Israel and the impulse within the sects, and
presumably also in the movement leading to their emergence,
to restore the past. Such tendencies are detectable in the
eschatological additions to the prophetic books. They clearly
ran counter to the increasing propensity of the religious leadership to limit itself to the temple-community around
Jerusalem, dictated largely but not exclusively by the need to
oppose Samaritan claims.[77] The all-Israelite ideal, at any rate,
seems to have permeated the thinking of the apocalyptic sects
known to us. One thinks of the Testaments of the Twelve
Patriarchs, the division of the Qumran community into
twelve tribes, their supreme council consisting of twelve
laymen and three priests (again, the prototypal or nuclear
people), the Judeo-Christian letter of James addressed to the
twelve tribes of the dispersion, the insistence in early Christianity on maintaining the apostolic cadre at twelve, and so
on.[78] It seems reasonable to conclude, then, that whoever

added this coda to the Prophets intended to present them as inculcating an observance of Torah which would not exclude the millenarian hope.[79] Thus, the tension which seemed to have been resolved in favor of the claims of the past at the end of the Pentateuch is now restored.

6: The Transformation of Prophecy

I. The Tripartite Canon

THE DESIGNATION OF CERTAIN WRITINGS AS CANON-
ical by a process of positive selection and equally positive
exclusion is an ideological factor in the great religious traditions and their modern secular counterparts such as Com-
munism. While the precise rationale for the choice of texts
will vary, the general intent is to fix and legitimate one form
of self-understanding and by implication to exclude others.
We have seen that the most basic and paradigmatic claim to
religious authority was that of the prophet, and that it had to
do with the mediation and interpretation of the shared tradition. It was this claim which evoked the official shaping of the
tradition in writing and which dictated that it could be done
only on prophetic warranty, namely, that of Moses as prophet
kat'exochen. In the course of time, and for reasons discussed in
the previous chapter, this original canon was extended to
include a collection of prophetic writings. The tensions which
only gradually came to the surface during the Second Temple
period can be best understood in relation to the interpretation
of prophecy. We see, in other words, the emergence of different kinds of theocratically acceptable "prophecy"; but we
also observe it being refashioned into their own image by
those elements which became increasingly disaffected from
the religious center. Thus the tensions which we have seen to
underlie the emergence of the Pentateuch itself still continued
to exist but in a different form, and the difference was due to

the fact that the words of the prophets were now available in writing.

This basic fact of early Jewish ecclesiastical history, the tension (as Plöger put it) between theocracy and eschatology, provides the clue to the existence of a tripartite rather than bipartite canon.[1] The fundamental issue, in other words, was still that of coming to terms with the prophetic claim and, therefore, of deciding between acceptable and unacceptable interpretations of the prophetic message. The third part of the canon provides a cross-section of the various ways in which prophecy was absorbed and transformed. It also contains one example of the "new prophecy" of apocalyptic but excludes a great number of similar works in circulation from the Seleucid down into the Roman period. The explanation is in general terms to be sought in positions assumed by an ascendant orthodoxy vis-à-vis those groups (later sects) which defined their own self-understanding in terms of prophetic eschatology. The question at issue was: which understanding of prophecy will prevail?

The title of the third part of the canon, "the Writings," is probably short for "the other writings," works, that is, over and above the Law and the Prophets which had achieved a certain popularity and authority. The perfect scribe, according to Jesus ben Sirach, devotes himself to the study of the Law, the wisdom of the ancients and the prophecies (Sir. 39:1). From indications eleswhere in his book we are led to conjecture that the author had in mind David as the composer of Psalms and Solomon as the author of Proverbs and perhaps also the Song of Songs, but this list would clearly not be exhaustive.[2] Interestingly enough, the order in which the various objects of study are mentioned here would suggest a Law-Writings-Prophets canon, but of course there is no indication that anything so definite as a tripartite canon had emerged at the time of writing (ca. 180 B.C.E.). This situation had not changed significantly a half century later when the author's grandson wrote a rather pedestrian prologue to the work. In it he refers to the law, the prophets and the other books of our fathers (*tōn allōn patriōn bibliōn*) or, alternatively, the law, the prophecies and the rest of the books (*ta loipa tōn*

biblíōn), neither of which gives an impression of a clearly
identifiable collection. The same conclusion is suggested by
the Greek translation of the Hebrew Bible, also from Egypt,
which has no special category for the Writings. The situation
was therefore quite open in the second century B.C.E. It is, in
fact, quite possible that Sirach's grandson was tactfully making
a bid for his grandfather's book to be granted authoritative
status alongside older compositions of the same kind.[3]

The success of the Maccabee rising must have given
additional impetus to the collection of writings over and
above the Law and the Prophets. Judas is said to have made
good the losses of scrolls during the persecution of Antiochus
IV (2 Macc. 2:14). Jewish communities in Egypt held in high
regard a wide range of writings including works mixing philosophy and piety like The Wisdom of Solomon and didactic
fiction like Tobit and Judith. The Qumran community
cherished a large number of works including, apparently, all of
the books later designated as *kᵉtûbîm* with the exception of
Esther, as well as other devotional and exegetical writings.
Early Christian communities also made use of such works as
the Assumption of Moses, the Apocalypse of Elijah, the Mar-
tyrdom of Isaiah and other works of edification which did not
find entry into any official list.[4] The situation, then, with
respect to writings over and above the Law and the Prophets
seems to have remained very fluid during the period beginning
with Seleucid rule and ending with the destruction of
Jerusalem. Even when we find definite lists being drawn up,
attested clearly only towards the end of the first century
C.E.,[5] there is no uniformity as to the number.

We may take it as very probable, then, that no definitive
list was drawn up either by Ezra and his Great Assembly, or
Nehemiah (2 Macc. 2:13) or the Maccabees, and that no such
list existed, none, that is, which could be called canonical,
before the end of the first century C.E. Consonant with this
reading of the evidence is the common practice of referring to
the Scriptures globally as "the Law and the Prophets."[6] It is
true that Lk. 24:44 speaks of "the Law of Moses, the Prophets
and the Psalms," reminiscent of Josephus' reference to the
additional books as "hymns and admonitions."[7] Such a prac-

tice may indicate that, due to liturgical usage, the book of Psalms already had a privileged status proceeding, as it was believed, from the prophetic inspiration of David.[8] There is, in addition, no evidence that the Jewish leadership at Javneh (Jamnia) fixed the canon once and for all, though discussion and debate about which books "soiled the hands," which were "outside" or "hidden" books, continued into the second century and beyond.[9] We are, therefore, led to think of a gradual process of acceptance and screening which was underway before the fall of Jerusalem and continued throughout the Javnean period and beyond the revolt against Hadrian (132–135).

While all this must be borne in mind, it is equally true and even obvious that the claims inherent in apocalyptic writings, especially when they based their authority on sages of greater antiquity than Moses, could not easily have been ignored by the official leadership. While many of these apocalyptic and Christian writings would have had a very limited circulation, some of them must have come to the attention of the Pharisaic-rabbinic leadership and would inevitably have been proscribed. In much the same way, a Christian canon first appeared in reaction to prophetic claims of Gnostics and Montanists.[10] Not that the apocalyptic element simply disappeared from Judaism after 70 C.E. The book of Daniel achieved and maintained canonical status, if only by title of antiquity, and was highly regarded by Josephus who could hardly be accused of partiality towards apocalyptic.[11] The exegetical schools of Akiba and Ishmael were far from renouncing the eschatological world-view, as an attentive reading of *Mekhilta* reveals. The same Akiba who is alleged to have banned apocalyptic writings supported the messianic claims of Simon bar Kochba.[12] Even after the disaster of the ensuing revolt it is far from clear that apocalypticism and messianism simply disappeared.[13]

For our present purpose, at any rate, the central issue in the long process which eventuated in a tripartite canon was still the understanding of and coming to terms with prophecy. With the exception of Daniel, which was included in spite of the injunction that it be kept secret and sealed (Dan. 12:4, 9), the Writings contain various forms of acceptable theocratic prophecy. All of those other works in circulation which tended towards an eschatological and millenarian interpretation of the prophetic legacy and, therefore, towards sectarianism, were either excluded—when they were not simply lost or destroyed—or went underground to feed the subterranean stream of esotericism and mysticism. As with the formation of the Torah-canon studied earlier, this development is inseparable from historical events which brought certain groups to power and deprived others of it. In both cases, moreover, we are dealing with the same classes of scribes and priests, ancestors of the rabbis who gave final sanction to the biblical canon. We shall deal with them in turn.

II. Scribal Prophecy

The common practice of referring to the Writings as "wisdom literature" is not very apt since, as vague as this expression is, it does not fit all of the $k^e t\hat{u}b\hat{i}m$. It is, nevertheless, significant in that it reflects the ascendancy of the sages in the Second Temple period and the success of their claim to mediate revelation in their own preferred literary forms and categories. The rabbinic dictum (Baba Bathra 12a) that prophecy has been taken from the prophets and given to the sages reflects the historical fact that the scribes who assumed the task of interpreting Torah could do so only by claiming an authority and inspiration comparable to those of the prophets. This in its turn led rabbinic orthodoxy to the indefensible but understandable position that, first, all of the Writings must have been composed within the normative epoch of revelation from Moses to Ezra and, second, that all of their authors must have been prophets. Thus (to follow the order of the Hebrew Bible) Psalms was composed by David,[14] Job by Moses,[15] Proverbs by Solomon,[16] Ruth by Samuel, the Canticle and Qoheleth by Solomon,[17] Lamentations by Jeremiah, Esther by Ezra's Great Assembly which included prophets,[18] Daniel by the sixth-century *gôlāh*-prophet of that name, Ezra, Nehemiah and Chronicles by Ezra, by some identified with

Malachi but in any case a prophetic as well as priestly and scribal figure.[19] Viewed in perspective, this is nothing more than a later extension of the process, examined in an earlier chapter, by which the Torah itself came to be endowed with prophetic credentials.

Even a cursory examination of some of the products of early Jewish scribalism will convince us that prophecy was in fact undergoing this metamorphosis during the post-exilic period. Thus the friends of Job, who are meant to represent the best wisdom available at the time, at least implicitly lay claim to an inspiration comparable to that of the prophets.[20] Ezra, who was both scribe and priest, succeeded in his mission because the hand of Yahweh was on him (Ezra 7:6, 28)—a phrase which comes directly from the old prophetic tradition.[21] His prophetic status is, of course, more explicit in the much later pseudepigraphal and apocalyptic Second Book of Esdras. Jesus ben Sirach compares his scribal teaching explicitly with prophecy (Sir. 24:33); and that this was not just a personal trait, but one considered characteristic of scribalism in general, can be deduced from his description of the ideal sage whose time is consumed in the study of Torah and prophecy. As a result of this study, he then becomes a source of revelation to others in his own right, filled as he is with the spirit of understanding.[22]

It will not escape us that this identification of prophecy with scribal activity marks a shift from direct revelation through the person of the prophet to revelation accruing from the inspired interpretation of biblical texts. In other words, the exegete or theologian is now the prophet. Here, too, a fundamental authority-claim is involved which has to do with the authorization to interpret Scripture which now includes prophetic texts. One way is taken by the Asideans and their presumed heirs including the early Pharisees, Essenes and Jewish Christians. With these, and no doubt other similar groups, the eschatological interpretation of prophetic texts leads directly to new forms of life and new understandings of what it means to be Israel. A quite different way is taken by the official representatives of the theocracy, and this leads to the institutionalization of exegesis as a constituent

element of rabbinic scholasticism. Naturally, such a polarization did not develop overnight. We do not, in fact, find the
lines clearly drawn before the crisis of Hellenization and the
"final solution" of Antiochus IV. Suffice it to note that Jesus
ben Sirach, perhaps a temple scribe but in any case no revolutionary, records the belief that Elijah will return at the appointed time (48:10) and prays for the fulfillment of the
prophecies (36:15–16).

The post-exilic scribes of whom we are speaking were the
first to elaborate what might be called a speculative theology.
Such a development was made possible by the availability of
categories which enabled them to give the Law a universal
significance detached from the historical particularities with
which it is associated in the tradition. The chief of these
categories was wisdom (*ḥokmāh*), and it was practically inevitable that it should come to be identified with Torah.[23] And
since *ḥokmāh* was regarded as transcending all creation, as the
first of all created things (Prov. 8: 22–31), it became possible
to affirm the primacy and absolute antiquity of Torah also.
This particular theological move, which was to become one of
the bases of later Jewish apologetics (e.g., in Josephus' tract
against Apion), served very opportunely to offset the claims of
the apocalypticists which were based on sources of revelation
of such unchallengeable antiquity as Adam, Enoch and Noah,
all of whom could claim precedence over Moses.

This first elaboration of a *ḥokmāh*-theology enabled the
scribes to accommodate prophecy within an inclusive scheme
of reference originating with themselves. In Prov. 1–9, for
example, Wisdom appears to act out the role of prophetess.
She is the source of revelation for others; she proclaims,
preaches, exhorts, threatens just as the prophets had done.
The identification of Wisdom with the divine Spirit may also
be understood in this context. For Sirach, for example, who
follows P rather closely here and elsewhere, Wisdom takes
over the role of the Spirit in the creation of the world (Sir.
24:3). In the book of Daniel and the *Wisdom of Solomon*,
works of profoundly different character which nevertheless
stand within the scribal tradition, wisdom is inseparable from
the prophetic calling and mission.[24]

What we are witnessing, then, is a progressive scribalization of prophecy which was to issue in very different though not totally incompatible positions. On the one hand the prophetic books were read for instruction and wisdom pertaining to the Law, as Sirach's grandson would put it. On the other hand their interpretation would lead to the "new prophecy" of apocalyptic which, with its secret books and tablets handed down from hoary antiquity, is eminently scribal. The issue of authority and legitimation is the same, only the ground over which it is fought has changed.

The presence of the Chronicler's work among the *kᵉtûbîm* reminds us that not only the exegete and teacher but also the historian came to be regarded as fulfilling a prophetic function. That prophecy and the writing of history were thought to belong in some way together is already apparent from the inclusion of the historical books in the prophetic canon. The traditional explanation is that they were composed by prophets; hence the writing of history was considered to be one form of prophetic activity. Josephus, himself a historian who laid claim to prophetic powers of sorts, states explicitly that in Judaism the writing of history was entrusted only to prophets since they had access to information about the past through divine revelation.[25] In point of fact, however, evidence is lacking either that the canonical prophets wrote history or that the historical books were written by prophetic authors. On the contrary, both direct inference from the Old Testament itself and analogy with other ancient Near Eastern cultures suggest that historiography arose and developed among the scribal and clerical classes. The explanation is rather that the sages' interpretation of the past, like their biblical interpretation, needed the kind of legitimation which prophetic status conferred.

Given this situation, it is no longer so surprising that the Chronicler, who rewrote the history of Israel from his own Jerusalemite and anti-Samaritan perspective, names prophets and seers among his historical sources with such frequency as to leave little doubt that he regarded the writing of history as a prophetic activity. Some of these sources are known to us and others are not. Their writings are variously described as rec-

ords (*dᵉbārîm*), prophecy (*nᵉbû'āh*), visions (*ḥᵃzôt*), treatise
(*midrāš*); some of which titles appear in superscriptions to
prophetic books and others do not.[26] While never so much
emphasized previously, this position was not entirely new. In
the Deuteronomic history, as we saw in an earlier chapter, it is
the relation between prophecy and fulfillment which makes
history intelligible. It is but a short step from this to the view
that prophets actually composed the history, being in the best
position, as they were, to understand its meaning. This is the
position of the Chronicler, and it goes far to explaining the
attribution to prophetic authorship of the national history.

III. Clerical Prophecy

In an earlier chapter[27] we saw that scribes and priests were
already closely associated classes in the pre-exilic period, that
scribes shared responsibility for the maintenance of the temple
and its functions, and that levitical scribes probably played an
important part in the production of Deuteronomy. The scribe
Shaphan, moreover, was very active in the religious reforms of
Josiah, one of his sons had a room in the temple (Jer. 36:10),
and his family continued to be active in religious affairs well
into the exilic period. It seems likely that with the collapse of
the state this kind of scribalism, which was a function of the
state-system, was merged with the priesthood. The kind
characteristic of the post-exilic period, the principal but by no
means unique function of which was the exposition of law, did
not, therefore, stand in direct line of descent from pre-exilic
scribalism but was rather a specialized function of the priesthood which came to achieve its own independent status.

From the time of Ezra, described as priest, scribe and expert
in Torah, the close associations between the two offices is
regularly attested. Jesus ben Sirach, the scribe *par excellence,*
shows a great interest in the temple liturgy and priesthood and
may have been a temple-scribe. During the Roman period
scribes were drawn from every level of the clergy as well as
from the laity.[28] They must have played an important role in
the education of the clergy and could be consulted on matters

pertaining to ritual law.[29] Josephus, himself both priest and scribe, uses the term *hierogrammateis*,[30] and the synoptic gospels refer routinely to the "chief priests and the scribes."[31] We would, therefore, not be surprised to find both classes sharing a similar ideology and, specifically, a similar understanding of prophecy.

Our brief study of the Priestly Work (P) in a previous chapter showed some of the ways in which the priesthood appropriated the prophetic claim to mediate revelation. It is probable that the high priesthood took over the oracular function from the prophets in a more or less conscious way as early as the Babylonian exile, principally by the manipulation of Urim and Thummim.[32] By the time of the Maccabees the combination of high priesthood and prophecy is amply attested. John Hyrcanus combined in his person the prerogatives of civic ruler, high priest and prophet, and by the time of Caiphas it was assumed that the high priest could exercise prophetic gifts.[33] It seems likely that, however we evaluate his claims, Josephus viewed his aptitude for prophesying as a function of his priestly and Hasmonean descent.[34]

More interesting for our purposes, however, are the prophetic and scribal functions of the lower clergy or Levites during the post-exilic period. They are listed among those who returned from exile under Cyrus but we hear little of their activity during the first century or so after the return. In preparation for his mission Ezra conscripted Levites from Casiphia in Babylon, one of the more important centers of the *gôlāh*, to instruct the people in the laws. The first named of these, a certain Sherebiah, is described as a man of understanding (*'îš śekel*), in other words, a sage.[35] Such a description is entirely consonant with what the Chronicler has to say about levitical scribes and "handlers of Torah," and it is clear that by his time these levitical scribes, of whom perhaps he himself was one, played a significant part not only in worship but the life of the community in general.[36] These people were above all inspired exegetes and artists, teachers and interpreters of Torah, and specialists in liturgical music and poetry.[37] In this last capacity they are described by the Chronicler as engaging in prophetic activity (1 Chron. 25:1ff.; 2 Chron. 20:14–17); a

hint, therefore, of the idea recurring in different cultures and
at different times that prophet and poet are essentially one.

The emphasis in the Chronicler's work on liturgical poetry
and music as an aspect of prophecy links up with the ecstatic
$n^e b\hat{\imath}$'$\hat{\imath}m$ in the early days of the monarchy who sang and
danced to the sound of pipe and drum in the country shrines
and, in due course, in the temple of Jerusalem.[38] The presence
of prophetic oracles in psalms and of psalms in prophetic
books, not to mention more direct references in the historical
books, puts it beyond reasonable doubt that cultic prophets
formed part of the temple staff during the pre-exilic period.[39]
This kind of liturgical prophecy persisted down into the
Roman period, being attested at Qumran and in early Christian communities.[40] It would seem, then, that some time
before the Chronicler wrote his work, Levites, organized in
different classes and guilds, had taken over the role of the
cultic prophets of the First Temple. One small but revealing
indication occurs in the Chronicler's account of Josiah's reform. Where his source (2 Kings 23:2) has Josiah accompanied by priests and prophets on his way to the temple, he
himself refers to priests and levites (2 Chron. 34:30).

If we exclude the genealogical prologue, the Chronicler
begins his history with the death of Saul and accession of
David. This decision, inspired by the polemical intent of
legitimating the Jerusalem community against Samaritan
claims to represent the true Israel of antiquity, resulted in a
great enhancement of the figure of David. It is he, rather than
Moses, who is represented as the founder of the ecclesiastical
community. More specifically, it is he who set up the whole
structure of temple worship. In keeping with the shift in emphasis in understanding prophecy, it is also David rather than
Moses who, by virtue of his poetic inspiration, is the prophet
par excellence.[41] Moreover, this prophetic gift was shared with
his colleagues, the founders of the levitical liturgical guilds
who are described as seers and sages.[42]

When we look back from the Chronicler's perspective to
the age of classical prophecy, it will be clear that much water
has flowed under the bridges. This should not, however, lead
us to conclude that his particular emphasis is purely arbitrary

or exclusively the outcome of his confessional and polemical stand. The attribution of prophetic characteristics to Levites, even where it was not based directly on ancient tradition, was not necessarily foreign to it. Much is obscure about this ancient order of *homines religiosi* and will probably remain so. We do know, however, that like the early nabis and Nazarites they were closely attached to the institutions of the tribal federation in the prestate period. Intimately associated with Moses, himself a Levite,[43] they were entrusted with the oracular Urim and Thummim which persisted as a primary symbol of sacerdotal prophecy well into the Roman period.[44] They were also active in the summons to and prosecution of the holy war,[45] and this aspect of their ministry was still there to be revived by the Chronicler in his retelling of the history and by the supporters of the Maccabees.[46] It, too, figured prominently in the Qumran community.[47] Links with the Deuteronomic corpus, which gives so much prominence to Levites, should also be borne in mind.[48]

The Levites, then, are of particular interest since it seems that they stood at the confluence of the priestly, scribal and prophetic movements in the period of the Second Temple. That is to say, as liturgists, teachers and exegetes they were represented, and probably thought of themselves, as heirs and successors of the prophets. In this capacity it is difficult not to think of them as contributing in a significant way to rabbinic scholasticism.[49] It is true, of course, that the Levites underwent many changes during the period of the Second Temple on which we are very poorly informed. To take only one example: at the beginning of this period the temple singers have not yet achieved levitical status while at the end of it they formed the upper stratum among the ranks of Levites.[50] There was also, as we have seen, considerable overlap between Levites and scribes, and it was no doubt the scribal and didactic element which contributed more directly to the main-line intellectual tradition.

The tendency for prophecy to be assimilated by the intellectual elite is not restricted to the religious establishment but appears also among the dissident groups once they begin to emerge clearly under Seleucid rule. Thus it is reasonable to ask

whether those *ḥᵃsîdîm* who resisted the overt campaign of
Antiochus IV, and presumably also the acceptance of Greek
ways which had been going on apace earlier, did not have ties
of some kind with the Levites. They are described in 1 Macc.
2:42–44 as mighty men of Israel who offered themselves
willingly for Torah; language reminiscent of the warlike Levites of ancient tradition. They accompanied or, more likely,
were actually identical with the group of scribes which approached the high priest Alcimus to negotiate terms (1 Macc.
7:12–14), which is significant in view of the close associations
attested in the books of Chronicles and elsewhere between
Levites and scribes. Since these people who formed the
backbone of religious resistance to hellenization are probably
connected with the *ḥᵃsîdîm* mentioned often in the Psalms, we
should also note that three psalms which mention *ḥᵃsîdîm* are
ascribed to Levitical authorship and that these *ḥᵃsîdîm* seem to
be thought of as both priestly and prophetic.[51] If the common
assumption that the book of Daniel comes from the same
group is correct, we may note further that in it the members of
the sect are called *maśkîlîm*, wise teachers, a term commonly
applied to Levites.[52] If this hypothesis makes sense, it may be
suggested that the term *ḥasîd* used by these people may have
been taken from the reference to Levi (rather than Moses[53])
in the Blessing of Moses as *'îs ḥᵃsîdekā*, thy devout-one (Deut.
33:8).

The prophetic character of the Levite as inspired interpreter
and instructor also finds some confirmation in the Qumran
scrolls. On this matter Geza Vermes has established a crucial
point. He argues that the Instructor (*maśkîl*), mentioned in the
Community Rule (1QS), the Damascus Document (CD) and
elsewhere, is identical with the Guardian (*mᵉbaqqēr*) and is a
Levite who functions alongside the priest. His duties were to
instruct, give spiritual counsel and supervise worship, and
there can be no doubt that the instruction which he imparted
was based on the study and interpretation of the Scriptures.[54]
He is, in fact, referred to as the Interpreter of the Law (*doreš
hattôrāh*) in the Community Rule and the Damascus Document; and we are at once reminded of the function of Levitical
maśkîlîm in the Chronicler's history.[55] Quite apart from this,

the Levites at Qumran have an important role to play in the eschatological holy war by sounding the alarm, summoning to battle and participating in the victory liturgy.[56] This, too, is based on ancient tradition and attested in the Chronicler's work.

The assumption and transformation of the prophetic prerogative by the clergy of both orders is therefore an incontrovertible and highly significant aspect of Second Temple religious history. Its beginnings were traced back in previous chapters to the book of Deuteronomy and the Priestly Work and we have seen it coming to clear expression in the historical work of the Chronicler. With the proscription of the Jewish religion by Antiochus IV we enter a decisively new phase. The main focus of resistance to cultural assimilation, even before the rise of the Maccabees, were those groups who go under the name of *ḥᵃsîdîm* or Devout. They and their predecessors referred to in certain cultic hymns thought of themselves as heirs of the prophets and may have belonged to the levitical class. The Maccabees themselves claimed descent from Levi and seem to have adopted the zealous Phineas, grandson of Aaron, as their eponym and patron saint.[57] They, too, appear to have been inspired by prophetic texts, to judge by the legend of Judas being visited by Jeremiah who presented him with a golden sword (2 Macc. 15:12–16). By the time of John Hyrcanus, however, the prophetic character of the Maccabean priest-kings was no more than a formal element of their official ideology. As such, it finds expression in the Testament of Levi in which the ancestor of the Hasmoneans foretells that one of his descendants will bear the title "Prophet of the Most High."[58] We have seen that this arrogation of the prophetic gift by the high priesthood outlived the Maccabees and persisted down to the destruction of the Temple.

Some time before Hyrcanus the *ḥᵃsîdîm* broke with the Maccabees, and this rupture is widely thought to have resulted in the well-known sects of Pharisees and Essenes and perhaps others less well-known. What we know of these suggests that, while severing themselves decisively from the civic and priestly leadership, they retained a strong clerical ethos; witness the devotion of the Pharisees to the laws of levitical tithing and the holiness laws and the priestly ethos of the Qumran community. That they also understood themselves to be successors of the prophets is about as explicit as it can be. It was among such groups, now removed from the center of power,[59] that apocalyptic came to its most characteristic expression. Apocalyptic is the child of prophecy, but prophecy which had already been taken over and transformed by priests and scribes. The writers of apocalypses claimed access to revelation not by virtue of direct communication from God, as did the classical prophets, but by access to the true meaning of prophetic texts and by possession of prophetic writings of even greater antiquity. In some groups, for example, Enoch was not only sage, scribe and priest but also a prophetic figure who knew divine mysteries and foretold the course of the future.[60]

Given the tendency for such claims to be translated into statements about ecclesiastical and civil polity, tension and conflict with the official leadership was inevitable. As is well known, the different understandings of prophecy we are discussing led directly to fundamental differences of attitude vis-à-vis the Roman occupying power and eventually to the disasters of the civil war and the catastrophes of 70 and 135 C.E. This did not lead to the outright proscription of apocalyptic writings, or at least we have no evidence that such a decision was made. We have noted that a strong eschatological undercurrent persists in Tannaitic exegesis and that the apocalyptic *Weltanschauung* became part of the esoteric tradition of which the rabbinic sages were carriers.[61] But the actual situation dictated that certain redefinitions of prophecy, and among them especially the exposition of law, should be officially and publicly validated and others should not.

7: The Canon and the Authority of the Bible

I. The Limitations of Canonicity

RENEWED HISTORICAL AND THEOLOGICAL INVESTIGA-
tion of the biblical canon is being forced on us by the methodological and conceptual impasse in which the study of the
Hebrew Bible now finds itself. As I suggested near the beginning of this study, there is a great deal of activity going on but
little overall sense of direction and purpose. It is well known
that the skills and techniques required for a critical reading of
these texts have been developed for the most part by Christian
scholars. The presuppositions which have colored much of
this work, especially during the formative period of Old Testament studies in the nineteenth century, go far to explain
why there has been so little dialogue between Christian and
Jewish scholars as they reflect on their work in this area. And
it is still the case that Christian Old Testament scholars,
where they venture beyond a purely descriptive approach to
their work,[1] tend to collapse the question of canon into the
other question of the relation between the testaments. Nothing has contributed so much as this to the evasion of the
ongoing existence of Judaism as a problem for Christian theology.

The general failure of biblical theology to give an adequate
account of its subject matter has been noted often in the
previous pages. It has been urged that if biblical theology
means a theology of the Bible it must take account of the Bible
in its final form and what that form means for theology. De-

spite their breadth and comprehensiveness, the systematic treatments—of which Eichrodt's is the most outstanding—hardly touch on this matter at all.[2] Even more telling has been the failure to isolate one principle of unity behind the heterogeneous mass of material of which the Hebrew Bible is composed. Critical study has made it clear that the viewpoints contained in these writings are just too diverse to yield to such a principle and, what is more important, that they are also at times mutually contradictory, and not only in matters of minor significance. If we are to find a unitary principle of interpretation it will not be by elevating one postulate to a unique status but by examining the relations between different postulates within the context of the canon as a whole.

While our concern has been exclusively with the Hebrew Bible, it may not be out of place to add that the same conclusion holds for the Christian Bible inclusive of early Christian writings. Attempts to discover in the New Testament *one* mandatory form of church government and ministry, for example, or *one* Christian understanding of the Law have all foundered on the same rock. In other words, a critical reading of the texts has made it impossible to ignore the fact that the viewpoints contained in them are not only diverse but also in some cases mutually exclusive. And we must add that where this is so it is not generally fortuitous but rather the result of a positive intention to exclude.[3]

Thus any attempt to elaborate a biblical theology on the basis of a "key concept" will inevitably fall short of being a theology of the Bible. It will not succeed, except by some implausible *tour de force,* in giving an account of all the material in the Bible. It will be even less able to deal with the inner contradictions and conflicts without explaining them away in the interests of convictional and confessional presuppositions. Most importantly, it will fail to account for the Bible in its overall structure and the internal relations between its parts which reveal the intentions and meanings which have gone into it.

It was also urged that the histories of the religion of Israel have likewise failed to satisfy in this respect despite contributions of high distinction. The most frequently voiced criticism is that many of them end up by imposing a preconceived pattern on the material inspired by the philosophical or religious presuppositions of the writer, and in some cases this is only too obviously the case. A question less often raised, however, is whether the material can be made to testify to a pattern of belief characteristic of Israel as a whole. In other words, the question we have to keep on asking is, "whose religion?" To study the formation of the canon is to be made aware that what these writings testify to *directly* is not the religion of Israel but of different individuals and groups attempting, with varying degrees of success, to make their vision prevail in the wider society. What they tell us *indirectly*, especially in the legislation, the historical narratives and prophetic denunciations, is that more often than not the "religion of Israel" was something quite different. This is not to deny the usefulness of accounts of festivals, calendars and the like, but it does imply that such descriptions will not amount to a history of the religion of Israel. For such a history would have to deal with the tensions between the popular cults, concentrated on the procreative and generative powers of nature, and the views of the prophets, priests and scribes who reworked the old traditions. It would also have to take account of the conflicts which arose within these groups themselves and the manner in which they were resolved. This means, in effect, that there can be no adequate history of Israel's religion which does not take account of the formation of the canon as a historical and theological problem.[4]

To introduce the idea of canonicity into biblical theology or theology in general does not at first sight seem very helpful. It may even seem more a hindrance than a help. The idea of locating authority in a book must be for many people today, including theologians, decidedly opaque. The reasons why some books were included and others omitted may also seem arbitrary or at least unimportant. Why make such a sharp distinction between canonical, apocryphal and pseudepigraphal writings? Why (to take an example from the Christian canon) include Jude and omit Didache? These, however, are relatively minor problems. More pressing would be the fear that to take the biblical canon seriously is altogether too committing. Not only does it oblige one to confer absolute validity on interpretative schemata, the relevance of which is no longer self-evident; it might also appear to risk ruling out other questions the theologian would like to ask.

However widespread these misgivings about the idea of canonicity may be, it is safe to say that the unity and authority of the Bible can no longer be taken for granted as central theological data. Since the collapse of neo-orthodoxy, based as it was on the authority of the biblical canon, no new synthesis has emerged in which the biblical canon has a determinative role. In this respect biblical theology has shared in the collapse of theology as a whole in the Christian and to a lesser extent the Jewish context. If no one talks much any more about the authority of the Bible, it is no doubt because the idea of authority has become problematic in theology, and indeed beyond theology;[5] which is to say that theology has become more than usually unsure about the source of its legitimacy. It is widely felt, in other words, that any arguments devised to support a claim to authority will reveal themselves on closer inspection to be relative, provisional and pragmatic. That religious bodies have not been exempt from this "crisis of authority" has become increasingly apparent these last several years to both Christian and Jew, nowhere more so than in the more authoritarian branches of the two faiths.

At first sight the present study would seem to add fuel to the fire by emphasizing the disunity rather than the unity of the Hebrew Bible and, by implication, the Christian Bible, too. And indeed it must be concluded that, if the argument advanced has any weight, the biblical canon cannot be taken as an absolute, in the sense of providing in a straightforward way a comprehensive legitimation or normative *regula fidei*. For the canon itself arose out of the need to resolve conflicting claims to authority in the religious sphere and the resolution did not come in the form of a final verdict. These claims, moreover, can be traced back to the prophets whose language about the nature and activity of God simply rules out the idea of a canon as it is generally understood.

If in view of arguments advanced in the preceding chapters we may speak of the Hebrew Bible as basically prophetic,[6] it would seem to follow that in the last analysis we cannot dissociate religious authority from personal experience. We must recall once again the accounts of prophetic callings and the many passages which speak of the "face-to-face" experience of Moses. To affirm this is not to fall back into the Wellhausian dichotomy between the living voice of prophecy and the dead institution. For it is inherent in prophecy of the Israelite kind to aspire towards a new community.

The problem of religious authority, therefore, seems to be inseparable from the kinds of problems which beset prophecy during the last years of the monarchy. The most obvious of these was the impossibility of establishing the prophetic claim in a convincingly objective and verifiable way. The prophet appealed to his inner sense of certitude, the inevitability and ineluctability of his own vision. He alone has stood in the councils of God. He derides other claims of access to the divine world—the consultation of the dead on behalf of the living, ghosts and familiar spirits that squeak and gibber, diviners, mediums and everything else that today goes under the rubric of the occult (Is. 8:19). His words are wheat compared with chaff, a fire that burns, a hammer that breaks up rocks (Jer. 23:25–32). Such a claim cannot be authenticated by objective criteria without handing over to others the power to judge it, and this would be a betrayal of the prophet's mission. Yet by the same token prophecy reveals its fragility and vulnerability, and nowhere more so than in those conflicts which arose within prophetic circles and which came to a climax during the last days of independent Judah. It is no accident that the same period witnessed the first attempts to control the free exercise of prophecy by elaborating objective and verifiable criteria.

The current tendency to overemphasize personal experience as against other factors makes it necessary to stress some other aspects of prophecy if we are to avoid a rather basic misunderstanding. The first is the sociological situation of the prophet which makes it impossible to view him in isolation, a "religious genius" in the Wellhausen sense. Study of prophetic material over the last few decades has obliged us to conclude that most of the prophets, while engaging in a radical critique of contemporary institutions including the cult, still retain

close connections with these institutions.[7] We cannot, therefore, subscribe to the image of the prophet as an anti-
establishment figure committed to the overthrow of these institutions, an image often projected in the ecclesiastical press
and the lecture rooms of the sixties. Quite apart from other
ambiguities inherent in this presentation, it was precisely the
"religious establishment" which provided the prophet with his
basic images and metaphors. The prophet, in other words,
drew on the tradition at the very heart of his message. He
should be thought of, therefore, not so much as an innovator
but as a renovator of the tradition.[8]

The same can be said *mutatis mutandis* of the "new
prophecy" of apocalyptic. The apocalypticists were also re-
novators of the tradition, the difference being that the tradition is now represented as available in written form and includes prophetic writings which call for inspired interpretation. In both cases, therefore, personal experience played a
decisive role without dismissing the claims of the past. What
was at issue in both the old and the new prophecy was a
personal experience of God working in and through the
transmitted metaphors and mediating past experiences and
disclosures in light of the contemporary situation.

The seriousness of the prophetic experience comes more
clearly into view when we consider how the prophetic calling
tended increasingly to involve the whole life of the prophet in
the message. The language of calling or vocation has been
somewhat dulled by ecclesiastical usage, and it goes without
saying that it can assume a wide variety of forms. The call of
Elisha, which was to become a basic paradigm for charismatic
succession, involved the transfer of spirit from master to disciple (1 Kings 19:19–21; 2 Kings 2:9–10). It is implied that this
act had to be verified by the disciple's prophetic colleagues
and validated by miracles. The call-experiences of the classical prophets were of a different kind since, as a general rule,
the commissioning occurred during a visionary experience.[9]
Unlike the priests and scribes, the prophets were not provided
with their audience by virtue of a legitimate and acknowledged office. They had to establish their own credentials and
stake their own claims by virtue of whatever self-
authenticating character their words possessed. It was, there-

fore, practically inevitable that this kind of calling introduced tension and conflict into the life of the community, as it did so often into the prophet's own life.

The call-narratives are clearly of great importance for the understanding of the nature of religious authority in the Hebrew Bible. Given the extraordinary nature of the experiences which they record, one question which they raise is whether the capacity for such experience was considered to be essential for legitimating the prophetic claim. In the earlier period war-ecstatics like Samson and Saul and the many dervish-like fraternities up and down the land clearly owed their prestige to visible and generally violent spirit-possession. This kind of legitimation through ecstasy is, moreover, widely attested in cultures otherwise quite different from ancient Israel.[10] It has become a commonplace of modern scholarship, however, to assert that these "plebeian technicians of orgiastics," as Max Weber called them,[11] have little in common with the so-called classical prophets beginning with Amos. This would be, if correct, an important point since it is meant to prepare for the assertion that the real basis for prophetic authority is not possession by the spirit but the word communicated by God to the prophet. It will be apparent that this polarity between spirit and word has played a major role in discussions on the canonical and inspired status of the Hebrew and Christian Scriptures.

It is true that the canonical prophets, with the exception of Ezekiel, make little use of the vocabulary of spirit, but it is far from clear that their kind of prophecy is quite independent of extraordinary states and experiences. Amos had five visions, Isaiah saw Yahweh seated on his heavenly ark-throne, Micah speaks of howling, wailing and going naked (1:8), Habakkuk solicits an oracle by keeping lonely vigil (2:1–3), as does an anonymous exilic prophet who waits fakirlike for a visionary intimation of the fall of Babylon (Is. 21:3–4, 8–9). These books also contain descriptions of the onset of trance and spirit-possession—trembling, dizziness, the wild beating of the heart (Jer. 4:19; Hab. 3:16). Ezekiel, who saw the vision of the spirit-powered chariot and the valley of dry bones, speaks all the time of the spirit entering him, falling on him, lifting him up.[12]

It would seem, then, somewhat oversimplified to distinguish between spirit-prophecy and word-prophecy as successive and discontinuous stages. The rubric "the word of the LORD" under which prophetic sayings regularly appear cannot be construed to refer to rational discourse as opposed to the nonrational utterance of the mantic. We have whole collections of sayings which are introduced simply as visions (as at the beginning of Isaiah, Obadiah and Nahum) or prefaced with the strange title, "the word which Isaiah (Amos, Micah, Habakkuk) saw." Without in any way rationalizing or scaling down the extraordinary nature of the prophetic experience (an obvious and banal temptation for those who do not share it), we may take these literary features as indicating that what the prophet says can only be validated in the last resort by the quality of his vision. Once again, therefore, we are brought up against the crucial dilemma of prophecy, that this self-authenticating quality of vision eludes the reach of extrinsic and objective criteria of discernment.

One of the more obvious differences between early Israelite prophecy and prophecy of the high period (eighth to the sixth century) is the shift in emphasis from the group to the individual.[13] This by no means implies that prophecy of the communal kind ceased to exist around the time of Amos, only that due to the changed situation the emphasis now lay elsewhere. With the demise of judgment-prophecy and the increasing polarization within the post-exilic community, however, the charismatic character and ascetic ideals of these orders of holy men ("sons of the prophets," Nazirites, Rechabites, Levites) began to find a new lease of life. However early we date the emergence of the sects, it seems clear that they looked back to the early history of prophecy for inspiration. This is particularly clear in the case of the Qumran community, Essenism in general, the encratite and ascetic elements in earliest Christianity, the Therapeutae of whom Philo speaks, and on to those early Christian monks who retired into the Egyptian desert to escape the corruption of the cities.[14] All of these groups, and others like them, illustrate the tendency for the prophetic and visionary to find embodiment in a community which perpetuates the prophetic claim.

The conclusion to which these considerations lead is that the canon is prophetic insofar as the claim to authority which underlies it in one way or another is the claim to a hearing actually staked by the prophets. This claim arises out of personal experience, often of an extraordinary nature, but always within the context of a community sharing a common memory and therefore mediating a common tradition. It also tends towards the formation of a new community which embodies the prophetic claim. To speak of the Bible as "the word of God" is to affirm or imply its authoritative and prophetic character. It is this which made it possible for the author of the Epistle to the Hebrews, for example, to refer to all previous revelations as God speaking to the fathers through the prophets (Heb. 1:1), and we have seen that the rabbis were in essential agreement. Such a claim, however, was made possible only by extending the concept of prophecy to cover all disclosures to the House of Israel, and in particular those communicated to it by Moses. But it is precisely in this redefinition of prophecy, documented in detail in the present study, that we are to locate the basic problem of canonicity. To repeat, the idea of a canon as generally understood is incompatible with the phenomenon of prophecy. Indeed, the emergence of a first canon with the book of Deuteronomy contributed greatly to the eclipse of prophecy. It is in this context, perhaps, that we can best grasp the force of the opposition between the letter and the spirit as enunciated by Paul.[15] Given the ways in which God chose to send his "discriminatory linguistic signals" to Israel, then, it is difficult to see how the canon can be given absolute status as rule of faith.[16] It seems that we could only do so at the price of ignoring the intentions and meanings to which the Hebrew Bible itself testifies.

II. The Uses and Abuses of Authority

One of the most pressing needs in biblical studies is for a thoroughly competent sociological examination of the phenomena which specialists in the field tend to look at only

from the religious perspective. The idea of a canon, in particular, would call for examination as an aspect of social history,
implying as it does claims to authority and comprehensive
attempts at legitimation on the part of different groups and
individuals. For the most part this work still remains to be
done,[17] and it is in no wise derogatory to the religious claims
being made to insist that it needs to be done. Nor is it inappropriate to suggest that the language of revelation which
occurs frequently in the Bible, especially in the prophetic
books, might be better understood by taking account, among
other things, of the sociology of knowledge.

A natural place to begin would be Max Weber's discussion
of authority in his *The Theory of Social and Economic Organization.* [18] Since Weber's typology is well-known, only the briefest
summary will be necessary. Following on his basic postulate of
the orientation of action to normative order, he differentiates
types of authority according to the nature of the claims which
they embody. The rational-legal type is characterized by
norms of law, clearly defined spheres of competence and juris-
diction, a fixed administrative hierarchy and the formulation
of all acts, decisions and rules in writing. Authority is not seen
to inhere in the individual as such but in the impersonal order
in the name of which all decisions are made and commissions
imposed. All-pervasive is the spirit of rational bureaucracy
and formalism which tend to exclude the arbitrary and unpredictable. Authority of the traditional type also appeals to an
impersonal order for its legitimation, the difference being that
it views this order as having always existed, or at least as
having existed from immemorial antiquity. What is important
is adherence to tradition and to norms handed down from the
past. No new norms may be introduced and no new laws
enacted; or, if they are, it will be in virtue of the fiction that
they are really ancient and have only now been rediscovered
or promulgated. The leadership will tend to de-emphasize its
executive role and recommend itself more by virtue of its
learning and wisdom.

It seems probable, though Weber does not say so explicitly,
that these two types correspond to successive stages in social
development, the trend being inexorably in the direction of

rational, bureaucratic organization. The charismatic type of authority would then correspond to the most primitive stage of organization. But charismatic authority, inherently unstable as it is, hardly merits a place alongside the other types since it cannot become the basis for established order without profound structural changes taking place.[19] Charisma, a term which Weber borrowed from Rudolph Sohm and ultimately from early Christian literature, signifies "a certain quality of an individual personality by virtue of which he is set apart from ordinary men and treated as endowed with supernatural, superhuman, or at least specifically exceptional powers or qualities."[20] Unlike the claims of traditional or bureaucratic leaders, that of the charismatic is legitimated only by recognition of his charisma. He is not designated, appointed or ordained but *called.*[21] If a community grows up around him, its character will likewise be exceptional, and it will be marked by the absence of many of the characteristics proper to a rational-legal bureaucracy.

As stated a moment ago, the most obvious characteristic of authority which claims this kind of legitimation is its instability. By its very nature such a claim soon finds itself in conflict with the established order based on either ancient tradition or an impersonal will. The testing point usually comes with the need to appoint a successor to the charismatic leader. This may be effected in one of several ways: the search for another charismatic leader, appeal to an oracle, designation of a successor in advance by the charismatic leader, and so on. In any event, the perseverance of the charismatic principle will at that point become problematic. The most likely outcome is that it will be embodied in concrete institutions and, of course, be profoundly altered in the process. A priesthood, for example, will claim to be charismatic by virtue of the act of consecration and by reference to a charismatic eponym. It goes without saying that the history of both Judaism and Christianity provides excellent examples of such lineage-charismata and office-charismata resulting from the routinization of the original charismatic impulse.

Critics of Weber have not been slow to point out that his theory of charisma is probably set too much in opposition to institutions and tied too exclusively to extraordinary individu-als.[22] While this criticism is undoubtedly well-founded in that Weber does present charisma as a socially marginal and ab-normal phenomenon, it needs to be said that he does not attribute it exclusively to individuals despite the definition quoted earlier. On the contrary, his concept of the routiniza-tion of charisma implies that the charismatic principle perse-veres, however transformed, in the fabric of institutions, providing them with an ultimate, nonrational basis for their existence.[23] This may help to explain the successive stages in the assimilation of prophecy, the end result of which was the tripartite canon. It remains true, however, that, as Weber also noted, this process is inseparable from conflict and tension.[24] A canon represents an attempt to construct and maintain one world of meaning by a dominant religious and intellectual elite. It can only do so by embodying a prophetic claim to legitimation, but it cannot prevent the original prophetic im-petus, given the appropriate circumstances, from showing up the impermanence of that world and the structures of meaning on which it is based.[25]

Weber's application of his theory to the situation of Israel and early Judaism is just as open to criticism as is the theory itself. We have to bear in mind that his brilliant and penetrat-ing survey entitled *Ancient Judaism* first appeared in 1917 and that a great deal has happened in Old Testament studies since then, particularly in our understanding of the prophets. Some of his emphases—for example, on the authoritarian character of Hebrew religion—will have to be toned down, and some of his distinctions—for example, between ecstatic-exemplary and communal-ethical prophecy—will have to be modified. But even granted the need for such revisions, it is remarkable how much light his theory can still throw on the fate of prophecy in Israel and the processes underlying the emergence of an authoritative written canon. As suggested earlier, these insights have not yet been seriously pursued, and there is an urgent need for more study and reflection in this area. Con-temporary sociologists and anthropologists, who tend to iden-tify prophecy with ecstatic cults and utopian and millenarian movements,[26] have on the other hand made significant contributions to our understanding of the "new prophecy" of apocalyptic. Perhaps because this is a more visible problem, and one deemed to be more relevant, it has received more attention in recent years.[27]

It should be obvious by now that the study of the canon is not just of historical, archeological or literary interest. On the contrary, it raises questions of rather basic significance for both synagogue and church. Not the least of these is the problem of keeping alive the prophetic-charismatic (Weber would say "nonrational") insight on which both are grounded. Here, too, Weber's work is of value despite all the reservations we have to make. If he is right, both synagogue and church will have to be more aware than they presently appear to be of the dangers inherent in intellectual rationalism and the drift towards bureaucracy which comes with quantitative growth.[28] It has generally been the case that such awareness has existed only at the periphery, finding expression in the formation of small-scale communities in a state of dubious belongingness vis-à-vis the official leadership. The aim of such communities, whether consciously formulated or not, is in essence that of rediscovering the genuine prophetic content of the parent body and embodying it in a shared sense of calling, a renewed conviction of personal salvation and a deeper involvement in the problems of society.[29] The hard question, then, is whether this awareness can exist in a state of tension at the center rather than at the periphery of large religious organizations. It seems to be a feature of religious groups organized bureaucratically (Weber called them hierocracies) to exclude the charismatic and seek complete control of the sources of power which, in the context, means access to the redemptive media. Weber did not answer this question, but the history of both Judaism and Christianity, and the emergence of authoritative canons as part of that history, confirm the essential accuracy of his analysis.

The canon, then, does not lend itself to a definitive solution of the problem of religious authority. The juxtaposition in it of law and prophecy suggests rather an unresolved tension, an unstable equilibrium, between rational order and the unpredictable and disruptive, between the claims of the past and those of the present and future. When emphasis is placed too much on the former the outcome is likely to be the conferring of absolute validity on present structures, bureaucratic paralysis and a drift to cultural assimilation.[30] When rational order is neglected in favor of the charismatic, the tendency will be towards disunity, disequilibrium and ultimately sectarianism. Prophecy is necessary if only to show up the precarious nature of all fixed orders and the claims to legitimacy which sustain them, but prophecy alone cannot build a lasting community. The canon does not contain its own self-justification but rather directs our attention to the tradition which it mediates. For to say the least which has to be said, without the tradition there is no shared memory and therefore no community. Our study of the canon has led to the conclusion that no one interpretation of the tradition can be accorded final and definitive status. The presence of prophecy as an essential part of the canon means that it will always be possible and necessary to remold the tradition as a source of life-giving power. It is this conclusion alone, it seems to me, which justifies our retention of the canon; for, as Kierkegaard said, it is not worthwhile to remember that past which cannot become a present.

Principal Abbreviations

Ab.	*Pirke Aboth* (The Chapters of the Fathers)
ABR	*Australian Biblical Review* (Melbourne)
ANET	J. B. Pritchard, ed., *Ancient Near Eastern Texts Relating to the Old Testament* (Princeton: Princeton University Press, 1955; 2nd ed.)
ANETS	J. B. Pritchard, ed., *The Ancient Near East. Supplementary Texts and Pictures Relating to the Old Testament* (Princeton: Princeton University Press, 1969).
Ant.	Josephus: *Antiquities of the Jews*
Ap.	Josephus: *Contra Apion*
ARN	*Abot d^eRabbi Nathan*
ASTI	*Annals of the Swedish Theological Institute in Jerusalem* (Leiden)
BASOR	*Bulletin of the American Schools of Oriental Research* (New Haven)
BWANT	Beiträge zur Wissenschaft vom Alten und Neuen Testament (Stuttgart)
BZ	*Biblische Zeitschrift* (Paderborn)
BZAW	Beihefte zur Zeitschrift für die Alttestamentliche Wissenschaft (Berlin)
CBQ	*Catholic Biblical Quarterly* (Washington)
CD	Damascus Document (Zadokite Work)
En	Enoch
FRLANT	Forschungen zur Religion und Literatur des Alten und Neuen Testaments (Göttingen)
Hist. Eccl.	Eusebius: *Historia Ecclesiastica*
HTR	*Harvard Theological Review* (Cambridge, Mass.)

IB	Interpreter's Bible (Nashville & New York)
IDB	*Interpreter's Dictionary of the Bible* (Nashville & New York)
Inter	*Interpretation* (Richmond, Virginia)
JBC	R. E. Brown, J. A. Fitzmyer, R. E. Murphy, eds., *The Jerome Biblical Commentary* (Englewood Cliffs: Prentice-Hall, 1968).
JBL	*Journal of Biblical Literature* (Philadelphia)
JJS	*Journal of Jewish Studies* (London)
JQR	*Jewish Quarterly Review* (Philadelphia)
JSS	*Journal of Semitic Studies* (Manchester)
LXX	Septuagint
m.	Mishnah
MT	Masoretic Text
NEB	New English Bible
NRT	*Nouvelle Revue Theologique* (Paris)
NTS	*New Testament Studies* (Cambridge, England)
OTS	*Oudtestamentische Studiën* (Leiden)
PRK	Pesikta d'Rab Kahana
1QH	The Hymns (*Hodayoth*) from the First Cave at Qumran
1QM	The War Scroll (*Milḥamah*) from the First Cave at Qumran
1QS	The Qumran Manual of Discipline (*Serek*)
RB	*Revue Biblique* (Jerusalem)
RGG	*Religion in Geschichte und Gegenwart* (Tübingen, 3rd ed.)
RSR	*Recherches de Science Religieuse* (Paris)
RSV	The Revised Standard Version
SDB	*Dictionnaire de la Bible. Supplements* (Paris)
SEA	*Svensk Exegetisk Årsbok* (Lund)
Sib	Sibylline Oracles
SVT	*Supplements to Vetus Testamentum* (Leiden)
TDNT	*Theological Dictionary of the New Testament* (ed. G. Kittel, trans. G. W. Bromiley; Grand Rapids, 1964–76)

Test. Levi	The Testament of Levi
ThZ	*Theologische Zeitschrift* (Basle)
TLZ	*Theologische Literaturzeitung* (Berlin)
t.	Tosefta
UM	Ugaritic Manual (C. H. Gordon; Rome, 1955)
VT	*Vetus Testamentum* (Leiden)
Wisd.	The Wisdom of Solomon
ZAW	*Zeitschrift für die Alttestamentliche Wissenschaft* (Berlin)
ZTK	*Zeitschrift für Theologie und Kirche* (Tübingen)

Abbreviations for tractates of Babylonian Talmud

b. BB	Baba Bathra
b. BM	Baba Mezia
b. Ber.	Berakhoth
b. Erub.	Erubin
b. Ket.	Kethubhoth
b. Meg.	Megillah
b. Pes.	Pesaḥim
b. RH	Rosh Ha-shanah
b. San.	Sanhedrin
b. Shab.	Shabbath
b. Sukk.	Sukkah
b. Yeb.	Yebamoth

Notes

CHAPTER 1: THE HEBREW CANON

1. Arnold Toynbee, *A Study of History* (revised and abridged edition; Oxford: Oxford University Press, 1972), pp. 65–69; see also Talcott Parsons, *Societies. Evolutionary and Comparative Perspectives* (Englewood Cliffs: Prentice-Hall, 1966), pp. 95ff.

2. See Hans von Campenhausen, *The Formation of the Christian Bible* (Philadelphia: Fortress Press, 1972).

3. Briefly, there is evidence in Jewish sources of discussion among Tannaim whether certain books, especially the Canticle and Sirach, "render the hands unclean" (e.g., m. Yad. 3:5), but nothing remotely comparable to a conciliar decision. The received view, repeated without question time out of number, seems to go back to H. E. Ryle's *The Canon of the Old Testament* (1892), pp. 171f.

4. Reference in Sanche de Gramont, *Claude Lévi-Strauss: The Anthropologist as Hero,* ed. E. N. and T. Hayes (Cambridge, Mass.: M.I.T. Press, 1970), p. 14.

5. Jer. 8:8–9, cf. 2:8. Both texts are discussed below, pp. 36ff.

6. On the theological treatment of this issue see G. von Rad, *Old Testament Theology* II (New York and Evanston: Harper & Row, 1965), pp. 3–5, and W. Zimmerli, *The Law and the Prophets* (Oxford: Blackwell, 1965). It is important and problematic to note that von Rad divides his work into the theology of Israel's historical traditions and that of her prophetic traditions. The rationale for this division lies in the typological re-actualization of the historical traditions in the prophets who thereby open them up to their fulfilment in Christ and the Church (pp. 428–429).

7. J. Wellhausen, *Prolegomena to the History of Ancient Israel* (New York: Meridian Books, 1957), pp. 3, 339, 505, etc.

8. *Ibid.,* pp. 398–399. This view remains very influential; to take only one example, see C. H. Dodd's *The Authority of the Bible* (London: Fontana Books, 1960, [first published 1929]), pp. 149ff. He actually uses the term "religious genius" of the prophet (p. 159).

9. This kind of formulary is not restricted to the Hittite treaties; further, it is apparent that some of the alleged borrowings are not very close at all. See, *inter alios,* D. J. McCarthy, *Treaty and Covenant* (Rome: 1963); F. Nötscher, "Bundesformular und 'Amtsschimmel,'" *BZ* 9 (1965), 181–214; G. Fohrer, *History of Israelite Religion* (London: S.P.C.K., 1973), pp. 80–81.

10. See G. Vermes, "Baptism and Jewish Exegesis: New Light from Ancient Sources," *NTS* 4 (1957–1958), 308–319.

11. G. von Rad, *The Problem of the Hexateuch and Other Essays* (New York: McGraw-Hill, 1966), pp. 1ff.
12. E.g., A. Weiser, *Introduction to the Old Testament* (London: Darton, Longman & Todd, 1961), pp. 83ff.
13. M. Noth, *A History of Pentateuchal Traditions* (Englewood Cliffs: Prentice-Hall, 1972).
14. Cf. the remarks of James Barr, *Old and New in Interpretation* (London: S.C.M. Press, 1966), pp. 18f., 74ff.
15. See B. S. Childs, *Biblical Theology in Crisis* (Philadelphia: Westminster, 1970); R. C. Dentan, *Preface to Old Testament Theology* (New York: Seabury, 1963²); J. Barr, pp. 15ff.
16. See G. E. Wright, *The Old Testament and Theology* (New York and Evanston: Harper & Row, 1969).
17. See note 15.
18. As we shall see in a later chapter, the decisive factor for the apocalyptic sects was the authority accorded to prophetic texts available in a written collection from about 200 B.C.E. For the role of priestly intellectuals in molding religious tradition, see Max Weber, *The Sociology of Religion* (Boston: Beacon Press, 1963 [first published 1922]), pp. 118ff. We must, therefore, be cautious about speaking without further qualification of the *community's* self-understanding reflected in the way it appropriates the tradition.
19. That is what early Christianity was in the context of Judaism of the Greco-Roman period. In Acts 24:5 the lawyer Tertullus speaks of "the sect (*hairesis*) of the Nazarenes."
20. Wright, pp. 9f., calls this "Christomonism" and refers to H. R. Niebuhr's use of the term "Christian henotheism." J. Barr, pp. 152ff., also criticizes an excessively Christocentric Old Testament exegesis.
21. J. A. Sanders, *Torah and Canon* (Philadelphia: Fortress Press, 1972).
22. *Ibid.*, p. 52. A *corrigendum* slip inserted into the book hastens to add that this must not be interpreted as a theological argument against the State of Israel! The text of p. 52 is altered, however, in the second printing (1974).
23. P. L. Berger and T. Luckmann, *The Social Construction of Reality* (Garden City: Doubleday, 1966).
24. Many of the viewpoints and even some of the terminology which I use are also found in John Gager's *Kingdom and Community: The Social World of Early Christianity* (Englewood Cliffs: Prentice-Hall, 1975), which I read only after completing all but the final revision of this book. Gager stresses the ambiguous role of the Christian canon as I do that of the Hebrew Scriptures. Canon in general is part of world construction and world maintenance. While it represents "an effort to sustain one interpretation of that world (i.e., the Christian world) against the threat of competition from within and without" (p. 11), it nevertheless preserves and even idealizes an image of the group's charismatic origins (p. 75).
25. See Ezra 4:1–3, where "the enemies of Judah and Benjamin" very probably include Samaritans. Whether the events referred to took place in

537 as the Chronicler suggests or in 520 during the ministry of Haggai and Zechariah need not be discussed. It is by no means clear that the impure people and nation of which Haggai speaks (2:14) refers to the Samaritans, and, therefore, we are not obliged to accept the classical thesis of J. W. Rothstein (*Juden und Samaritaner*, 1908) that the twenty-fourth day of the ninth month of 520 marks the birthday of Judaism. For recent discussion of Hag. 2:10–14, see K. Koch, "Haggais unreines Volk," *ZAW* 79 (1967), 52–66, and H. G. May, "'This People' and 'This Nation' in Haggai," *VT* 18 (1968), 190–197.

26. The question cannot be settled exclusively with reference to use of the term $y^e h \hat{u} d \hat{\imath}$, Jew (or Judahite) which begins before the Exile, e.g., Jer. 32:12; 34:9; 38:19.

27. Lucy S. Dawidowicz, *The War against the Jews 1933–1945* (New York: Holt, Rinehart & Winston, 1975), pp. 23–47, has a brief and impressive account of the growth of antisemitism in nineteenth-century Germany and Austria.

28. See H-J Kraus, *Geschichte der Historisch-kritischen Erforschung des Alten Testaments* (Neukirchen: Verlag der Buchhandlung des Erziehungsvereins Neukirchen Kreis Moers, 1956), pp. 235–249; L. Perlitt, *Vatke und Wellhausen* (BZAW 94; Berlin: Töpelmann, 1956).

29. Kraus, p. 248.

30. The virulent anti-Judaism of Hegel's earlier writings, never disavowed, entitles him to be considered one of the founders of modern intellectual anti-semitism; see the brief but telling remarks in Kraus, pp. 177f., and Emanuel Hirsch, *Geschichte der neuern evangelischen Theologie* IV (Gütersloh: C. Bertelsmann Verlag, 1952), pp. 469f.

CHAPTER 2: DEUTERONOMY: THE FIRST STAGE

1. *Prolegomena to the History of Ancient Israel* (New York: Meridian, 1957), p. 362.

2. The name derives from the inelegant *deuteronomion* of LXX at Deut. 17:18. The Hebrew *mišneh hattorah hazo't* means "a copy of this law," not a second law.

3. Deut. 31:26ff. stipulates that the law book be deposited in the sanctuary where, according to the Deuteronomic historian, it was found, and 31:10ff. requires that it be publicly read at Sukkot every seven years. 4:2 and 12:32 contain a solemn prohibition of adding to or subtracting from the law.

4. See Ex. 24:4, 12; 31:18; 32:15–16; 34:1, 27–28.

5. The law code of Lipit-Ishtar contains the same prohibition as Deuteronomy accompanied by blessings and curses (*ANET*, 161). The famous law code of Hammurabi was inscribed on a stele which was set up in a public place so that people could refer to it. It, too, was not to be altered under pain of falling subject to curses (*ANET*, 178f.). The prologue to the

treaty between Suppiluliumas and Mattiwaza also forbids anyone to change the wording of the tablet (id., 205).

6. Later on, we have the unnamed royal scribe (*soper hammelek*) during the reign of Joash (2 Kings 12:10ff.), Shebnah scribe of Hezekiah (2 Kings 18:18, 37; 19:2), Shaphan scribe of Josiah (2 Kings 22:3ff.) and one later on named Jonathan (Jer. 37:15ff.).

7. 2 Sam. 15:12, etc. See P. A. H. de Boer, "The Counsellor," *SVT* 3 (1955), 42ff.

8. Is. 9:5; 11:2, on which see W. McKane, *Prophets and Wise Men* (Naperville: A. R. Allenson, 1965), p. 110. The phrase *rûaḥ ḥokmah* is also used of Joshua by the Priestly Writer at Deut. 34:9.

9. McKane, pp. 47f. On the theme of suspect wisdom see also J. Blenkinsopp, "Theme and Motif in the Succession History (2 Sam xi 2ff.) and the Yahwist Corpus," *SVT* 15 (1966), 44ff.

10. See 2 Chron. 30:26; 32:27–29, cf. Is. 38:9; on which see R.B.Y. Scott, "Solomon and the Beginnings of Wisdom," *SVT* 3 (1955), 277.

11. b. BB 15a.

12. Cf. the tablet with the name of the prophet's son written on it (Is. 8:1–4) and Jeremiah's symbolic act of buying a parcel of land and having the deed of purchase solemnly witnessed (Jer. 32).

13. Hab. 2:2f.; Jer. 30:2; 36:2ff., 27–32; 45:1; 51:60f.

14. J. Fichtner, "Jesaja unter den Weisen," *TLZ* 74 (1949), 73ff., and R. J. Anderson, "Was Isaiah a Scribe?" *JBL* 79 (1960), 57f., argue inconclusively that he had been a scribe or counsellor.

15. See also Is. 29:14–16 and 30:1–5, and cf. his references to the *ḥᵃkāmîm* of other countries, Is. 19:11 (cf. Jer. 9:22) and 30:9 (cf. v.1).

16. See the important article of J. S. Holladay Jr., "Assyrian Statecraft and the Prophets of Israel," *HTR* 63 (1970), 29ff. His main point concerns more the addressees of the prophets who, beginning in the Assyrian period, direct their message not to individuals so much as to the entire people; but the insistence by the Assyrians on carrying on negotiations in public may well help to explain why we have a book of Amos but not of Elijah, Elisha or Micaiah.

17. While accepting the historical value of the account in Kings and (with some reservations) in Chronicles of Hezekiah's reforming activity, H. H. Rowley denied that it could have been based on the Deuteronomic law since there occurs no mention of a written law in these accounts, and if the law book had existed so early we would expect to hear of it before the eighteenth year of Josiah; see his essay, "Hezekiah's Reform and Rebellion," in his *Men of God: Studies in Old Testament History and Prophecy* (London: Nelson, 1963), pp. 126ff., and "The Prophet Jeremiah and the Book of Deuteronomy" in his *From Moses to Qumran: Studies in the Old Testament* (New York: Association Press, 1963), pp. 190f. Such an argument *e silentio* has some force but it would also work against Rowley's own hypothesis that Deuteronomy was first put together during the reign of Manasseh. The point of our discussion here is not, however, about the date of the book but rather the origins of the movement or school within which the book took shape.

18. 2 Kings 11–12. 2 Chron. 15:12, 14f., speaks of covenant-making during the reign of Asa and 2 Chron. 29:10 implies that Hezekiah also made a covenant.

19. First advanced by Burney, this view has been recently restated by E. W. Nicholson, *Deuteronomy and Tradition* (Philadelphia: Fortress, 1967).

20. Liturgical functions: Deut. 10:8–9; 17:12; 18:1ff.; 21:5; 26:3–4; custodianship of the law book: 31:9, 25; judicial function: 17:9; 19:17; 21:5; 24:8; 27:9; responsibility vis-à-vis the king: 17:18.

21. Deut. 12:12, 18, 19; 14:27, 29; 16:11, 14; 18:6; 26:11, 13.

22. Here we find the prototype for the covenant ceremony in the Qumran Manual of Discipline (1QS I–II) in which the priests recite the blessings and the levites, as *clerus minor*, the curses.

23. This was argued convincingly by J. A. Emerton, "Priests and Levites in Deuteronomy," *VT* 12 (1962), 128ff., against the position of G. E. Wright, "The Levites in Deuteronomy," *VT* 4 (1954), 325ff. See also A. H. J. Gunneweg, *Leviten und Priester* (Göttingen: Vandenhoeck & Rupprecht, 1965), pp. 26, 69ff., 126ff.

24. See G. von Rad, "The Levitical Sermon in I and II Chronicles," in *The Problem of the Hexateuch and Other Essays* (Edinburgh and London: Oliver & Boyd, 1965), pp. 267–280 and cf. *Studies in Deuteronomy*, pp. 66–68. In Deuteronomy itself, however, only one very short sermon is attributed to the Levites and Moses, i.e., 27:9–10. There is also the difficulty of dissociating oneself from the Christian ecclesiastical connotations of the word "preaching." Von Rad, in fact, speaks with approval of the "protestant" atmosphere of the book (*Studies in Deuteronomy*, p. 68).

25. Unless there is a confusion of names here; cf. Jer. 36:10.

26. As argued by M. Weinfeld, *Deuteronomy and the Deuteronomic School* (Oxford: Clarendon, 1972), pp. 158ff.

27. Ezra 7:6, 10f.; Neh. 8:1, 4, 9, 13; 12:26, 36.

28. See especially the levitical scribe Shemaiah at the time of David (1 Chron. 24:6) and levitical scribes who instructed the people during the reign of Josiah (2 Chron. 34:13; 35:3).

29. Deut. 1:9ff., cf. Num. 11:14–17 and Ex. 18:13–27. It is worthy of note, incidentally, that Deut. 1:9 ff. does not mention elders ($z^e q\bar{e}n\hat{\imath}m$) who were among those to whom the law was entrusted (31:9). There seems to have been a close association between elders, priests and sages in the Kingdom of Judah (see Jer. 18:18 and cf. Ezek. 7:26).

30. These are presented fairly exhaustively by Weinfeld, pp. 171–178, 320–365 and *passim*.

31. Weinfeld's arguments (pp. 51ff.) against the possibility of levitical composition of Deuteronomy are not particularly convincing. One is that the book never speaks of Levites writing the law; but, as he himself observed earlier (p. 6), the book carefully avoids anachronisms, assuming that the address comes directly from Moses. He adds that in pre-exilic Israel instruction was the task of priests. This is true but beside the point if there was no *essential* distinction between temple and country clergy with respect to status. The old argument, repeated by Weinfeld, that by authoring

Deuteronomy the Levites would be cutting off the branch they were sitting on, overlooks the fact that the book makes provision for their participation in the Jerusalem cultus (18:6–8).

32. Especially A. Bentzen, *Die josianische Reform und ihre Voraussetzungen* (Copenhagen: G. E. C. Gadd, 1926), pp. 58ff; G. von Rad, *Studies in Deuteronomy*, pp. 66–68.

33. While the Deuteronomic historian (2 Kings 22–23) gives the impression that reforming activity began only after the discovery in the temple, the Chronicler dates it six years earlier (2 Chron. 34:3ff.) which makes it likely that its inception coincided with the death of Ashurbanipal in 627. It is clear, at any rate, that the religious reform goes in tandem with aspirations to political emancipation, and it is highly probable that the extension of reforming activity into the territories north of Judah was contingent on Josiah's political ambitions in that area. For a recent discussion see S. Herrmann, *A History of Israel in Old Testament Times* (Philadelphia: Fortress, 1975), pp. 263–273.

34. Of the many studies on *tôrāh*, G. Östborn, *Tōrā in the Old Testament* (Lund: Ohlsson, 1945), is still useful and has an ample bibliography. W. Gutbrod's treatment in *TDNT*, Vol. 4, 1036ff., is not one of the better articles in the Dictionary.

35. E.g., Hos. 4:5; 5:1; 6:9; 8:4; Mic. 3:11; Jer. 18:18; Zeph. 3:4; Ezek. 22:26; Hag. 2:11; Mal. 2:6ff. See J. Begrich's study in *Gesammelte Studien* (Munich: Kaiser, 1964), pp. 232–260.

36. Is. 8:3; Mic. 4:2.

37. E.g., Prov. 1:8; 4:2; 6:20.

38. E.g., Prov. 3:1; 7:2; 12:15; 14:24; 15:2, 7.

39. "... whether they walk in my *torah* or not" in Ex. 16:4 occurs in the account of the manna composed or edited by P. In Ex. 24:12 the phrase "with the *torah* and the commandments" was probably inserted by an editor to explain what was written on the tablets; on which see M. Noth, *Exodus: A Commentary* (Philadelphia: Westminster, 1962), pp. 133, 200.

40. The phrase $v^e z\bar{o}'t$ *tôrat 'ādām* (2 Sam. 7:19), whatever it means, has no relevance to the present discussion.

41. Leaving aside Am. 2:4, which belongs to the editorial history of the book, we have two passages in Hos. in both of which (4:6; 8:1) the word would more naturally mean "teaching" or "instruction" than "law."

42. E.g., Deut. 27:3, 8, 26. See B. Lindars, "Torah in Deuteronomy," in *Words and Meanings*, ed. P. Ackroyd and B. Lindars (Cambridge: Cambridge University Press, 1968), pp. 128f. and *passim*. E. W. Nicholson, *Preaching to the Exiles* (New York: Schocken Books, 1970), p. 124, also rightly attributes to the Deuteronomic circle the decisive development in the use of *tôrāh*.

43. E.g., Deut. 1:5; 28:61; Jos. 1:7; 8:32; 2 Kings 22:8. The more compendious phrase "the book of the Torah of Moses" occurs at Jos. 8:31 and 1 Kings 2:3.

44. Jer. 20:6; 28:17.

45. Thus the term is not necessarily pejorative as might appear in transla-

tion; it is more of a *terminus technicus*, cf. other cases where *tāpaś* in partici-
pial form with substantive occurs: wielders of the harp (Gen. 4:21), shield
(Jer. 46:9), sickle (Jer. 50:16), oar (Ezek. 27:29), sword (Ezek. 38:4), bow
(Am. 2:15). In all cases the phrase connotes possession of a particular skill.

46. Jer. 10:7; 49:7; 50:35; 51:57.

47. E.g., Jer. 6:19; 26:4; cf. Is. 1:10; 8:16–20; Zech. 7:2–14. See
Östborn, p. 57.

48. A state of tension is "characteristic of any stratum of learned men
who are ritualistically oriented to a law book as against prophetic charismat-
ics," Weber, *Ancient Judaism* (New York: The Free Press, 1952), p. 395. See
also chapters 4 and 8 of his *The Sociology of Religion* (London: Methuen,
1965).

49. E.g., Jer. 30:2; 36:2ff.; 51:60.

50. A selective polling of scholarly opinion would give some idea of the
difficulties involved, including those which derive from denominational
presuppositions.

51. E.g., in Mal. "sons of Levi" is synonymous with "priests" (2:1, 4; 3:3)
and the condemnation of the prophet in Zech. 13:2 ff. seems to presuppose
Deut. 13:1–5. For Nehemiah's legislation cf. Neh. 13:1ff. with Deut. 23:3ff.
and Neh. 10:31 with Deut. 15:2.

52. On which see M. Noth, *Uberlieferungsgeschichtliche Studien*
(Tübingen: Mohr, 1957²), pp. 12ff., 16. While there probably existed a
pre-exilic draft of the history, I cannot agree with Frank Moore Cross,
Canaanite Myth and Hebrew Epic (Cambridge, Mass.: Harvard University
Press, 1973), p. 289, that it is "essentially . . . a work of the late kingdom."
It seems to me that the pattern of judgment and grace in Judges, the
emphasis on the Davidic dynasty and the Jerusalem cult and the high praise
of Josiah are perfectly understandable in the context of the exilic period. It
also seems unnecessary to suppose that the final notice in the history, the
paroling of the exiled Davidic king, was added subsequently.

53. The pattern for which is, however, already laid down in the wilderness period (Deut. 1:26ff.; 9:7ff.; 31:27).

54. See especially Deut. 4:25–31, beginning as a conditional threat but
ending as an unconditional prediction of exile (v. 30); 29:22–28, which
again refers explicitly to exile; 30:1ff.; 31:16–18, 20–21; 32–33. Predictions
of exile are found frequently in the prophetic books beginning with Amos
and probably reflect Assyrian practice. We may add that the predictions of
well-being conditional on observance of the law provide a valuable insight
into *shālôm*-prophecy so often castigated by the canonical prophets.

55. The Deuteronomic representation of Moses as prophet may have
drawn on Hos. 12:13; cf. Num. 12:6ff. and the title of the "Blessing of
Moses," Deut. 33:1, where he is described as "man of God."

56. The following verbs are used: *dibbēr* (1:4; 4:45; 5:1, 27), *hîgîd* (5:5),
bē'ēr (1:5), *lāmad* (4:1, 5; 5:31; 6:1), *ṣivvāh* (1:18; 11:22).

57. On his intercession see Deut. 3:23–25; 9:18–20, 25–29. He fasted
forty days and nights on the mountain (9:9). It is noteworthy that the

intercessory function of the prophet comes to the fore during the last days of the Kingdom of Judah and during the exile. There is a close thematic similarity between the Deuteronomic Moses, the Jeremiah of the "Confessions" and the Servant of the LORD of the exilic Isaiah; see von Rad, *Old Testament Theology* II (New York and Evanston: Harper & Row, 1965), pp. 261–262, 275ff.; W. Zimmerli, *The Law and the Prophets* (Oxford: Blackwell, 1965), pp. 88–89.

58. Deut. 5:5, 22–27 cf. the tradition in Ex. 20:18–21 which also appears at Deut. 18:15–18.

59. 13:2–6, 7–12, 13–19. The concluding formula, "you shall purge the evil from your midst" (*ûbi'artā hārā' miqqirbekā*) is used with casuistic laws calling for the death penalty: 13:6; 17:7; 17:12 (. . . *miyyiśrā'ēl*); 19:19 (application of *lex talionis* rather than death penalty); 21:9; 21:21; 22:21, 24; 22:22 (. . . *miyyiśrā'ēl*); 24:7.

60. For the association between prophet and dreamer see also Num. 12:6 and Jer. 23:25ff. Deut. 18:22 speaks more accurately of the prophet's *word* not coming true. While 13:2–6 assumes that a prediction of a non-Yahvistic prophet may come true, in 18:22 the nonfulfillment of a prediction is taken as sufficient evidence that it does not come from Yahveh.

61. Quoted from A. Klostermann by von Rad, *Studies in Deuteronomy*, p. 15.

62. Since 17:8–13 is a casuistic law calling for the death penalty (see n. 59), it does not belong form-critically with the other pericopes.

63. See especially 17:14 and 18:9. 17:9 speaks of the judge who will be in office "in those days."

64. It is noteworthy that both king (17:15) and prophet (18:15) must be of Israelite descent (*miqqirbgᵉkā mē'aḥêkā*).

65. See H. M. Teeple, *The Mosaic Eschatological Prophet* (Philadelphia: Society of Biblical Literature Monographs, 1957).

66. *Deuteronomy: A Commentary*, p. 123; *Old Testament Theology* II, p. 261.

67. One might be tempted to find some kind of allusion to Joshua. The Deuteronomist stresses the similarities between Moses and Joshua and represents him as promulgator and guardian of the law and mediator of the covenant. He is also identified as the Mosaic prophet in Jewish tradition (Teeple, pp. 11, 49–50). Other candidates (among biblical figures) proposed by modern exegetes are Elijah and Jeremiah.

68. E.g., S. R. Driver, *Deuteronomy* (Edinburgh: T. & T. Clark, 1895), p. 227; H. Wheeler Robinson, *Deuteronomy and Joshua* (Edinburgh: T. & T. Clark, 1907), p. 149; G. A. Smith, *The Book of Deuteronomy* (Cambridge: The University Press, 1918), p. 233; A. C. Welch, *Deuteronomy: The Framework to the Code* (Oxford: 1932), p. 25; A. Clamer, *Le Deutéronome* (Paris: 1946), p. 633; H. Cunliffe Jones, *Deuteronomy* (London: S.C.M., 1951), p. 113; G. E. Wright, "The Book of Deuteronomy" in IB, Vol. 2, 448ff.; G. von Rad, *Deuteronomy: A Commentary*, pp. 122–125; J. Blenkinsopp, "Deuteronomy," *JBC*, 113; W. Moran, "Deuteronomy," *A New Catho-*

lic Commentary on Holy Scripture (London: Nelson, 1969), p. 270; G. Henton Davies, "Deuteronomy," *Peake's Commentary on the Bible,* (London: Nelson, 1962), p. 278.

69. By the time of Deuteronomy the ambiguities attending prophecy had become clear, especially in the conflicts which arose within prophecy in the late period of the kingdom. On this subject see especially James L. Crenshaw, *Prophetic Conflict* (Berlin: de Gruyter, 1971).

70. Terms used by H-J Kraus, *Die Prophetische Verkündigung des Rechts in Israel* (Zurich: Zollikon, 1957), pp. 15–16.

71. The tradition in Ex. 20:18–21, usually assigned to E, is placed so as to separate the Ten Words from the individual stipulations of law, the *deḇārîm.* In Deut. 18:21–22 "the word" of the prophet has a quite different connotation.

72. Alt, *Essays on Old Testament History and Religion* (Oxford; Blackwell, 1966), pp. 79ff.

73. See on this subject, much discussed in recent decades, E. Würthwein, "Der Ursprung der prophetischen Gerichtsrede," *ZTK* 44 (1952), 1ff.; F. Hesse, "Wurzelt die prophetische Gerichtsrede im israelitischen Kult?," *ZAW* 65 (1953), 48ff.; H. Graf Reventlow, "Prophetenamt und Mittleramt," *ZTK* 58 (1961), 280ff.; *Das Amt des Propheten bei Amos* (FRLANT 80; Göttingen: 1962); H. E. von Waldow, *Der traditionsgeschichtliche Hintergrund der prophetischen Gerichtsreden* (Berlin: Töpelmann, 1963); H-J Kraus, *Die prophetische Verkündigung des Rechts in Israel,* pp. 29f., has pointed out the methodological weakness of arguing from a cultic *Sitz im Leben* of the prophetic doom oracle to conclusions re the status of the speaker; another example of the over-extending of form criticism. On Kraus' own views on the office of *Bundesmittler* see his *Worship in Israel* (Richmond: John Knox Press, 1966), pp. 106ff.

74. "Canon of the OT," *IDB* Vol. I (Nashville and `New York: Abingdon, 1962), p. 503.

75. Noth, *Uberlieferungsgeschichtliche Studien* (Tübingen: Mohr, 1957²).

76. Weinfeld, pp. 320–365 provides a practically exhaustive tabulation of Deuteronomic terminology.

77. See Noth, pp. 19ff.

78. For a sampling of critical opinion see H. Wheeler Robinson, *Deuteronomy and Joshua,* p. 256; M. Noth, *Das Buch Josua* (Tübingen: Mohr, 1953²); J. Bright, "The Book of Joshua," IB II, 541–546; J. Gray, *Joshua, Judges and Ruth* (London: Nelson, 1967), pp. 1–3, 8–11; J. A. Soggin, *Joshua: A Commentary* (Philadelphia: Westminster, 1970), pp. 3–7.

79. Jos. 1:1–9, cf. Deut. 3:28; 31:7–8, 23; 2 Kings 2:9ff.

80. Judg. 2:10–23, cf. 10:6–16. In 6:7–10, a brief sermon by an anonymous prophet, the rather different theological pattern for the monarchic period is anticipated; cf. 1 Sam. 2:27–36.

81. Jerubbaal, Barak, Jephthah, Samuel (1 Sam. 12:11). Note that 13:1 contains a typically Deuteronomic *incipit* for a reign, the first of a long series.

82. The verb *hēqîm* is used of judges in 2:16, 18 and saviors in 3:9, 15,

both referring to the same category, i.e., charismatic warlords. The same verb is used by the Deuteronomists for prophets (Deut. 18:15, 18; Jer. 29:15; Am. 2:11). The verb connotes an election, a divinely bestowed charisma, and its use in these cases is an important pointer to the Deuteronomic "theology" of institution and the place of prophecy within it. Being raised up leads to possession of the spirit: Judg. 3:10 (Othniel); 6:14 (Gideon); 11:29 (Jephthah); 13:25; 14:6, 19; 15:14 (Samson).

83. M. Noth, "Das Amt des Richters Israel," *Bertholet Festschrift* (Tübingen: Mohr, 1950), pp. 404ff.; *Uberlieferungsgeschichtliche Studien*, p. 49; "Office and Vocation in the Old Testament," *The Laws in the Pentateuch and Other Essays* (Edinburgh & London: Oliver & Boyd, 1966), pp. 242–245. Noth has made a valuable contribution to the general problem under discussion by emphasizing the charismatic element in the field of law.

84. Judg. 10:4 and 12:14 speak of their sons, thirty and forty respectively, who rode on asses. At that time the ass bore the tribal levy into battle (cf. Judg. 5:10).

85. The late passage 1 Sam. 7:2–14 which has him defeating the Philistines is transparently unhistorical and is in fact contradicted by the subsequent narrative.

86. Martin Noth, *Uberlieferungsgeschichtliche Studien*, p. 48, suggested that the Deuteronomic editor first brought the two functions together under the rubric *šopeṭ*.

87. He is listed among the judges (1 Sam. 12:11), defeats the Philistines and so saves Israel (7:2–14), administers justice (7:15–17), is a prestigious seer (9:5ff.) and prophet (1:1–4:1).

88. The intervention of an anonymous man of God at Shiloh who predicts the extermination of the Eli priesthood (2:27–36), and the prophetic oracle given Samuel (3:11–14) show signs of Deuteronomic editing; phrases like *v°zeh-l°kā hā'ôt* (2:34), *vahᵃqîmotî lî kohēn ne'°mān* (v. 35), *t°ṣillênāh š°tē 'oznâv* (3:11, cf. 2 Kings 21:12) are of Deuteronomic vintage. 1 Kings 2:27 verifies the prediction against the Shiloh priesthood in the Deuteronomic manner. See M. Noth, *Uberlieferungsgeschichtliche Studien*, pp. 54ff.; W. McKane, *I & II Samuel* (London: 1963), pp. 28f.; J. Mauchline, *1 and 2 Samuel* (London: 1971), p. 31.

89. I Sam. 8:1–3. They did not dispense *mišpaṭ-ṣedeq* as required by Deut. 16:18; with *vayyiqhû-šoḥad* and *vayyaṭṭû mišpāṭ* cf. Deut. 16:19.

90. Most scholars agree that the various *incipits* and archival lists and notices are Deuteronomic (1 Sam. 13:1; 14:47–51; 2 Sam. 2:10a, 11; 5:4–5; 8:15–18; 20:23–26; 1 Kings 2:27b; 4:2–6).

91. On this important passage L. Rost, *Die Uberlieferung von der Thronnachfolge Davids* (Stuttgart: 1926), pp. 47ff., should be consulted. R. E. Clements, *Prophecy and Covenant* (Naperville: A. R. Allenson, 1965), p. 56, gives more recent bibliography.

92. As von Rad in particular has pointed out, the "Name theology" of Deuteronomy is one of the book's most distinctive features.

93. H. W. Wolff, "Das Kerygma des deuteronomistischen Ges-

chichtswerks," ZAW 73 (1961), 171–86 [=*Gesammelte Studien* (Munich) Kaiser, 1964), pp. 308–324], examines Deut. 4:29–31 and 30:1–10, together with similar passages in the historical work, and finds in them counsel to the exiled community to pray to the LORD and attend to his words communicated through prophets. This is questionable not only for the reason stated, that prophets are not mentioned in these passages except when referring to the past, but also because it seems to imply that for the Deuteronomists the exile was just one in a series of disasters. This was clearly not the case.

94. 1 Kings 10:23, cf. Deut. 17:17 (wealth); 1 Kings 10:26–29, cf. Deut. 17:6 (horses); 1 Kings 11:1ff., cf. Deut. 17:17 (women).

95. The list of these linked texts is given by von Rad, *Studies in Deuteronomy*, pp. 78–81. Some are particularly noteworthy in that they lead to deeper reflection on the cause of Israel's failure. In addition to 2 Kings 17:7–23 see 21:10–16 and 1 Kings 8:24 where the causal link is expressed metaphorically as the relation between the mouth (i.e., the word) and the hand (i.e., the power to act) of the LORD.

96. As seen earlier, *'ebed* occurs as a synonym for *nābî'* in Deuteronomic writings and *"bādâv hannᵉbî'îm* stands for the prophetic succession as a whole (1 Kings 14:18; 15:29; 18:36; 2 Kings 9:7, 36; 10:10; 14:25; 17:13, 23; 21:10; 24:2; Jer. 7:25; 25:4; 26:5; 29:19; 35:15; 44:4). Am. 3:7 looks like a Deuteronomic insertion into the poem which shifts the emphasis from the ineluctability of prophecy to the typically Deuteronomic idea that the disasters in store for Israel must have been foretold by the prophets, in this instance the prophet Amos.

97. Scholarly debate on this question goes back to Sigmund Mowinckel's study, *Zur Komposition des Buches Jeremiah*, published in 1914. A recent contribution is that of E. W. Nicholson, *Preaching to the Exiles* (New York: Schocken Books, 1970), who tends to defeat his purpose by attributing too much to the Deuteronomists without too rigorous a set of criteria. The unpublished Hebrew University dissertation *mᵉgillôt lig'ûlāh bidvārē yirmᵉyāhû* of Jerry Unterman (1975) discusses the problem perceptively and has a bibliography updated to 1975.

98. E.g., Jer. 26:2ff. reminiscent of Deut. 18:15–18; 44:10; 11:1–17 in which he is commissioned as agent in renewing the covenant, reading the law publicly and emphasizing the gravity of the curses attached to it.

99. 14:11–16; 23:25–40; 27:9–10, 14–15; 28 (the encounter with Hananiah); 29:17–19, 23. These naturally bring to mind Deut. 13:2–6 and 18:20–22. On this matter of criteria see J. L. Crenshaw, *Prophetic Conflict* (Berlin: de Gruyter, 1971), pp. 49–61.

100. Against Nicholson, pp. 82ff., 138 n. 1.

101. In "The Word of God in the Book of Ezekiel," *History and Hermeneutic*, ed. R. W. Funk (New York: Harper, 1967), p. 13, W. Zimmerli speaks of "a curious and strange formulation of *sola gratia*" in Ezekiel who goes further than Jeremiah in speaking of the need for a new heart and spirit and of the Spirit of God as the agent of transformation (Ezek. 11:19; 18:31; 36:26–27; 37).

CHAPTER 3: THE PRIESTLY WORK (P): THE SECOND STAGE

1. J. Wellhausen, *Prolegomena to the History of Ancient Israel* (New York: Meridian, 1957), pp. 82, 150, 422, etc.

2. This will be apparent on consulting any major critical Introduction to the Old Testament. One of the more interesting alternatives, Yehezkel Kaufmann's *The Religion of Israel from Its Beginnings to the Babylonian Exile*, trans. and abridged by Moshe Greenberg, (New York: Schocken Books, 1972), dates P before the reign of Hezekiah.

3. A point well made in Frank M. Cross, *Canaanite Myth and Hebrew Epic* (Cambridge, Mass.: Harvard University Press, 1973), pp. 294, 301ff.

4. Especially the fragmentary Atramhasis myth, a translation of which is available in *ANET*, cols. 104–107 and *ANETS*, 512–514.

5. It is also possible that Gen. 5:24 stands not at the beginning but within an Enoch tradition cherished by priests from an early period. Despite the difference in dates a more detailed comparative study of P and Berossus would be worth undertaking.

6. E.g., the well-developed cartography in Gen. 10, the exact dimensions of the ark (Gen. 6:15) and the wilderness sanctuary (Ex. 25:10ff.). The building of the latter calls for wisdom in the sense of technical expertise (Ex. 31:2–6).

7. *Prolegomena*, pp. 297f.

8. E.g., Job 28; Prov. 8:22–31; Sir. 24:3ff. (note the parallelism between cosmos and sanctuary, v. 10). See G. von Rad, *Wisdom in Israel*, (New York and Nashville: Abingdon, 1972), pp. 144ff.

9. Mal. 1:8, 13, cf. Lev. 22:18–21.

10. See Eissfeldt, *The Old Testament: An Introduction* (New York: Harper & Row, 1965), p. 208; G. von Rad, *Old Testament Theology*, Vol. I, pp. 347ff.

11. Ezra 7:1–6, 10, 25; 8:15–20; Neh. 8:4–12.

12. As is well known, the difficulty of determining the date arises out of the uncertainty as to which Artaxerxes reigned when Ezra came to Jerusalem (Ezra 7:7–8). If it was Artaxerxes Longimanus the date would be 458, if Artaxerxes Mnemon, 398; assuming, of course, that the Chronicler is correct at this point.

13. Ezra 8:15–20, where the term *hammāqôm* (meaning "place" but also used of a "holy place") is used rather obtrusively of Casiphia, thus giving rise to the suspicion that the exiles worshipped there; and we are also told that there were trained Levites to be found there under the direction of a certain Iddo, presumably a priest. A. Lods, *The Prophets and the Rise of Judaism* (London: Routledge & Kegan Paul, 1955), p. 218, held that there was a temple there and suggested that it was to discuss the feasibility of building such a temple (contrary to the Deuteronomic law) that the elders came to consult with Ezekiel. The place near the river Chebar (Ezek. 1:3; 3:15) may also have been a place of worship legitimated by the appearance of the *kābôd*.

14. The analysis of G. von Rad, *Die Priesterschrift im Hexateuch* (BWANT IV 13, Stuttgart: 1934), who divided the *Grundschrift* into two strands has been particularly influential. For the following see my paper "The Structure of P," *CBQ* 38 (1976), 275–92.

15. The important issue of P's exegetical methods has never been adequately dealt with; e.g., is the identifiable P material in Ex. 19–24 to be read as supplementary to JE (as suggested by von Rad, *Old Testament Theology*, I, p. 234, n. 101) or as correcting it?

16. E.g., *kᵉkol 'ašer* or, more rarely, *lᵉkol 'ᵃšer* for *ka'ᵃšer, dibbēr* for *ṣivvāh*, etc.

17. *Tabnît* (model), used of the sanctuary and its appointments in Ex. 25:9, 40 and of the altar in Jos. 22:28; *mar'eh* (form, appearance), of the menorah in Num. 8:4.

18. E.g., Gen. 1:28 and parallels studied by W. Brueggeman, "The Kerygma of the Priestly Writer," *ZAW* 84 (1972), 397ff.

19. Cf. the conclusion of the command to build the sanctuary and set up the cult (Ex. 29:45–46) and the conclusion of the Holiness Code (Lev. 26:45). Some commentators stress the occupation of the land as a major theme of P—e.g., K. Elliger, "Sinn und Ursprung der priesterschriftlichen Geschichtsschreibung," *ZTK* 49 (1952), 121–143 [= *Kleine Schriften*, 1966, pp. 174–198]. J. Roth, "Thèmes majeurs de la tradition sacerdotale dans la Pentateuque," *NRT* 90 (1958), 696–721, prefers to see the essential object of the covenant in P as God making himself present to his people. The point being made here is that these two themes should not be separated.

20. Besides the introductions and commentaries, see W. Beyerlin, *Origins and History of the Oldest Sinaitic Traditions* (Oxford: Blackwell, 1965); W. Zimmerli, "Sinaibund und Abrahambund," *ThZ* 16 (1960), 268ff.; K. Koch, "Die Eigenart der priesterschriftlichen Sinaigesetzgebung," *ZTK* 55 (1958), 36–51.

21. The provenance of this passage about Moses' shining face has been long in dispute. Many of the older commentators including Wellhausen ascribed it to P and several read it as continuing on from Ex. 31:18. Under the weighty influence of Martin Noth, *Exodus: A Commentary*, p. 267, this judgment is now often called into question. However, *luḥot hā'ēdut* (v. 29, cf. 31:18) and the role of *kol-hannᵉśi'ê ha'ēdāh* (v. 31) indicate at least editing by P. See the thorough but inconclusive discussion in B. S. Childs, *The Book of Exodus* (Philadelphia: Westminster, 1974), pp. 609–610, 617–619.

22. According to the itinerary in Num. 33, usually attributed to P, the Israelites departed from Rephidim, camped in the Sinaitic wilderness and departed thence for Kibroth hattavah (vv. 15–16); no mention is made of Mount Sinai or events alleged to have taken place there. It is possible that in this respect the itinerary may reproduce an ancient stage of tradition before the inclusion of the Sinai pericope. It is generally held, at any rate, that if P ever had an account of covenant-making at Sinai it has not survived (e.g., M. Noth, *Exodus*, pp. 17, 200), though H. Cazelles, "Pentateuque: Textes Sacerdotaux," *SDB* 39 (Paris: 1964), 829, 834, ascribes 19:3b–8b to P and maintains that this source does speak of a Sinaitic

covenant. It is always possible, of course, that P has touched up some of the older traditions. I suspect, for example, that the account of the theophany granted to Moses, Aaron, Nadab, Abihu and the seventy elders owes a debt to P. *kᵉmaʿᵃśēh libnat hassappîr* (24:10) recalls *kᵉmarʾeh ʾeben sappîr* of Ezekiel's theophany (1:26, cf. 10:1) and *kᵉʿeṣem haššāmayim laṭohar* sounds distinctly priestly; phrases with *ʿeṣem* occur with notable frequency in P (Gen. 17:23, 26; Ex. 12:17, 41, 51; Lev. 23:14, 21, 28, 29, 30; Deut. 32:48; Jos. 5:11) as in Ezekiel (2:3; 24:2; 40:1), while *ṭohar* occurs elsewhere only at Lev. 12:4, 6.

23. *Prolegomena*, pp. 338f., 385.

24. Ex. 31:12–17; cf. Ezek. 20:12. The injunction not to gather the manna on the seventh day (Ex. 16:5, 22–30) may be taken as a dramatic anticipation.

25. We shall have further occasion to note the tremendous theological emphasis which P places on the primeval history of mankind. Following the ancient Sumero-Akkadian scribal tradition, P has an intense interest in dividing the past into historical epochs, the object being to show how Israel fits in with the primal and unconditional design of grace which God has for the world. The elucidation of P's learned historiography is, unfortunately, not nearly so clear. One suspects that the key is to be found in the P chronology which, however, has proved resistant to interpretation, not to mention the textual problems involved. J. Hempel, "Priesterkodex," *Paulys Realencyclopädie der classischen Altertumswissenschaft* XXII, 2 (Stuttgart: 1954), 1948, followed by P. R. Ackroyd, *Exile and Restoration* (Philadelphia: Westminster, 1968), p. 91, concludes that creation to exodus takes in two-thirds of a span, the end of which lay for the writer in the future. A. Jepsen, "Zur Chronologie des Priesterkodex," *ZAW* 47 (1929), 251–255, thought that it ended with the rebuilding of the temple, while G. Fohrer, "Priesterschrift," *RGG*³ V (Tübingen: 1961), 568–569, found four periods (creation to deluge, deluge to the fathers, the fathers to exodus, exodus on), the first three of which prepare for the fourth and last which contains laws for Israel alone. Whatever the correct interpretation, it will not be over- looked that in this respect as in others P represents an important step in the direction of apocalyptic.

26. It should be noted that the spirit and the word play a simultaneous creative role in Ezek. 37, the vision of the valley of dry bones.

27. *ruaḥ* occurs elsewhere in P in the phrase *ʾelohê harûhôt lᵉkol-bāśār*, Num. 16:22 and 27:16.

28. The text from the Greco-Syrian period is in *ANET*, 331–334.

29. On the P version of the deluge see C. Westermann, *Genesis* (Neukirchen-Vluyn: 1966), pp. 39ff, 66ff., who, however, denies that P contains any vestige of creation as combat. He makes the important point that in this version the emphasis is on salvation from a sinful situation which, given the historical milieu of P, inevitably ties in with the experi- ence of exile.

30. Ezek. 30:1–32:32. Judgment on Egypt will include darkness over the land (30:18; 32:7–8, cf. Ex. 10:21–9) and the filling of the watercourses and

the whole land with blood (32:6, cf. Ex. 7:19, 21); in P, as opposed to JE, blood is over the whole land, not just in the water. The typically Ezekielan *šᵉpāṭîm* is also used in both passages for divine acts of judgment (30:14, 19, cf. Ex. 6:6; 7:4; 12:12) as also the declarative formula "then they will know that I am the LORD" (30:19, 25; 32:15, cf. Ex. 12:12).

31. The classical treatment of this theme is still that of Gunkel, *Schöpfung und Chaos in Urzeit und Endzeit* (Göttingen: 1895).

32. L. R. Fisher, "The Temple Quarter," *JSS* 8 (1963), 40–41 and "Creation at Ugarit and in the Old Testament," *VT* 15 (1965), 313–324.

33. *De Dea Syra*, p. 13.

34. See Henri Frankfort and others, *Before Philosophy* (Baltimore: Penguin Books, 1949), pp. 59ff.

35. *YHWH lammabbûl yāšāb*, Ps. 29:10. M. Dahood, *Psalms I* (Garden City: Doubleday, 1965), pp. 175 and 180, translates "from the flood," but a temporal sense is not dictated by *parallelismus membrorum*. The preposition can mean "on" in Ugaritic (137:23; UM 282).

36. A selection of quotes can be found in Raphael Patai's *Man and Temple in Ancient Jewish Myth and Ritual* (New York: Ktav, 1967²), pp. 54ff.

37. The generations series or *tôlᵉdôt* in P which begin with the heavens and earth (Gen. 2:4) and end with the Aaronite priesthood (Num. 3:1) reflect faintly creation as procreation or theogony. Whether or not there ever existed a separate *seper tôlᵉdôt*, as they now occur in P they serve the purpose of linking the primeval history with the later history of mankind and, within it, of Israel. In something of the same way Hesiod's *Theogony* begins with Chaos, Erebos, etc., comes down to legendary figures such as Herakles and then to historical figures like king Aietes. Thus the *tôlᵉdôt* may be taken to reflect a kind of demythologized theogony; see Westermann, pp. 9, 11; Cross, pp. 302ff.

38. In "The Unknown Prophet of the Exile," *Scripture* 14 (1962), 81–90, 109–118, I argued for thematic association between Is. 40–55 and the *akitu* festival.

39. As argued by Koch, "Die Eisgenart" (see n. 20 above), pp. 40f. It should also be borne in mind that P's version of the promise to the fathers speaks of kings among their descendants (Gen. 17:6, 16; 35:11).

40. *Ant.* III 7 7; *Wars* V 5 5. The symbolic correspondence between cosmos and temple has long been recognized and discussed, especially by proponents of the "Myth and Ritual" school. Patai's treatment (see n. 36 above) is particularly full, and the matter is dealt with briefly by W. F. Albright, *Archaeology and the Religion of Israel* (Baltimore: Penguin Books, 1942), pp. 144–150 and by R. E. Clements, *God and Temple* (Philadelphia: Fortress, 1965), pp. 65ff.

41. *taḥtiyyim, šᵉniyyim, šᵉlišîm* (Gen. 6:16 P); *taḥtonāh, tîkonāh, šᵉlišît* (1 Kings 6:6).

42. The following are either certainly or very probably from P: twelve stones set up in the Jordan (4:9), the date of the crossing of the Jordan (4:19, cf. Deut. 1:3), the celebration of Passover according to the P chronology (5:10–12), one strand of the Gibeonite covenant narrative (9:15–21), com-

pletion of the conquest (11:15, 20), introduction to distribution of territory (14:1–5), setting up of the wilderness sanctuary at Shiloh (18:1), completion of the work of distribution (19:51), allotment of levitical cities (21:1–8), decision about the altar of the Transjordanian tribes (22:10–34), the death of Phineas (24:33).

43. *Introduction to the Old Testament,* p. 306.

44. Koch, "Die Eigenart," p. 42, speaks of concentric circles of holiness, but of course the camp was square, P giving great significance to the cosmic number four.

45. Jos. 22:10–34 deals with an objectionable altar set up by the tribes east of the Jordan; in the absence of information on Jewish settlements in the area contemporary with P it will probably remain obscure. It is unclear whether the altar in question was on the east or the west bank. Since we are not obliged to conclude that *ᵃšer bᵉ'ereṣ kᵉnāʿan* (v. 10) is a gloss, and since it was assumed that their land was unclean, and therefore not fit for an altar (v. 19), very probably the west bank. The idea of ritual impurity attaching to land is not exclusive to P (cf. Am. 7:17, cf. Ps. 137:4) but becomes a central concept in it.

46. No one has succeeded in making out a convincing case for P material after Jos. M. Haran, "Shiloh and Jerusalem: The Origin of the Priestly Tradition in the Pentateuch," *JBL* 81 (1962), 20–21, believes P edited Judg. 19–21 and finds the last traces of the source at 1 Kings 8:4. H. Cazelles, *Introduction à la Bible,* ed. A. Robert and A. Feuillet, (Tournai: Desclée, 1959²) , p. 376, finds traces of P as late as 2 Sam. 20:23–26.

47. J. G. Vink, *The Date and Origin of the Priestly Code in the Old Testament* (Leiden: Brill, 1969), is over-ingenious in explaining individual passages in P from the exilic perspective.

48. Jer. 14:13, cf. Hag. 2:9; Jer. 28:2–11, cf. Hag. 2:6–8. It goes without saying that prophecies of well-being are not considered to be *ipso facto* false. Jeremiah himself spoke such a word (42:11, cf. Hag. 1:13; 2:4) at the right moment.

49. In the superscription to the book (Zech. 1:1) Zechariah is the grandson of Iddo. A Zechariah, son of Iddo, is listed among priestly families in the early Restoration period (Neh. 12:16, cf. 12:4). He is not identified positively as the prophet in the canon but it seems highly probable that he was.

50. E. Hammershaimb, *Some Aspects of Old Testament Prophecy from Isaiah to Malachi* (Copenhagen: Rosenkilde & Bogger, 1966), pp. 91–112, is one of the few Old Testament scholars who have made this point, i.e., that structural changes in society removed the prerequisites for the exercise of prophecy.

51. "Parable monger" is a translation of *mᵉmaššēl mᵉšālîm,* Ezek. 20:49 (MT 21:5); cf. words attributed to his hearers at 33:32–33 which also acknowledge his literary skill. For examples of *mᵉšālîm, ḥîdôt* and *qînôt* in Ezek., see 12:21–25 (cf. 18:1–3); 15:1–8; 16:1ff. (see v. 44); 17:1–10; 19:1–9; 19:10–14; 23:1ff.; 24:3–5; 26:17–18; 27:2–9; 32:2–8, 32:12–16.

52. See especially Ezek. 14:12–20; 18:5–29; 33:1–20. His severing of the

link of moral causality between the members of three generations corrects the Deuteronomic doctrine of retribution as found in Deut. 5:9 (cf. Ex. 20:5).

53. The visionary city is set on a high mountain (Ezek. 40:7) reminiscent of the mountain of God on which the first man was placed (28:14). The cherubim mentioned in both these passages (41:18–20; 28:14) recall the decorative cherubim of Solomon's temple (1 Kings 6:23ff.) and the figures which guarded Eden (Gen. 3:24). The cosmic stream issues from the temple at the center of the world (47:1ff.) as the life-giving water of Eden flowed to the four quarters of the world (Gen. 2:10–14).

54. The term clearly belongs to the vocabulary of the cult. Ezekiel's vision is of the *kābôd* in the temple (1:28, etc.); the LORD will set up his *kābôd* among the nations, referring to worship in the *gôlāh* (39:21, cf. Num. 14:21 P, all the world will be filled with his *kābôd*); the *kābôd* will return to the future temple (43:2–5, cf. 44:4).

55. Ex. 6:2, 6, 7; 7:17; 14:4, 18; 16:6 (all P); Ezek. 5:13; 6:2, 6, 7, 10; 7:5; 30:8; 32:15; 37:6, etc.

56. Ezek. 14:14; 28:3 (Noah, Danel, Job); 27:3–9; 28:2–19; 31:15–18; perhaps also 38–39 (Gog and Magog).

57. Ezek. 22:6–12, 26. "I will sprinkle clean water upon you, and you shall be clean from all your impurities" (36:25) recalls the importance attached to lustrations in P, e.g., Ex. 40:12; Lev. 8:6; Num. 8:6.

58. Emphasized rightly by W. Zimmerli, *Ezechiel* (Neukirchen-Vluyn: Neukirchener Verlag, 1969), p. 79* and *passim.*

59. The prophetic idea of the remnant appears at Ezek. 6:8–10; 11:13; 12:16; 20:28. It is implicit in P's deluge story and in the *tôlᵉdôt.* It will be noted that the community of the once-exiled, the *bᵉnê haggôlāh* of Ezra, is identical with the "remnant of the people" (*šᵉ'ērît hā'ām*) of Hag. 1:12, 14; 2:2, cf. Zech. 8:6, 11.

60. Jer. 29:1; Ezek. 7:26; Lam. 1:19; 4:16; Ezra 5:5, 9; 6:7, 8, 14; 10:8.

61. Ex. 24:9 (cf. Deut. 5:23f.; Is. 24:23); Num. 11:16ff.

62. In Ezek. 7:26 counsel (*'ēṣāh*) belongs not to the sages as in the parallel Jer. 18:18 but to the elders. From Jer. 29:1 we learn that together with priests and prophets they formed the leadership of the exiled communities.

63. As stated by Mircea Eliade, *Cosmos and History* (New York: Harper & Row, 1959), p. 104.

64. Here, too, P is close to Ezekiel, who, in speaking of Israel's history as one of failure, takes the story from Egypt (20:5–9) through the wilderness period (vv. 10–26) to the occupation of the land and no further (vv. 27–31).

65. In Deuteronomy itself the reference to Aaron at 10:6 is an editorial addition and 32:50 is from P; this leaves 9:20 in which Aaron is saved from the divine wrath by the intercession of Moses. Apart from references to his descendants, the only allusions to him in the Deuteronomic history are at Jos. 24:5 and I Sam. 12:6, 8.

66. Cf. the periodizing of history in Ezek. 20 (n. 64) and the introductory exhortation to the Damascus Rule (CD I 3–12) which dismisses the period of monarchy as one of infidelity, attributing Israel's survival to the covenant which God made with the fathers and which he remembered during the exile.

67. On this incident see H. S. Nyberg, "Korah's Uppror," *SEA* 12 (1947), 230ff.; G. Hort, "The Death of Korah," *ABR* 7 (1959), 2ff.; S. Lehming, "Versuch zu Num. xvi," *ZAW* 74 (1962), 291ff.; A. H. J. Gunneweg, *Leviten und Priester* (Göttingen: 1965), pp. 82ff., 171ff.

68. According to Ezra 2:63 (=Neh. 7:65), disputed priestly genealogies were decided in this way; cf. Num. 27:21 where the priest Eleazar consults Urim and Thummim for Joshua.

69. Consult Eliade's treatment of eschatology and cosmology in *Myth and Reality* (New York: Harper & Row, 1963), pp. 54ff.

70. In P, God does not renew the covenant but *remembers* it, especially during the Egyptian and Babylonian exiles; see Gen. 8:1; 19:29; Ex. 2:24; 6:5; Lev. 26:42, 45.

71. *ANET*, 68f., on which see E. Burrows in *The Labyrinth*, ed. S. H. Hooke (London: S.P.C.K., 1935), pp. 65ff., and for other examples of this motif, M. Eliade, *Cosmos and History*, pp. 6ff.

72. Ex. 25:9, 40, cf. 1 Chron. 28:11–12, 18–19, where David gives the *tabnît* of the temple to Solomon; Ezek. 43:10, cf. *ḥôtēm toknît* at 28:12 which unfortunately is also textually uncertain. Ezek. 40:2 refers to something like the structure of a city (*kᵉmibnēh-ʿîr*) and 43:11 to the *tᵉkûnāh* (arrangement, disposition) of the temple.

73. *Ant.* VII 90ff., cf. VII 334; VIII 114.

74. *Ant.* IX 7ff.; X 168–169.

75. Num. 16:18–19. In Ex. 16:9ff. the Israelites saw the *kābôd* in the wilderness since the sanctuary had not yet been built. In the early traditions the Israelites were guided by the ark (Num. 10:33–36), in P by the *kābôd* (Ex. 40:36–38; Num. 9:15–23).

76. M. Haran, "The Nature of 'Ohel Mo'edh' in Pentateuchal Sources," *JSS* 5 (1960), 52ff.

77. In Ex. 33:11 Joshua is Moses' *mᵉšārēt* (minister, assistant) a term used elsewhere of royal officials (e.g., 1 Kings 10:5), cultic people (Jer. 33:21; Is. 61:6; 1 Chron. 16:4; 2 Chron. 23:6) and a prophet's acolyte (2 Kings 4:43; 6:15). It is regularly used, and is used here, of Joshua in relation to Moses (Ex. 24:13; Num. 11:28; Jos. 1:1). In itself the use of this word is inconclusive but the analogy of Samuel in the shrine at Shiloh is suggestive since he is described as *mᵉšārēt 'et-pᵉnê YHWH* (1 Sam. 2:18). In the same verse he is also described as *naʿar*, like Joshua in Ex. 33:11. This last is taken by F. Dummermuth, "Joshua in Ex. xxxiii, 7–11," *TLZ* 19 (1963), 161–168, to be a technical term for cultic ecstatic, the idea being that Moses obtained oracles through Joshua rather as the prince of Byblos did through his possessed youth in the story of Wen-Amon (*ANET*, 26). Two texts not discussed by Dummermuth might have helped him make out a better case. 1

Sam. 1:24, v^e*hanna'ar na'ar,* is usually emended but perhaps could be translated, "and the youth (i.e., Samuel) was an ecstatic"; 2 Kings 9;4, *vayyelek hanna'ar hanna'ar hannābî'*, may perhaps likewise be translated, "so the youth, the ecstatic prophet (i.e., Gehazi), went. . . ." Further, the Levite in the service of Micah and the Danites is regularly described as *na'ar* (Judg. 17:7, 11–12; 18:3, 15) and Levites are, of course, involved in the cult (they are m^e*šārtîm* in the Chronicler's work). All of this is, of course, no more than hypothetical.

78. With Ex. 3:12, *'ehyeh 'immāk,* cf. Jer. 1:8, *'itt^ekā '*ʾ*nî*; on the form-critical question consult N. Habel, "The Form and Significance of the Call Narratives," *ZAW* 77 (1965), 301ff.

79. The description of Moses as *nābî'* became of central importance to the Deuteronomists but did not originate with them; we might compare the similar characterization of Mohammad as the Prophet. Moses, Aaron and Miriam belong to a levitical family, and it may be reasonably surmised that this points to association with the oracular and mantic Levites established at the Kadesh oasis. There are indications linking the early Levites with this place, including the oracle at Deut. 33:8–11 and the fact that Miriam died there (Num. 20:1). Moses also sacrifices, gives oracular guidance and is described as priest *tout court* in Ps. 99:6. The priesthoods at Dan (Judg. 18:13) and Shiloh (1 Sam. 2:27) were also traced back to him.

80. The genealogy at Ex. 6:14–25 serves the purpose of enhancing the importance of Aaron by revealing Aaron's seniority and remaining silent on Moses' descendants. O. Eissfeldt, "Toledot," *Texte und Untersuchungen* 77 (Berlin: 1961), pp. 1–8, made out a good case that the last of the *tôl^eTôt* ("These are the generations of Aaron and Moses," Num. 3:1) originally stood before this genealogy, which would make the point even more clearly. That "Aaron's rod" originally belonged to Moses is clear from Ex. 7:15.

81. We are to think of the role of the *nāśî'* in Ezek. 40–48, the reworking of Zech. 6:9–14 making it refer not to Zerubbabel (as in its original form) but to Joshua the high priest, and the problem of dyarchic rule in the post-exilic period in general.

82. Consult the commentaries on Ex. 28 and 39:1–31, especially M. Noth, *Exodus,* pp. 217–227. In addition, the robe (*m^e'îl*) is also worn by high dignitaries including kings and the only non-priestly reference to a girdle or sash (*'abnēṭ*) is at Is. 22:21 where it belongs to a royal official. The oracular connotations of the ephod and Urim and Thummim, the latter kept in the priestly breastpiece, should be kept in mind; on which consult M. Haran, "The Ephod according to Biblical Sources," *Tarbiz* 24 (1954/55), 380–391; K. Elliger, "Ephod und Choshen. Ein Beitrag zur Entwicklungsgeschichte des hohepriesterlichen Ornats," *VT* 8 (1958), 19–35.

83. Another indication can be found in the priestly laws governing the nazirate, Num. 6:1–21, which were closely associated with early prophecy (note, for example, the parallelism between n^e*zîrîm* and n^e*bî'îm* at Am. 2:11–12).

CHAPTER 4: NO PROPHET LIKE MOSES

1. Taken as a whole, it belongs to the *genre* of valedictory which, as comparable examples (e.g., Gen. 49) show, consists in a prophetic oracle.

2. "I firmly believe that the prophetic revelation of Moses was direct, and that Moses was the father of all prophets before and after him." Taken from M. Friedlander, *Die jüdische Religion* (Basel: 1971²), p. 106. It may be noted also that the first Christian canon, that of Marcion, was assembled according to the criterion of inspiration by the Holy Spirit; see F. W. Beare, "Canon of the New Testament," *IDB* I (1962), 520ff.

3. b. Ber. 5a.

4. Moses' age is given twice (31:2; 34:7), as is also the command not to cross the Jordan (31:2; 34:4, cf. 1:37; 3:27; Num. 20:12). There are several predictions of successful conquest and subsequent apostasy (31:3, 4–6, 16–18, 20–21, 27–29) and both the song (31:30–32:44) and the final blessing (33) are predictive. Dispositions with respect to the law book (31:9–13, 24–26) and the commissioning of Joshua (31:7, 14–15, 23; 34:9) are also repeated.

5. This summary should be checked against the standard introductions and commentaries. For the P affinities of 31:14–15, 23 see M. Noth, *A History of Pentateuchal Traditions* (Englewood Cliffs: Prentice-Hall, 1972), p. 176.

6. The ensuing awkwardness is betrayed at Num. 31:2, ". . . *and then* you will be gathered to your father's kin."

7. It will be seen that the two sections in Deut. were separated when the Blessing of Moses (chapter 33) was inserted. Deut. 34:1 is also generally assigned to P.

8. Deut. 1:37; 3:27; 31:2; 34:4; cf. Num. 20:12 (P).

9. There is here no official act; only a characteristically worded exhortation to be strong and resolute. See Deut. 3:28; 31:7–8, 23; cf. Jos. 1:1–9.

10. See his well-known treatment of the routinization of charisma in *The Theory of Social and Economic Organization* (New York: The Free Press, 1964), pp. 363–373.

11. With the exception of 2 Chron. 29:23, which depends on P, all cases of the laying on of hands in the Hebrew Scriptures occur in P. Hands are laid on the sacrificial animal (Lev. 1:4; Num. 8:12), perhaps as a symbol of ownership or for some other reason not apparent. The only exception is the ordination of Levites (Num. 8:10), but even here the context suggests the sense of a sacrificial dedication.

12. This is, therefore, one of several instances, of which the theophany at Horeb is the most obvious (1 Kings 19:9–18; Ex. 34:5–6), of the influence of Elijah on the developing Moses-tradition. It is not surprising then that Moses and Elijah are closely associated in Mal. 3:22–24 and in subsequent Jewish and Christian tradition. According to the earlier sources Moses died in the land of Moab and was buried there by the LORD himself in an unknown grave (Deut. 34:5–6). This, too, may depend on the tradition of

the marvelous passing of Elijah (2 Kings 2:11–12). In speaking of the last dispositions and death of Moses, the Targum of Pseudo-Jonathan refers to a place where the prophet Moses is hidden and to 42,000 chariots of fire which he had seen; see J. W. Etheridge, *The Targums of Onkelos and Jonathan ben Uzziel on the Pentateuch* (London: Longman, Green & Co., 1865), pp. 679, 683. To judge by the lost *Assumption of Moses*, the belief that he, too, was taken up into heaven was held by some groups during the Roman period and perhaps earlier.

13. *Ancient Judaism* (New York: The Free Press, 1952), p. 388.

14. As at 2 Chron. 13:20, "Jeroboam never again recovered his power during the lifetime of Abijah." Other instances are: Ex. 2:3; Jos. 2:11; 5:1, 12; Judg. 2:14; 1 Sam. 1:18; 2 Sam. 3:11; 14:10; 1 Kings 10:5, 10; 2 Kings 2:12; 1 Chron. 19:19; 2 Chron. 9:4; Jer. 44:22; Ezek. 33:22.

15. Cf. 2 Kings 23:25, the statement that no king like Josiah arose after him (*wᵉ'aḥᵃrâv lo'-qām kāmohû*). This is easier to grasp since we know who these kings were and when the historian was writing.

16. Apart from the fact that these are the only two passages in the book which refer to Moses as *nābî'*, the similarities in vocabulary are convincing: *qām*, cf. *'āqîm*, *yāqîm* (18:15, 18); *bᵉyśrā'ēl*, cf. *miqqirbᵉkā mē'aḥēkā* (18:15); *kᵉmošeh*, cf. *kāmonî*, *kāmôkā* (18:15, 18).

17. This was pointed out succinctly by S. R. Driver, *Deuteronomy* (Edinburgh: T. & T. Clark, 1895), p. 425.

18. See above, p. 48. Note, too, that Jesus ben Sirach refers to him as "the successor of Moses in prophesying" (Sir. 46:1).

19. 1 Macc. 4:46. See also 11:27 and 14:41 which testify to the expectation of a righteous prophet at that time.

20. Suggested not only by the association between the two figures in later tradition (see n. 12) but by their juxtaposition in this text and the phrase *mal'ak habbᵉrît* (3:1) indicating a mediatorial function.

21. See pp. 120–3 where this question is discussed at greater length.

22. The Samaritans identify the Mosaic prophet with the *Tahev* (Restorer) who, like the "messenger of the covenant" of Mal. 3:1, will reinstitute the sacrificial cult.

23. "Signs and wonders," "a mighty hand," "great terror," "which he did in the land of Egypt . . . in the sight of all Israel . . . to Pharaoh and all his servants . . . to all his land" are all Deuteronomic clichés; see especially Deut. 4:34; 6:22; 7:19; 11:3; 26:8; 29:1–2.

24. Driver, p. 425. A. C. Welch, *Deuteronomy. The Framework to the Code*, p. 185, held that the book ended originally with the phrase *pānîm 'el pānîm*.

25. M. Buber, *Moses: The Revelation and the Covenant* (New York: Harper, 1958), p. 155.

26. Num. 12:8. The occurrence of the divine name in *oratio recta* together with prosodic irregularity strongly suggest that this verse has been added.

27. See Deut. 4:12, 15 which leads into the tradition about the people's request for a covenant mediator (Ex. 20:18–21), the tradition appealed to in Deut. 18:16 as proof that such a function must always be present in Israel.

The association between this tradition and God's face-to-face knowledge of Moses is explained by the fact that both are rooted in the cult.

28. See especially H-J Kraus, *Worship in Israel*, pp. 101–112; G. von Rad, *The Problem of the Hexateuch and Other Essays* (Edinburgh & London: Oliver & Boyd, 1966), p. 30.

29. Reading *mar'eh* with MT or *bᵉmar'eh* following LXX. "Openly" is probably correct since contrast with speaking in riddles is called for. There is probably no significant difference between "face to face," "mouth to mouth" and "eye to eye." This last occurs at Num. 14:14: the Egyptians have heard that Yahweh is with the people of Israel and is seen "eye to eye" (NEB has "face to face"). Here, too, the context refers us to the Tent of Meeting. It is of interest to note that at Num. 12:8 the Targum of Pseudo-Jonathan, no doubt offended by the apparent anthropomorphism, substituted "word to word" adding "the voice of the Word was heard, but the majesty of the Presence was not seen" (Etheridge, I, 555, cf. II, 685 on Deut. 34:10).

30. It was seen that *tᵉmûnāh* and *pānîm* have to be understood against the background of the cultic theophany. To seek or see the Face connotes participation in worship, as is clear from Ps. 24:6; 27:8–9; 42:3; 143:7 and *passim*.

31. See M. Noth, *Exodus: A Commentary* (Philadelphia: Westminster, 1968), p. 96.

32. On this passage see Buber, p. 169. Many of the commentators identify the "back" as part of the *kābôd*, but there is no justification for this in any description of the *kābôd* in the Hebrew Scriptures. It may be of interest to note that all other occurrences of the word *'aḥor* have some connection with the sanctuary. Onkelos seems to render the sense well by contrasting the front (*dᵉqādāmay*) with the back (*dᵉbātray*), in other words, what precedes with what follows the *kābôd* or Shekinah as it passes (Etheridge, I, 424). Pseudo-Jonathan substitutes "the border of the tefillah of my glorious Shekinah" for "my back" (Etheridge, I, 556).

33. See, for example, Eissfeldt, *The Old Testament: An Introduction*, p. 189, and Noth, *Exodus. A Commentary*, p. 267.

34. b. Ber. 7a; *Midrash Rabbah Exodus* III 2; XLVII 6; *Midrash Rabbah Lev.* XX 10; *Midrash Rabbah Deut.* XI 3.

35. As suggested by Buber, p. 162.

36. E.g., the high priest Simon (t. Soṭah 13:7) and John Hyrcanus (Josephus, *Ant.* XIII 282–283; b. Soṭah 33a) as also the priest Zechariah in Lk. 1:8ff.

37. That the Bible itself contains midrash should no longer occasion surprise. As G. Vermes puts it, "Post-biblical midrash is to be distinguished from the biblical only by an external factor, canonization" (*The Cambridge History of the Bible*, I [eds.P. R. Ackroyd and C. R. Evans; Cambridge: Cambridge University Press, 1970] p. 199). The pioneering article on the study of biblical midrash is that of Renée Bloch in *SDB* V (Paris: Letouzey & Ane), cols. 1263–1281. More recently, S. Sandmel, "The Haggada within Scripture," *JBL* 80 (1961), 105–122, raises some interesting possibilities though without the rigorous criteria with respect to dating, literary form and

the like which are called for. It may be added that this text (Ex. 34:29–35) seems in its turn to have evoked a Christian midrash in II Cor. 3:7–18. The account of the transfiguration of Jesus is also in some way based on it.

38. See below, pp. 120–123.

39. A phrase which occurs in Gershom Scholem's stimulating essay, "Revelation and Tradition as Religious Categories in Judaism," in *The Messianic Idea in Judaism* (New York: Schocken Books, 1971), p. 295.

CHAPTER 5: THE MAKING OF THE PROPHETIC CANON

1. b. BB 14b–15a.

2. *Contra Ap.* I 37–41; see also *Ant.* X 35.

3. E.g., Lk. 24:44; Mt. 23:35 = Lk. 11:50–51; Philo: *De Vita Continentiae* 25.

4. Sir. 48:22–25; 49:10.

5. Otto Plöger, *Theocracy and Eschatology* (Richmond: John Knox Press, 1968), pp. 24–25, argues that its omission was probably deliberate since the apocalyptic circles from which the book derives were precisely those responsible for the collecting and editing of the Latter Prophets. The book of Daniel was put together during the persecution of Antiochus, in or about the year 165 B.C.E.

6. See O. Eissfeldt, *The Old Testament: An Introduction*, p. 565; E. Sellin and G. Fohrer, *Introduction to the Old Testament*, p. 486; R. Pfeiffer, "The Canon of the Old Testament," *IDB* I (New York and Nashville, Abingdon, 1962), p. 508.

7. D. N. Freedman, "The Law and the Prophets," *SVT* 9 (1963), 250–265; "Son of Man, Can These Bones Live?" *Inter* 29 (1975), 181–182. He follows W. F. Albright in putting both the Deuteronomic history and P in the late pre-exilic period; see W. F. Albright, *From the Stone Age to Christianity* (Garden City: Doubleday, 1957²), pp. 345–346.

8. Suggested also by the appendices in Isaiah and Jeremiah (Is. 36–39; Jer. 52) taken over from the Deuteronomic History.

9. The attempts of W. H. Schmidt, "Die deuteronomistische Redaktion des Amosbuches," ZAW 77 (1965), 168–193 and E. W. Nicholson, *Preaching to the Exiles* (Oxford: Blackwell, 1970), call for careful scrutiny.

10. See above, p. 52.

11. F. Crüsemann, "Kritik an Amos im deuteronomistischen Geschichtswerk," in H. W. Wolff, ed., *Probleme biblischer Theologie* (G. von Rad Festschrift; Munich: 1971), pp. 57–63, makes the interesting suggestion that 2 Kings 14:27 may be aimed at Amos.

12. See E. Auerbach, "Die grosse Überarbeitung der biblischen Bücher," *SVT* 1 (1953), 1–10.

13. Hag. 2:6–9, 20–23; Zech. 6:12–13; 8:11–13, 22–23.

14. Is. 41:25–29; 44:8, 24–25; 46:8–11; 48:3–5. The "former things" (ri'šonôt, 41:22; 42:9; 43:9, 18–19; 46:9; 48:3) refer to predictions of earlier

prophets now seen to be fulfilled or about to be fulfilled. See G. von Rad, *Old Testament Theology* II, p. 265; M. Haran, "The Literary Structure and Chronological Framework of the Prophecies in Is. xl–xlviii," *SVT* 9 (1963), 127–55.

15. Is. 43:14; 45:1–3 (referring to Cyrus); 46:10–11; 47:1–15; 48:3, 5, 6, 14.

16. Israel (Jacob) at 41:8–9; 44:1–2, 21; 45:4; 48:20; 49:3; those addressed by the prophet at 43:10, cf. 54:17; the anonymous Servant at 42:1–4; 49:3 (cf. Jer. 1:4; Is. 50:7); 50:10; 52:13; 53:10–11. Note also 42:19 where *'ebed* and *mal'āk* are synonyms.

17. See above, pp. 35ff., 73.

18. E.g., the elucidation of text-critical problems in the judgment-oracle at Is. 2:6–22 must not be allowed to obscure the important datum that exegetical expansions are to be found *within* the poem. While I hope to deal with this in detail in a later study, it may be noted by way of illustration that vv. 18 and 20 appear to be theological glosses of a sharply eschatological character on v. 8 (cf. Is. 30:22; 31:6–7) reminiscent of the anti-idolatry polemic in Second Isaiah; vv. 19 and 21 may be taken as alternative versions of v. 10 (significantly absent from 1QIsᵃ), while vv. 11 and 17 (cf. 5:15) should stand in the margin opposite v. 12. The final v. 22 was perhaps added later than LXX from which it is absent except as a note in the margin of one MS. At 1QS V 17, it is quoted as a sectarian admonition to dissociate from non-members, and it is not impossible that it came into the Isaiah text from such a source.

19. Introduced by *maśśā'*, 13:1; 14:28; 15:1; 17:1; 19:1; 21:1, 11, 13; 22:1; 23:1.

20. Plöger, *Theocracy and Eschatology* (Richmond: John Knox Press, 1968).

21. Perhaps no more than the addition of the phrases "David their king" and "in the latter days" at 3:5. For a different view, see R. E. Wolfe, "The Editing of the Book of the Twelve," *ZAW* 53 (1935), 90–129.

22. Mic. 1:10–15, cf. Is. 10:27–32; Mic. 2:1–3, cf. Is. 5:8–10; Mic. 4:5, cf. Is. 2:5; Mic. 4:1–3, cf. Is. 2:2–4; Mic. 5:9–14, cf. Is. 2:6–8.

23. G. Scholem, *The Messianic Idea in Judaism* (New York: Schocken Books, 1971), p. 295.

24. With few exceptions the history of post-exilic prophecy is skimped in works on prophecy, histories of Israelite religion and theologies of the Old Testament. A reason for this state of affairs has already been suggested, i.e., that modern critical scholarship has concentrated on the recovery of the message of the "classical" prophets, after which high point the religion of Israel had nowhere to go but down. In one respect or another the following are useful: A. Jepsen, *NABI. Soziologische Studien zur alttestamentlichen Literatur und Religionsgeschichte*, pp. 217ff., 237ff.; A. Lods, *The Prophets and the Rise of Judaism* (London: Routledge & Kegan Paul, 1937); A. R. Johnson, *The Cultic Prophet in Ancient Israel* (Cardiff: University of Wales Press, 1962²), pp. 65ff.; T. Chary, *Les Prophètes et le Culte à partir de l'Exil*

(Tournai: Desclée, 1955); J. Lindblom, *Prophecy in Ancient Israel* (Oxford: Blackwell, 1962), pp. 403ff.; E. Hammershaimb, *Some Aspects of Old Testament Prophecy from Isaiah to Malachi* (Copenhagen: Publications de la Société des Sciences et des Lettres d'Aarhus, 1966), pp. 91–112.

25. Ezra 5:2 speaks of "the prophets of God," Zech. 7:2–7 refers to temple prophets and 8:9 to prophets who had been preaching since the foundations of the temple were laid.

26. Is. 66:1–4.

27. The central importance of control of the cult in these tensions and conflicts is stressed—in very different ways—by Paul D. Hanson, *The Dawn of Apocalyptic* (Philadelphia: Fortress Press, 1975) and Morton Smith, *Palestinian Parties and Politics that Shaped the Old Testament* (New York: Columbia University Press, 1971).

28. See Martin Hengel, *Judaism and Hellenism. Studies in their Encounter in Palestine during the Early Hellenistic Period* (Philadelphia: Fortress Press, 1974), pp. 212ff.

29. Neh. 6:10; 'āṣûr may, but need not, imply this meaning.

30. Zech. 13:2–6. This interpretation, followed by NEB, depends on *hiqnanî* (v. 5) with the meaning of "lusting" and *bēt me'ah*abāy* (v. 6) meaning "the house of my lovers." This sense is quite appropriate in the context given the association between idolatry and sexual deviation.

31. Lam. 2:9; Is. 63:7ff.; Ps. 74:9.

32. The activity of temple musicians is described as prophesying (1 Chron. 25:1, etc.) but they are not called prophets.

33. *Old Testament Theology* II (New York and Evanston: Harper & Row, 1965), pp. 301–308; *Wisdom in Israel* (Nashville & New York: Abingdon Press, 1972), pp. 269–283.

34. *Old Testament Theology* II, p. 308. It is strange that von Rad omitted to mention those cases where the prophet is admitted to the heavenly court (or temple) to receive revelations concerning the course of the future; e.g., 1 Kings 22:19–22; Is. 6:1–13; 40:1–11.

35. *Ibid.*, pp. 306–308.

36. E.g., Klaus Koch, *The Rediscovery of Apocalyptic* (Naperville: Alec R. Allenson, n.d.), pp. 42–47; W. Schmidtals, *Die Apokalyptik* (Göttingen: Vandenhoeck & Rupprecht, 1973), pp. 96–99.

37. Rowley, *The Relevance of Apocalyptic* (London: Lutterworth Press, 1947²), pp. 11–50.

38. E.g., that they wrote for different audiences, with the classical prophets for the most part addressing the entire people and the apocalypticists their own groups; *ibid.*, pp. 13, 21.

39. *Ibid.*, pp. 31, 41; cf. D. S. Russell, *The Method and Message of Jewish Apocalyptic* (Philadelphia: Westminster, 1964), pp. 88ff. Rowley did not consider the possibility that some of the Enoch literature may antedate the book of Daniel.

40. Cross, "New Directions in the Study of Apocalyptic," R. W. Funk (ed.), *Journal for Theology and the Church. 6: Apocalypticism* (New York: Herder & Herder, 1969), pp. 157–165; "A Note on the Study of Apocalyptic

Origins," *Canaanite Myth and Hebrew Epic* (Cambridge, Mass: Harvard University Press, 1973), pp. 343–346.

41. Hanson, "Jewish Apocalyptic against Its Near Eastern Environment," *RB* 78 (1971), 31–58; "Old Testament Apocalyptic Re-examined," *Inter 25* (1971), 454–479; "Zechariah 9 and the Recapitulation of an Ancient Ritual Pattern," *JBL* 92 (1973), 37–59; *The Dawn of Apocalyptic* (Philadelphia: Fortress, 1975).

42. "Jewish Apocalyptic against Its Near Eastern Environment," p. 47 (the exilic period or a little earlier); cf. W. F. Albright, *From the Stone Age to Christianity* (Garden City: Doubleday, 1957²), p. 331 (fifth or sixth century). No reasons are given in either case.

43. "Old Testament Apocalyptic Re-examined," p. 468; *The Dawn of Apocalyptic, passim.*

44. The term was, apparently, first suggested by Cross. One takes the point, but the confusion caused by introducing the term "proto-Gnosticism" ought to be borne in mind.

45. A surprising omission in view of the fact that he dates these chapters, again without supporting arguments, to the late sixth or early fifth century; see "Old Testament Apocalyptic Re-examined," 471.

46. *Theocracy and Eschatology.* (Richmond: John Knox Press, 1968).

47. *Ibid.,* p. 115.

48. *Ibid.,* pp. 44, 113.

49. Mal. 1:2; 2:17; 3:13–15.

50. Plöger, p. 109; also his article "Prophet und Priester," *ZAW* 63 (1951), 189ff.

51. *Theocracy and Eschatology,* p. 109.

52. Moses received Torah from Sinai; he delivered it to Joshua, Joshua to the elders, the elders to the prophets and the prophets to the men of the Great Assembly; thence it passed to the "pairs" of whom Hillel and Shammai are the best known; m. Abot I:1; *ARN* (Recension A) I:3; b. Meg. 17b; b. Yoma 9b; in m. Peah II:6 the links are: Moses at Sinai, prophets, pairs, rabbis. See W. Bacher, *Tradition und Tradenten in den Schulen Palästinas und Babyloniens* (Leipzig: G. Fock, 1914); E. S. Bikerman, "La Chaîne de la Tradition pharisienne," *RB* 59 (1952), 44–54.

53. Their teaching could, therefore, be described as *dibrē qabbālāh* (Words of tradition), b. RH 7a. See Bacher, pp. 2, 23ff.

54. b. San. 11a; b. Yoma 9b; b. Soṭah 48b; t. Soṭah 12:2ff. Where it occurs in these texts, *rûaḥ haqqodeš* is in effect synonymous with *rûaḥ hann*bû'āh.*

55. "Until then (i.e., the time of Alexander) the prophets prophesied in the Holy Spirit; from then on 'incline thine ear to hear the words of the sages,'" *Seder Olam Rabbah* 30. In b. Meg. 15a Malachi is identified with Ezra.

56. For details see my article "Prophecy and Priesthood in Josephus," *JJS* 25 (1974), 250–251.

57. See J. Levy, *Wörterbuch über die Talmudim und Midrashim* III (Darmstadt: Wissenschaftliche Buchgesellschaft, 1963), pp. 323–325.

58. b. BB 12b. The Holy Spirit and the Urim and Thummim were two of the five realities present in the first and absent from the second temple; see b. Soṭah 48a and b. Yoma 21b. On the midrash of the "five things" consult P. Schäfer, *Die Vorstellung vom Heiligen Geist in der rabbinischen Literatur* (Munich: 1972), pp. 89–93.

59. There were, of course, many charismatic figures like Honi the Circle-Drawer, Hanina ben Dosa and Eliezer ben Hyrcanus who performed healings, exorcisms and other wonders, but the tradition does not apply to them the term "prophet"; see b. Yeb. 121b; b. Ber. 34d; b. Erub. 63a, and on Hanina G. Vermes, "Hanina ben Dosa," *JJS* 23 (1972), 28–50; 24 (1973), 51–64. It may be noted further that the same reserve was practiced by Josephus; for concerned as he was with the phenomenon of prophecy and prepared as he was to stigmatize certain of his contemporaries as *pseudoprophētai*, he used the term *prophētēs* only of the canonical prophets. E. E. Urbach, "When did Prophecy cease?" (in Hebrew), *Tarbiz*, 17 (1945/46), 1ff., misrepresented Josephus' position by failing to note the significance of his use of *prophētēs* and *theion pneuma*.

60. b. Yeb. 49b; *Wayyiqra' Rabbah* I:14.

61. b. RH 21b. Cf. Josephus: *Ant.* IV 303, 313–314.

62. *Mekhilta: Baḥodesh* IX 62–8 (Lauterbach ed., II 270–271); *Exodus Rabbah* 42:8 (on Ex. 32:7); cf. *Exodus Rabbah* 28:6 where Isaiah is represented as having been present at Sinai. In b. Ber. 5a a piece of exegetical virtuosity attributed to the third century Rabbi Shimeon ben Lakish establishes that Prophets, Writings, Mishnah and Gemarah in addition to Torah were given at Sinai.

63. *Sifra* 115d (on Lev. 27:34); b. Meg. 14a. In cases where it might seem that prophets had made innovations, e.g., the recitation of the Hallel and the institution of the "four kinds" at Sukkot, these had been revealed to Moses but subsequently forgotten, b. Pes. 117a; b. Sukk.44a. The principle stands: no prophet is at liberty to introduce anything new, b. Meg. 2b–3a, cf. b. Ber. 14a.

64. See especially b. Ber. 5a.

65. *War* IV 385–6; Test. Levi XVI 2; CD VII 17–18.

66. See Blenkinsopp, "Prophecy and Priesthood in Josephus," p. 245.

67. E.g., Justin, *Trypho* 82; Origen, *Contra Celsum* VII:8.

68. b. BB 12b. The similarity between this logion and Sir. 51 has also been noted; see the commentaries and W. D. Davies, *Paul and Rabbinic Judaism* (London: S.P.C.K., 1958²), pp. 156–158.

69. Gershom Scholem has long maintained that apocalyptic elements survived in a transformed state in the various schools of mysticism; see his *Major Trends in Jewish Mysticism* (New York: Schocken Books, 1961), and several of the essays in *The Messianic Idea in Judaism* (New York: Schocken Books, 1971).

70. *Shirata* III 28ff. (Lauterbach ed., II 58).

71. *Shirata* VII 17ff. (Lauterbach, II 58). The use of the future tense at Ex. 15:1 (*yāšîr*) points prophetically forward to the song Israel will sing at the resurrection, *Shirata* I 8–10 (Lauterbach, II 1).

72. The eschatological application of *ius talionis* is found often in *Mekhilta*, as it is in the New Testament; see Judah Goldin, *The Song at the Sea* (New Haven: Yale University Press, 1971), pp. 135, 143, 165; E. Käsemann, "Sätze heiligen Rechtes im Neuen Testament," *NTS* 1 (1954/55), 248–260; "The Beginnings of Christian Theology," R. W. Funk, ed., *Journal for Theology and the Church*, Vol. 6: *Apocalypticism*, pp. 21–22.

73. b. BB 12a.

74. Ezra 7:1, 9, 28; Sir. 24:33, cf. Wisd. 7:27. In rabbinic writings scribalism also qualifies one for the prophetic gift: Job is *nābî'* as well as *hākām* (b. BB 15b); the scribe is even greater than the prophet since the latter needs the seal of God evidenced through signs and miracles while the former proves himself through Torah alone (y. Ber. 17:11, cf. b. BB 12a and b. Ber. 34d)—a curious reversal of the usual process of legitimation!

75. In the famous story about the oven of Aknai (b. BM 59b) R. Eliezer is defeated, even though supported by a *bath qol*, by appeal to Deut. 30:12. The story ends with God smiling and saying, "my children have defeated me."

76. A similar suggestion was made in passing by G. Östborn, *Cult and Canon* (Uppsala: 1950), p. 44, though in other respects his explanation of the prophetic canon is very different from mine.

77. See, e.g., the Chronicler's frequent use of "Judah and Benjamin" and Sirach's disparaging references to the Samaritans (50:25–26).

78. Worthy of further consideration is the idea that the Twelve stand for the prophetic and eschatological plenitude of Israel, in keeping with the title *apostolos*, a synonym for "prophet." They are called, endowed with the Spirit, charged with preaching to an unresponsive public, bear the revelation available through Jesus, and in the new world will sit in eschatological judgment (Mt. 19:28 = Lk. 22:30, cf. Sib. III 781), an evident reference to Dan. 7. The Twelve-tribal motif in Revelation, the only explicitly prophetic book in the New Testament, is also noteworthy in this regard.

79. It is also possible that Mal. 3:23–24 refers to Elijah as "prophet like Moses" (Deut. 18:15–18). In later tradition Elijah is a high priestly figure associated with Phineas, no doubt because of the zeal which they had in common.

CHAPTER 6: THE TRANSFORMATION OF PROPHECY

1. According to the view which became official, the Law and the Prophets really form only one corpus since the prophets' essential task is to continue the work of Moses. Correspondingly, there is one epoch of revelation from Moses to the death of the last prophet or, alternatively, to Ezra.

2. Sir. 44:3–5; 47:8–9, 15, 17. Apart from these, none of the *ketûbîm* is mentioned in Sir.

3. "So my grandfather Jesus, who had applied himself industriously to the study of the law, the prophets, and the other writings of our ancestors . . . was moved to compile a book of his own . . . so that, with this further help,

scholars might make greater progress in their studies by living as the law directs"; "Not only with this book, but with the law, the prophets, and the rest of the writings, it makes no small difference to read them in the original."

4. See, e.g., 1 Cor. 2:9 (Apocalypse of Elijah?); Heb. 11:37 (Ascension of Isaiah); Jude 9 (Assumption of Moses); Jude 14–16 (Enoch).

5. Josephus, *Ap.*, I 8, gives the number as twenty-two, as do the early ecclesiastical writers Melito and Origen (Eusebius: *Hist. Eccl.* IV 26; VI 25), whereas II Esd. 14:44–45 has twenty-four. The discrepancy may be due to the desire to tally with the number of letters in the Hebrew and Greek alphabets, respectively.

6. See, e.g., t. BM 11:23; 1QS I 2–3; Mt. 5:17; 7:12; 11:13; 22:40; Lk. 16:16; Jn. 1:45.

7. *Ap.*, I 8; cf. Philo: *De Vita Contemplativa* 3, who also speaks of law, prophets and psalms.

8. The prophetic status of David is assumed in the psalm at 2 Sam. 23:1–7, a late insertion into the narrative, as it is by the Chronicler (1 Chron. 17:17; cf. 2 Chron. 8:14 and Neh. 12:24, 36 where he is called *'îš 'elohîm*, man of God). The Psalms Scroll from Qumran (11QPs^a) attributes to him 4,050 hymns which "he spoke by means of the prophecy (*n^{e}bû'āh*) which was given him by the Most High." On this last, see J. A. Sanders, *Discoveries in the Judaean Desert of Jordan: IV. The Psalms Scroll of Qumran Cave 11 (11QPs^a)* (Oxford: Oxford University Press, 1965), pp. 137ff.

9. On the meaning of these terms: *m^{e}ṭamm'îm 'et-hayyādayim, s^{e}pārîm hiṣônîm, g^{e}nûzîm*, see the encyclopedias and standard works of reference. Some very recent literature on the subject is discussed in A. J. Saldarini, "Apocalyptic and Rabbinic Literature," *CBQ* 37 (1975), 348–358.

10. H. von Campenhausen, *The Formation of the Christian Bible*, especially chapter 5.

11. J. Blenkinsopp, "Prophecy and Priesthood in Josephus," *JJS* 25 (1974), 244–245.

12. On the difficult question of the relation between Akiba and Bar Kochba, see E. Schürer, *The History of the Jewish People in the Age of Jesus Christ (175 B.C.–A.D. 135)* I (revised ed.; eds. G. Vermes and F. Millar; Edinburgh: T. & T. Clark, 1973), pp. 543–544.

13. The rabbinic tradition about Jonathan ben Uzziel being restrained from writing a targum on the *k^{e}tûbîm* on the grounds that they revealed the date of the Messiah points in the same direction; see above, p. 118. On the connections between apocalyptic and mysticism, see Gershom G. Scholem, *Major Trends in Jewish Mysticism* (New York: Schocken Books, 1961), pp. 40–79.

14. On David as prophet, see n. 8 above.

15. This rabbinic attribution (b. BB 15a) may be quite old, as is perhaps suggested by the fact that Job fragments from Qumran were written in the archaic Hebrew script. It may be explained by the tradition of a patriarchal sage of that name as attested at Ezek. 14:14, 20, but we cannot be sure. The attribution proves nothing, of course, on the antiquity of the book itself.

16. Solomon's authorship of Proverbs is also suggested by Sir. 44:5 and 47:17.

17. Cf. Sir. 47:17.

18. b. Shab. 104a; Meg. 2a. An alternative way of solving the problem of Esther, which seemed to lack prophetic authorship, was to suppose that either Esther herself or perhaps Mordechai was a prophetic figure; see *Seder Olam Rabbah,* ch. 30.

19. The identification with Malachi is found at b. Meg. 15a.

20. Eliphaz describes in some detail the supernatural source of his insights, 4:12–16; see too 15:17 (also Eliphaz); 32:8, 18; 33:15–16; 36:1–4 (Elihu).

21. See especially Ezek. 1:3; 3:22; 33:22; 40:1.

22. Sir. 39:1–11; cf. 44:3 where we read that the sage counsellors of yore spoke out with prophetic power. The colophon to Hosea (14:10) also suggests scribal study and appropriation of prophecy, and we recall that Baruch, Jeremiah's amanuensis, was a scribe.

23. Sir. 24:23, cf. 1:26–27; 15:1; 21:11; 34:8.

24. Dan. 5:11, 14; Wisd. 7:27; 11:1.

25. *kata tēn epipnoian tēn apo tou theou, Ap.* I 37.

26. For the list of prophetic sources see J. M. Myers, *I. Chronicles* (Garden City, New York: Doubleday, 1965), p. xlvii.

27. See above, pp. 31f.

28. See the articles in standard works of reference under "scribe"; also J. Jeremias, *Jerusalem in the Time of Jesus* (Philadelphia: Fortress Press, 1969³), pp. 233–245.

29. E.g., sacrifice and food-offerings, b. Ket. 106a.

30. *War* VI 291.

31. Mk. 8:31; 10:33; 11:18, 27; 14:1; 15:31; Mt. 2:4; 21:15; Lk. 22:66; 23:10.

32. See, e.g., Ezra 2:63 = Neh. 7:65 and cf. Ex. 28:30; Lev. 8:8.

33. On Simon the Just and John Hyrcanus, see b. Soṭah 33a and for the latter also Josephus, *Ant.* XIII 299. Caiphas' prophecy is mentioned at Jn. 11:49–52, on which see E. Bammel, "ARCHIEREUS PROPHETON," *TLZ* 79 (1954), 353 and C. H. Dodd, "The Prophecy of Caiphas. John xi 47–53," *Neotestamentica et Patristica* (Leiden: Brill, 1962), pp. 134–143.

34. Blenkinsopp, "Prophecy and Priesthood in Josephus," pp. 250–255.

35. Ezra 8:18, *śekel* belongs to the vocabulary of the wisdom schools, cf. Prov. 12:8; 16:22; 19:11; 23:9; Job 17:4.

36. Most frequently used are the verbs *haśkîl* and *mēbîn* referring to proficiency in instruction and worship; see, e.g., 1 Chron. 15:22; 25:8; 2 Chron. 30:22; 35:3; Neh. 8:9. Levitical scribes are referred to at 1 Chron. 24:6 and 2 Chron. 34:13.

37. On their liturgical function see 1 Chron. 6:31–48; 15:16–24; 2 Chron. 7:6; 20:19–20; 29:25–30. At 1 Chron. 15:22, 27 S. Mowinckel, *The Psalms in Israel's Worship* II (New York and Nashville: Abingdon Press, 1967), p. 56, finds a reference to a levitical office of "master of the oracle." While it may seem more natural to translate *śar hammaśśā'* "precentor" or "di-

rector of music," the use of a term (*maśśā'*), which generally means "oracle," may well point to the prophetic or inspired character of liturgical music.

38. 1 Sam. 10:5, 10; 2 Kings 3:14–15, etc.

39. H-J Kraus, *Worship in Israel*, pp. 101–112; S. Mowinckel, pp. 53–73 (on prophetic oracles in psalms); A. R. Johnson, *The Cultic Prophet in Ancient Israel* (Cardiff: University of Wales Press, 1962²).

40. See especially 1QH (*Hôdāyôt*) and 1 Cor. 14. The giving of a liturgical blessing is attributed to the spirit of prophecy in Jub. 25:14 and 31:12–17 with which cf. Lk. 1:67–79. See the brief observations on liturgical, hymnic prophecy of W. H. Brownlee, *The Meaning of the Qumran Scrolls for the Bible* (New York: Oxford University Press, 1964), pp. 271–273.

41. See n. 8 above.

42. 1 Chron. 25:1–31, cf. 2 Chron. 20:14–17. On the levitical eponymi see 1 Chron. 25:5; 2 Chron. 29:30; 35:15.

43. Ex. 2:1; Aaron also, Ex. 4:14. In the golden calf incident Moses addresses them in the prophetic manner (Ex. 32:27) and they answer the call.

44. Deut. 33:8–11; 4QpIs^d I 5; 1QM IV 6, 23; XVIII 29; b. Yoma 73d.

45. Gen. 49:5; Ex. 32:25–29; Num. 25; Judg. 19:29–30.

46. 2 Chron. 13–14; 20:14–22: an inspired Levite prophesies victory and liturgical singing plays the decisive role in defeating the enemy. The Maccabees took the priest Phineas as their model, as is clear from 1 Macc. 2:26, 54. Contrary to what is often stated, there is no evidence that the *ḥ^{a}sîdîm* were pacifists who took up arms only reluctantly and as a last resort. That they refused to fight on sabbath (1 Macc. 2:32–38, if the people here referred to are indeed *ḥ^{a}sîdîm*, which is by no means assured) certainly does not prove this. On the contrary, they are described as warriors (1 Macc. 2:42, presumably *gibbôrîm*) and Alcimus alleges, probably quite correctly, that they were at the center of armed resistance to the Syrians (2 Macc. 14:6). We might compare Ps. 149:5–9, which speaks of *ḥ^{a}sîdîm* both praising God and engaging in the holy war.

47. Especially in the War Scroll (1QM).

48. For the holy war in Deuteronomy see G. von Rad, *Studies in Deuteronomy*, pp. 45–59.

49. M. Gertner, "The Masorah and the Levites. An Essay in the History of a Concept," *VT* 10 (1960), 241–284, advances the view that the levitical scholars combined midrash and mesorah, or exegesis and mastery in reciting the biblical text. As such, they were the ancestors of the medieval Masoretes.

50. Jeremias, *Jerusalem in the Time of Jesus*, p. 213. The only Levite named in the New Testament, Joseph Barnabas the Cypriot, was a church leader, prophet, teacher and missionary; see especially Acts 13:1ff.

51. Priests are paired with *ḥ^{a}sîdîm* at 2 Chron. 6:41 and Ps. 132:9, 16. *'ebed*, synonymous with *nābî'*, is in parallelism with *ḥasîd* at Ps. 79:2; 86:2 and 116:15–16. Pss. 50, 79 and 85, all of which speak of *ḥ^{a}sîdîm*, are ascribed to Asaphite or Korahite Levites.

52. Dan. 11:33, 35; 12:3, 10, cf. 9:22 (Gabriel comes to instruct him, lᵉhaśkîlkā).

53. If the words "give to Levi" are to be supplied from LXX, which seems likely, Levi wold be in parallelism with 'îš hᵃsîdekā.

54. G. Vermes, *The Dead Sea Scrolls in English* (Harmondsworth: Penguin Books, 1968), pp. 22–25.

55. See n. 36 above.

56. 1QM I 2; VII 14–16; VIII 9; XIII 1; XV 4; XVI 7; XVIII 15.

57. 1 Macc. 2:26, 54. In later Jewish tradition, beginning with Pseudo-Philo, Phineas is identified with Elijah. David Clark has examined this tradition in an unpublished University of Notre Dame Ph.D. dissertation, "An Investigation of the Priestly Office and Duties of Elijah."

58. Levi in this work is a prophetic figure and a visionary filled with the spirit of understanding. He foretells the future and declares mysteries concerning the last age; see Test. Levi II 3, 5ff., 10; VIII 1ff.; X; XIV–XVI. On the *triplex munus* see VIII 11–15. Note that the tripartite office attributed to Simon in 1 Macc. 13:42 does not yet include prophecy.

59. This is demonstrably the case with the Qumran community, less clearly so with the Pharisees due to the difficulties involved in reconstructing their history during the Greek period and identifying their writings, if indeed any have survived from that time. While their popular appeal was considerable, they experienced increasing difficulties under the later Maccabees, especially Alexander Jannaeus.

60. Enoch was the first scribe (En. IV 17) and was adept at natural science, onomastics and parables (II 1–V 3; XLI 3–9, etc.). His access to and participation in heavenly liturgies (LXXI 5ff., etc.) imply priestly status, and we have seen that Gen. 5:21–4 (P) suggests that the Enoch tradition was carried by priestly-scribal groups. Apocalyptic writing of the Enoch type, characterized by visions, first emerges in the work of prophets who are also priests, i.e., Ezekiel and Zechariah. For the prophetic character of Enoch see especially I 2; LXXI 11; XCI 1.

61. See n. 13 above; also, J. Jeremias, *Jerusalem in the Time of Jesus*, pp. 237–243.

CHAPTER 7: THE CANON AND THE AUTHORITY OF THE BIBLE

1. See the comments of James D. Smart, *The Strange Silence of the Bible in the Church* (Philadelphia: Westminster Press, 1970), pp. 77ff.

2. While not treating of the canon, Eichrodt does have one remark on the subject of our discussion worth quoting: "By taking the prophets as well as the legal writings into the canon, the community of the Law ensured that its thinking would be constantly cross-fertilized by a thoroughgoing theonomy. Alongside the great mainstream of the ethic of the Law the currents of prophetic thought flow on, and prevent a total silting up by

external legalism." *Theology of the Old Testament* II (Philadelphia: Westminster Press, 1967), p. 348. The section from which this passage is taken betrays an unfortunately all too common lack of appreciation for the specifically Jewish understanding of Torah. Comparison between Eichrodt's idea of the "silting up" (*Versandung* in the original) of genuine Israelite religion and Wellhausen's idea of congealment (*Erstarrung*) may help to reveal the source of this prejudice.

3. For the situation in various sectors of early Christianity, including Jewish Christianity, see the important work of Walter Bauer, *Orthodoxy and Heresy in Earliest Christianity* (Philadelphia: Fortress Press, 1971), inclusive of the appendix by Georg Strecker.

4. In Georg Fohrer's *History of Israelite Religion* (London: S.P.C.K., 1973), the most recent to appear in English at this writing, the only reference to the canon is a brief mention of the role of the Deuteronomists (p. 300).

5. See J. D. Smart, op. cit., pp. 90ff., and *The Interpretation of Scripture* (Philadelphia: Westminster Press, 1961), pp. 197–231; also James Barr, "The Old Testament and the New Crisis of Biblical Theology," *Inter* 25 (1971), 38–39, and *The Bible and the Modern World* (New York: Harper & Row, 1973), pp. 23–30.

6. C. H. Dodd's *The Authority of the Bible* (London: James Nisbet & Co., 1928), p. 154, came to the same conclusion but in the radically different form proposed by Wellhausen. His reference to the Law as "the bony skeleton which supported the warm flesh and blood of prophetic religion" puts this beyond doubt. See the criticism of this approach by Smart, *The Interpretation of Scripture*, pp. 216–219.

7. Which does not oblige us to subscribe to the view that prophets like Amos were originally cultic personnel; see, for example, E. Würthwein, "Amos-Studien," *ZAW* 62 (1949/50), 10–52, who holds that ʾAmos previous to his mission had been a *shālôm*-prophet at the Bethel sanctuary.

8. K. Burridge, *New Heaven, New Earth* (Oxford: Blackwell, 1969), pp. 32, 91, 98, arrives at a similar understanding of prophecy though working with very different material.

9. Here, too, however, we should avoid making too absolute a distinction since the differences can to some extent be explained by the need of the later prophets to establish their authority not just in the eyes of their prophetic colleagues but of the nation as a whole. On the call-narratives consult J. Lindblom, *Prophecy in Ancient Israel*, pp. 182–197; G. von Rad, *Old Testament Theology II*, pp. 50–69; N. Habel, "The Form and Significance of the Call Narrative," *ZAW* 77 (1965), 297–323.

10. For examples, see I. M. Lewis, *Ecstatic Religion* (Harmondsworth: Penguin Books, 1971), pp. 27, 34, etc.

11. "Major Features of World Religions," Roland Robertson (ed.), *Sociology of Religion* (Baltimore: Penguin Books, 1969), p. 21, where he is speaking of Sufism; cf. his remarks on the plebeian status of early Israelite nebiism in *Ancient Judaism* (New York: The Free Press, 1952), pp. 96ff.

12. Ezek. 2:2, 5; 3:12, 14, 24; 8:3; 11:1, 5, 24; 37:1. This revival of

spirit-language by Ezekiel may perhaps be explained by his evident interest in prophecy of the archaic period; cf., for example, the fiery chariots seen by Elijah and Elisha with Ezek. 1, the levitations to which both Elijah and he were subject, the posthumous miracle worked by Elisha when a corpse came to life after touching his bones (2 Kings 13:21) which may have inspired the vision of the valley full of dry bones in Ezek. 37.

13. Here again, however, this should not be overstressed since most of the classical prophets must have had a discipleship even though this is not always mentioned.

14. See M. Black, *The Scrolls and Christian Origins* (New York: Charles Scribner's Sons, 1961), pp. 75–88.

15. Rom. 7:6; 2 Cor. 3:6. This dichotomy has often been used in speaking of the fate of prophecy, generally in a way which reflects the confessional presuppositions of the writer; e.g., J. Skinner, *Prophecy and Religion: Studies in The Life of Jeremiah* (Cambridge: The University Press, 1922), p. 190; A. Lods, *The Prophets and the Rise of Judaism* (London: Routledge & Kegan Paul, 1937), p. 205.

16. See von Rad, *Old Testament Theology* II, pp. 62–63. The phrase in inverted commas is from James Barr, *Old and New in Interpretation* (London: S.C.M., 1966), p. 22.

17. See, however, Salo Baron, *A Social and Religious History of the Jews* I (New York: Columbia University Press, 1952²), pp. 85ff., and Simon M. Dubnov, *History of the Jews* I (South Brunswick, N.J.: T. Yoseloff, 1967), pp. 25ff., 311ff. The essay of Peter L. Berger, "Charisma and Religious Innovation: The Social Location of Israelite Prophecy," *American Sociological Review* 28 (1963), 940–950, is one of the rare attempts (apart from Weber's) to take the specialist literature on prophecy seriously.

18. *The Theory of Social and Economic Organization* (New York: The Free Press, 1964), pp. 324–423.

19. *Ibid.*, pp. 363ff.

20. *Ibid.*, pp. 358–359.

21. On Weber's more specific treatment of prophecy see *Ancient Judaism*, pp. 267ff. and *passim*, and *The Sociology of Religion* (London: Methuen, 1965), pp. 46–59.

22. Talcott Parsons' Introduction to *The Theory of Social and Economic Organization*, pp. 75–76 and to *The Sociology of Religion*, xxxiii–xxxviii; Dorothy Emmett, "Prophets and Their Societies," *Journal of the Royal Anthropological Institute* 86 (1956), 13ff., who finds that his doctrine of charisma smacks too much of the *Führerprinzip* and the mystique of great men and overstresses the irrational and socially deviant aspects; David Little, "Max Weber and the Comparative Study of Religious Ethics," *The Journal of Religious Ethics* 2 (1974), 5–40, who also questions his position on the charismatic-irrational basis for action as well as other aspects of his thinking.

23. On the routinization of charisma, see *The Theory of Social and Economic Organization*, pp. 363–373.

24. *Ibid.*, p. 370.

25. Stressed by Peter L. Berger, *The Precarious Vision* (Garden City: Doubleday, 1961), and P. L. Berger and T. Luckmann, "Sociology of Religion and Sociology of Knowledge," in R. Robertson, ed., *Sociology of Religion*, pp. 61–73 ("all universes, as meaning structures, are precarious," p. 66).

26. E.g., L. Festinger, H. W. Riecken and S. Schachter, *When Prophecy Fails* (New York: Harper & Row, 1964); K. Burridge, *New Heaven, New Earth* (Oxford: Blackwell, 1969); S. L. Thrupp, *Millenarian Dreams in Action* (New York: Schocken Books, 1970); P. Worsley, *The Trumpet Shall Sound* (New York: Schocken Books, 1968²).

27. See, e.g., John G. Gager, *Kingdom and Community. The Social World of Early Christianity* (Englewood Cliffs: Prentice-Hall, 1975). Brian W. Kovaks has made a significant methodological contribution in a paper written for the Consultation on the Social World of Ancient Israel held at the Society of Biblical Literature meeting in St. Louis, October 1976, under the title "Contributions of Sociology to the Study of the Development of Apocalypticism. A Theoretical Survey."

28. Weber considered intellectual rationalism to be inherently hostile to prophecy; see *Ancient Judaism*, pp. 285–286; "The Economic Ethic of the World Religions," R. Robertson, ed., *Sociology of Religion*, p. 33.

29. For the social function of small communities embodying what he calls "the mystical power of the weak," see Victor Turner, *The Ritual Process* (Chicago: Aldine Publishing Co., 1969), pp. 131ff.

30. Otto Plöger, *Theocracy and Eschatology*, pp. 44, 113, comments on the correlation between neglect of eschatological prophecy and cultural assimilation during the Second Commonwealth; for the present situation, see especially Thomas Luckmann, *The Invisible Religion* (New York: Macmillan, 1967).

Index of Modern Authors

Index of Books
in the Hebrew Bible